Radical Cartographies

Radical Cartographies

Participatory Mapmaking from Latin America

EDITED BY
BJØRN SLETTO
JOE BRYAN
ALFREDO WAGNER
CHARLES HALE

University of Texas Press   Austin

Publication of this book was made possible in part by support from the Pachita Tennant Pike Fund for Latin American Studies.

Copyright © 2020 by the University of Texas Press
All rights reserved
Printed in the United States of America
First edition, 2020

Requests for permission to reproduce material from this work should be sent to:
    Permissions
    University of Texas Press
    P.O. Box 7819
    Austin, TX 78713-7819
    utpress.utexas.edu/rp-form

∞ The paper used in this book meets the minimum requirements of ANSI/NISO Z39.48-1992 (R1997) (Permanence of Paper).

Library of Congress Cataloging-in-Publication Data

Names: Sletto, Bjørn, editor. | Bryan, Joe (Joseph H.), editor. | Almeida, Alfredo Wagner Berno de, editor. | Hale, Charles R., editor.
Title: Radical cartographies : participatory mapmaking from Latin America / edited by Bjørn Sletto, Joe Bryan, Alfredo Wagner, Charles Hale.
Description: First edition. | Austin : University of Texas Press, 2020. | Includes bibliographical references and index.
Identifiers: LCCN 2019030455 (print) | LCCN 2019030456 (ebook)
    ISBN 978-1-4773-2088-4 (cloth)
    ISBN 978-1-4773-2089-1 (library ebook)
    ISBN 978-1-4773-2090-7 (non-library ebook)
Subjects: LCSH: Human geography—Latin America. | Cartography—Social aspects—Latin America. | Communities—Latin America. | Indigenous peoples—Latin America—Ethnic identity. | Ethnosociology.
Classification: LCC GF514 .R33 2020 (print) | LCC GF514 (ebook) | DDC 304.2089/0098—dc23
LC record available at https://lccn.loc.gov/2019030455
LC ebook record available at https://lccn.loc.gov/2019030456

doi:10.7560/320884

CONTENTS

Introduction: Radical Social Cartographies   1
BJØRN SLETTO

PART I.

1. Oral Narratives in the Rincón Zapoteco:
   A Cartography of Processes   19
   MELQUIADES (KIADO) CRUZ

2. Social Polygraphy: Territory as a Living Memorial
   to Culture and Nature   35
   ÁLVARO CÉSAR VELASCO ÁLVAREZ

3. Emulating Kuyujani: Boundary Making in
   the Caura River Basin, Venezuela   45
   NALÚA ROSA SILVA MONTERREY

PART II.

4. Revealing Territorial Illusions and Political Fictions
   through Participatory Cartography   65
   WENDY PINEDA

5. Mapuche Cartography: Defending *Ixofillmogen*   81
   PABLO MANSILLA QUIÑONES AND MIGUEL MELIN PEHUEN

6. The Ethnocartography of *Sumak Allpa*:
   The Kichwa Indigenous Community of Pastaza, Ecuador   97
   ALFREDO VITERY AND ALEXANDRA LAMIÑA

7. Social Cartography and Territorial Planning
   in Robles, Colombia   115
   CARLOS ALBERTO GONZÁLEZ

PART III.

8. New Social Cartography and Ethnographic Practice — 131
   ALFREDO WAGNER BERNO DE ALMEIDA

9. Social Cartography and the Struggle for Multiethnic, Urban Indigenous Lands: The Case of the Beija-Flor *Aldeia* in Rio Preto da Eva, Brazil — 145
   EMMANUEL DE ALMEIDA FARIAS JÚNIOR

10. Participatory Cultural Mapping in Nvwken, Mapuce Territory, Argentina: Exploring Other Forms of Territorial Representation — 163
    MARÍA LAURA NAHUEL

11. Political Appropriation of Social Cartography in Defense of Quilombola Territories in Alcântara, Maranhão, Brazil — 183
    DAVI PEREIRA JÚNIOR

    Commentary: What Sort of Territory? What Sort of Map? — 203
    JOE BRYAN

    Afterword — 217
    CHARLES R. HALE

    Contributors — 221

    Index — 227

Introduction

Radical Social Cartographies

BJØRN SLETTO

Map production and distribution are no longer the sole purview of the state. Over the past two decades, Indigenous, Afro-descendant, and other traditional peoples across the Americas have used participatory mapping tools and internet-based technologies to assert their own territorial rights. Coupled with advances in international law, such as the adoption of the ILO Convention 169 (International Labour Organization's Indigenous and Tribal Peoples Convention, 1989) and attendant recognition of the rights of traditional peoples throughout the region, this "countermapping" (Peluso 1995) has contributed significantly to important territorial gains for Indigenous peoples by providing cartographic documentation of traditional land and resource uses.

However, participatory mapping has now entered a new phase we call "radical social cartographies." This new phase is characterized by a much wider diversity of purposes and techniques, taking us beyond the view of participatory mapping as merely a tool to contest dominant state-endorsed and state-produced maps. These diverse mappings represent the radical edge of a new social cartography with significant lessons for marginalized communities across the globe.

Beyond making claims on the state, Indigenous and Afro-descendant communities appropriate participatory mapping technologies to strengthen self-determination, local governance, and resource management within their own territories; to document and represent their own conceptions of time, place, and space; to defend existing territorial and other resource rights against new actors, including agroindustry, extractive industries, and global processes associated with climate change legislation; and to critically engage in reproductions and imaginaries of selves and community in postdevelopment contexts. We are increasingly seeing Indigenous and Afro-descendant uses of participatory mapping to survey, document, and monitor the activities of the state and of corporate actors, thus using the surveillance power of cartography in the struggle for justice.

This fundamental rethinking of the role of maps and the different ways they can be created, analyzed, and remade is driven in large part by inhabitants of the territories themselves, rather than by Western scholars or NGOs. It is these voices that are represented in this book. In their own language and on their own terms, these authors from the margins critically explore the creative processes of describing and depicting the natural and built environments emerging from Indigenous, Afro-descendant, and other traditional groups in Latin America. They demonstrate that these radical mapping practices are as varied as the communities in which they take place, dispelling any notions of an essential quality to mapping. They underscore that mapping as a practice of making, reading, and exploring maps constitutes a powerful analytical and political vehicle for their communities. As they do so, they engage in a unique conversation with critical academic discourse by exploring the intersection of technology and representation with issues of Indigenous and Afro-descendant identity and space in a postdevelopment context.

This book is the product of a community of scholars, intellectuals, activists, and practitioners that has been formed and sustained through collaborations in field research, personal and professional engagements in international conferences and other encounters, and friendships and mentoring relationships in which maps and mappings have played a variety of roles. We have all sought to better understand the current trends in participatory mapping as we engage with these technologies both in practice and in theory. The implications for communities and their territories of recent movements in participatory mapping have been poorly documented, and theoretical engagement with this work has been largely limited to inaccessible and often English-language academic discourse. Reflective dialogue about this phenomenon is lacking between Indigenous and Afro-descendant populations, scholars, and practitioners, and critical thinking about the politics, potentials, and pitfalls of these technologies is spotty and uneven. Despite the innovations in uses and conceptualizations of maps and mappings emerging from Indigenous and Afro-descendant communities, participatory mapping is still predominantly thought of in Cartesian and empirical terms as a means to an end, whether this is from a developmentalist worldview or from a territorial rights perspective.

The intent of this edited volume, then, is to foster such a dialogue between scholars and community leaders who engage with these radical new social cartographies as observers, critics, and practitioners, and to shed light on innovative uses of participatory mapping emerging from Latin America's marginalized communities. We seek to describe and critically assess not merely what mapping in the singular can "do" in empirical, Cartesian, developmentalist, or political terms within a nation-state context but also what maps and mappings in the plural mean for the reproduction of places, natures, and identities in a region characterized by political and economic experimentation. In doing so, the authors in this volume assume a critical stance toward expert-driven mapping. Instead of seeking to define best practices in Cartesian terms, the authors explore situated practices of analyzing, navigating, and refusing power as it takes form in their respective contexts.

While the professional and personal relationships among many of us reach back years and even decades, the early beginning of this edited volume was a two-day workshop on participatory mapping, climate change, and forest rights organized by a team of UT-Austin faculty members and graduate students in collaboration with the Rights and Resources Initiative (RRI) at the University of Texas at Austin (UT-Austin) in November 2010. At the time, UT-Austin faculty members and students had already been working with RRI to develop the concept for an international forum on participatory mapping focusing on the role of such mappings for forest rights in Latin America and elsewhere.

The Forum on Participatory Mapping and Forests Rights took place at the Universidad de los Andes in Bogotá, Colombia, in May 2011. Hosted by Claudia Leal and her colleagues in the Department of History and co-organized with faculty and staff from UT-Austin, the forum was sponsored by the RRI with additional funding assistance from UT's Lozano Long Institute for Latin American Studies (LLILAS) and the New Social Cartography Project of the Amazon (PNCSA). The forum facilitated discussion among more than fifty representatives of global funding institutions, including the Ford Foundation; the academic community in the United States and Latin America; and Afro-descendant and Indigenous communities who are involved in issues of climate change, land rights, and forest reform (Sletto et al. 2013). Several participants were asked to provide "anchor papers," which served to frame the separate panels and were later revised and included in the conference proceedings.[1] The conference also included an exhibit of participatory mapping projects and speakers from the Democratic Republic of Congo, Indonesia, Liberia, and the Philippines who are also engaged in participatory mapping and forest rights struggles. In fall 2012, many of the participants in the Bogotá conference were reunited at the Universidad Nacional de Rosario in Argentina, where Carlos Salamanca and colleagues with the interdisciplinary center Spaces, Politics, and Societies organized a conference that further explored issues of participatory mapping and Indigenous territorial rights (Sletto et al. 2012).[2]

This series of presentations and encounters at UT-Austin, Bogotá, and Rosario gave rise to the idea of this edited volume. The co-editors and other participants in this transregional conversation considered how to build on this dialogue and develop a trilingual edited book that would incorporate theoretical contributions as well as case-based experiential chapters by Indigenous and Afro-descendant scholars, practitioners, and activists. To make such a plural, regional, and transdisciplinary publication possible, in 2014 many of the authors in this volume (Alfredo Vitery, Álvaro Velasco, Carlos González, María Nahuel, Melquiades (Kiado) Cruz, and Wendy Pineda) traveled to UT-Austin with funding from LLILAS to work jointly with co-editors to prepare chapters for publication but also to engage in open-ended critical reflections about participatory mapping.

The workshop represented a transdisciplinary and multilingual process of coproduction of knowledge that was new to us and that ultimately took many forms. Prior to the workshop, most of the writers had shared drafts of their chapters with co-editors; transcribed recordings of their verbal presentations from the 2011 Bogotá forum were also available to serve as a basis for the development of the chapters. During the workshop, authors and editors worked in groups of two or three, discussing, outlining, revising, and writing each chapter. At various moments, the group convened as a whole to discuss overarching themes that united us but also demonstrated the diversity of experiences and perspectives within the group.

Following the workshop, writers submitted revisions of their chapters, which were then further developed in collaboration with editors. This work took place in person during the first editor's stay in Manaus, Brazil, in 2013; through the first editor's regular discussions with the authors Alexandra Lamiña and Davi Pereira, who are both currently PhD students in LLILAS, and co-editor Joe Bryan's ongoing dialogues with the authors Melquiades (Kiado) Cruz and Pablo Mansilla Quiñones; and through discussions and virtual writing sessions between authors and the first editor via Skype or e-mail. Some chapters were developed primarily on the basis of spoken presentations given at the forum in Bogotá, others emerged through cowriting during the UT-Austin workshop, and others were written almost in their entirety by authors while in their home country. Chapters were subsequently translated from their original Spanish or Portuguese by Ava Hoffmann with Davi Pereira (chapters by Wagner and Farias in Portuguese), by Joe Bryan (chapters by Melquiades [Kiado] Cruz and Pablo Mansilla Quiñones in Spanish), by Bjørn Sletto (remaining chapters in Spanish), and then were proofread by the editors as well as the UT-Austin alumnus Caroline Daigle. Finally, the translated chapters as well as accompanying illustrations were reviewed and approved by the authors.

Our collaboration could be considered an intertextual approach to knowledge production (Dowling et al. 2012) within an informal and fluid writing community (R. Parker 2009). As we gave and responded to presentations, engaged in dialogue, and shared and commented on drafts, our own critical understanding of Indigenous cartographies grew in depth and nuance through our engagements with other participants in our writing community. However, although our intertextual engagement was critical for the knowledge production reflected in this volume (Ward and West 2008), we have inevitably failed to reproduce the dynamic, critical dialogue and diverse coproduction of texts that went into developing the present volume. Even though the chapters here represent an unusually wide range of styles to reflect differences between authors, the format of a printed book will always do violence to complex Indigenous ontologies and forms of representation (Hunt 2014). In spite of our shared commitment to decolonial research methodologies, collective projects such as these, prompted and driven from privileged positions within Western academia, will inevitably and inextricably be linked with colonialism (see, for example, de Leeuw et al. 2012; Hale 2006).

To be sure, even this introduction constructs an overarching narrative of radical Indigenous cartographies that inevitably blunts contrasts; reduces nuance; and glosses over the visceral moments of joy, frustration, memory performance, storytelling, and discovery that always accompany such situated and experiential mapping processes. Some of the writers in this volume have faced violence and dispossession of their traditional lands but have also experienced the emotional resonance of mapping workshops and imagined the anticolonial possibilities (Coombes, Johnson, and Howitt 2012b) of these tools.

However, as we developed this volume, we strove to guard against romanticizing what are complex and evolving Indigenous and Afro-descendant geographies and relationships to land and environments (Coombes, Johnson, and Howitt 2012a). Indigenous and Afro-descendant production of critical thought has long been subalternized and invisibilized in favor of colonial science and knowledge regimes that are reproduced through the political-economic structures of Western academia (Walsh 2007), and personalized narratives may buttress long-held biases against Indigenous and

Afro-descendant knowledge formations. Critical perspectives originating from Indigenous and Afro-descendant intellectual communities are discounted and negated in Western academia (Perry and Rappaport 2013) as local, embodied, situated, and "political," which is said to limit its generalizability and hence its value as objective knowledge production. Instead of seeking to make the Indigenous and Afro-descendant communities presented in this book navigable or understandable, therefore, ours is a modest attempt to give voice to very real experiences and visceral optimism about the potential of radical social cartographies while also reflecting critically on the inherent limitations of such Cartesian technologies.

Intellectual pursuits surrounding questions of space and identity are of course inherently and deeply political. From the perspective of postcolonial thought, Indigenous and Afro-descendant intellectuals are simultaneously knowledge producers and political actors (Perry and Rappaport 2013, 30), and any critical thinking around the mapping of spaces and identities can never be divorced from issues of rights, authority, and justice. But the politics of knowledge production extends beyond Indigenous and Afro-descendant communities. The political is not simply a feature of the mapping process that can be disciplined through scholarly discourse. Instead, feminist science studies remind us that there are no invisible lines separating the laboratory or the scholar's office from the sites where research is conducted, belying simplistic distinctions between the "field" of scholarship and the "home" of scholarly production, and any simplistic dualism between the subject and the researcher (Katz 1994). Instead, knowledge emerges from experiments, tensions, encounters, and dialogues across spaces, time, and communities, as in the case of this volume. And knowledge production is always political, whether it occurs in a Skype conversation, in a seminar room at UT-Austin or Uniandes, or in a community meeting space.

This is particularly true for cartography, which has a troubled history as a technology of power. Cartography has served as a tool of colonization, imperialism, and the global development project, erasing Indigenous landscapes through Cartesian ordering and Western conceptualizations of space and place and providing rhetorical support for development and conservation interventions of various sorts (Barr 2011; Biggs 1999; Bryan 2011; Craib 2000; Rundstrom 1990, 1991, 1993; Sletto 2009a, 2009b; Sparke 1998; Winichakul 1994; Wood 2010). Work in critical cartography starting with J. B. Harley (1989) has understood maps as ideological representations that support the interests of their developers, which reflect the social contexts in which they are produced, and which derive their authority from a veneer of scientific objectivity (Crampton 2001, 2010; Pickles 2004; Sparke 1998).

Participatory mapping can, from the perspective of critical cartography, be understood as a means to leverage the power of maps to further the interests of subaltern groups. While Indigenous peoples throughout the Americas have produced maps on paper and in ephemeral media for centuries, the more recent boom in participatory mapping emerged with the shift toward participatory research and development, which especially took hold in the 1980s. Such mapping projects conducted by scholars with the participation of Indigenous and Afro-descendant groups in Mexico, Central America, and South America sought to enlist community members in documenting land-use and conservation practices and designing conservation and management plans. In the process, such participatory mapping would ostensibly lead to the devolution of authority and control over development and conservation decision-making to local communities, affording a measure of self-determination (see, for example, Chapin, Lamb, and Threlkeld 2005; Chapin and Threlkeld 2001; Herlihy 2003; Herlihy and Knapp 2003; Parker 2006; Poole 1995; Sletto 2010). At the same time, the Indigenous and Afro-descendant rights movement enlisted academic collaborators in projects Peluso (1995) labeled "countermapping," which sought to produce alternative knowledge representations in contradiction to development projects or to directly support Indigenous and Afro-descendant territorial and other rights claims.

However, as participatory mapping matured into a genre of its own and earned its place in the standardized toolsets of global development institutions, it increasingly became subject to critique. While participatory mapping has been premised on making Indigenous and Afro-descendant spatialities visible as a means to press claims ranging from participation in decision-making to territorial rights, this visibilization has been effected under the terms of Western cartography and within the strictures of Cartesian structure. This mainstreaming of participatory mapping as its own genre within the development project has led to calls for "an ongoing attentiveness to avoiding misappropriations of knowledge, understandings, and perspectives" through participatory mapping (Pearce and Louis 2008, 123). "The problem that faces Indigenous peoples worldwide is to find a way to incorporate Western [geospatial technologies] and cartographic multimedia while minimizing the mistranslations, recolonizations, and assimilations of conventional technoscience" (Pearce and Louis 2008, 123).

As an epistemologically and politically problematic project, participatory mapping may therefore have unexpected implications, due not only to its erasures but also to its visibilizations. Concerns have been raised that such mappings have served to erase dynamic Indigenous conceptions of space and time (Rocheleau 2005; Sletto 2009c); impose Western forms of boundary making and territorialization (Bryan 2011; Parker 2006; Sletto 2009a, 2009b); appropriate Indigenous knowledge for the benefit of development institutions (Hodgson and Schroeder 2002); support imperialist and often military ambitions (Bryan 2011); and facilitate capitalist expansion in Indigenous lands (Wainwright and Bryan 2009). Although this volume focuses on Indigenous and Afro-descendant mappings in Mexico, Central America, and South America, research on Cartesian epistemic violence, Indigenous geographies, and Indigenous map production in North America have also contributed to critiques of the heroic assumptions of earlier participatory mapping (see, for example, Barr 2011; de Leeuw 2017; de Leeuw, Cameron, and Greenwood 2012; Hunt 2014; Larsen and Johnson 2012; Louis, Johnson, and Pramono 2012; Palmer 2012; Pearce and Louis 2008; Rundstrom 1990, 1991, 1993; Sparke 1998). As Radcliffe (2012) suggests, participatory mapping may be one person's Cartesian vehicle for rights claims and another's neoliberal tool.

On the other hand, the recent postrepresentational turn in geography and other social sciences has drawn further attention to the socially contingent and iterative process of mapmaking to challenge any easy assumption about the ontological stability and hence mimetic power of maps (Kitchin and Dodge 2007; Sletto 2015; see also Thrift 2003, 2004, 2007). The postrepresentational perspective on participatory mapping leads us to question the assumption, derived from the Harleyan viewpoint on the discursive power of maps, that countermaps will inevitably impose new social and spatial relations because they draw their authority from Cartesian cartography. Instead, the postrepresentational view holds that maps are in fact inherently unstable and representationally fragile social productions (see, for instance, Della Dora 2009; Kitchin and Dodge 2007, Kitchin, Gleeson, and Dodge 2013; Perkins 2008; Young and Gilmore 2013). The postrepresentational turn in cartography calls for a renewed focus on mappings as performative, situated, and contested practices intimately implicated in complex social processes and as rhizomatic formations that emerge through embodied and contingent forms of storytelling (Caquard and Cartwright 2014; Hirt 2012; Sletto 2014, 2015; Vermeylen and Davies 2012).

The present volume seeks, then, to make a contribution to the work in decolonizing methodologies and postcolonial scholarship that challenges the subalternization of Indigenous and Afro-descendant critical thought, and in so doing, to introduce conceptualizations of participatory mapping that perhaps move us beyond these social science debates. Rather than framing the chapters around these theoretical conversations, we have therefore structured the chapters in accordance with the lived experiences and concerns of the authors and the communities they represent. In that way, we sought to make visible the contributions of critical thinking from (what has long been produced by Western academia as) the margin of scholarly discourse to the development of new perspectives in a field that has long been defined by Western-dominated scholarship and practice.

We begin with a section devoted to different perspectives of space, place, and landscapes, which, rather than being obscured by a heavy-handed Cartesian approach to cartography, have emerged and become visualized through participatory mapping. We start the section with a chapter by Melquiades (Kiado) Cruz, a community organizer, communication technology innovator, and Indigenous scholar from the Zapotec community of Yagavila in the Rincón de la Sierra Norte of Oaxaca, Mexico, who has long been engaged as an activist in the development of community organizations oriented toward conservation of traditional culture and knowledge, and who has been a critic of Western-driven cartographic projects in Indigenous lands in southern Mexico. His chapter examines the fraught relationship between Western and Indigenous views of land and environment. Moving beyond two-dimensional understandings of space, Cruz uses an exploration of group activities such as quilt making and storytelling to imagine deeper ways of mapping that include the elements of memory and emotional attachment that are linked with territory.

Writing from his experience with participatory mapping in the Cauca Valley in Colombia, Álvaro Velasco is a lawyer and professor of environmental studies at the University of Nariño, Colombia, and founder and director of the Fundación Fundaminga. As founder of Fundaminga, he was an early proponent of participatory mapping in Colombia and has decades of experience collaborating with Indigenous groups. His chapter develops the concept of "social polygraphy," a form of participatory research premised on developing insights from unstructured processes of conversation and depiction, including "speaking maps." Drawing on extensive experience with Indigenous community members, Velasco grounds the chapter in critical reflections on the ways natural and built environments are made and understood through alternative mappings across time and place.

Third, Nalúa Rosa Silva Monterrey, currently director of the Centro de Investigaciones Antropológicas de Guayana at the Universidad Nacional Experimental de Guayana, Venezuela, has worked extensively for the last three decades with Indigenous people of eastern Venezuela, including on territorial demarcation projects with Indigenous Ye'kwana collaborators. Her chapter critically explores the complex roles of Western location-based technologies for development of new conceptualizations of land and self in an area undergoing rapid social change under a socialist governing experiment.

She considers the complex role of coproduction involving Western-trained anthropologists and Indigenous peoples, critically assessing the complex understandings of landscapes brought to the fore via participatory mapping.

The second section turns from the complex meanings of landscapes to the persistent and visceral threats from state- and private-sector-led interventions in Indigenous and Afro-descendant lands. These threats from extractive industries and other capital-intensive state-building projects remind us that despite advances in Indigenous territorial rights, participatory mapping projects continue to be carried out from a sense of urgency. Despite scholarly critiques of participatory mapping, such maps are still seen as potentially powerful means to assert rights and further claims, precisely because of their Cartesian representational weight.

First, Wendy Pineda, a specialist in geoinformatics and Geographic Information Systems and advisor to a number of Indigenous organizations in the Peruvian Amazon, examines the role of participatory mapping to surveil and contest encroachments by the oil industry. With her collaborators, Pineda uses participatory mapping methods and GPS to document petroleum exploitation and its cultural, health, and environmental impacts in order to pressure the government to begin effective remediation of contaminated lands and waters. In her chapter, she critically reviews the challenges of deploying such cartographic tools in these traditional communities. She focuses on the complex relationships between the three Indigenous groups, revealing how cultural and political practices specific to these groups have impacted map production, how mappings have overlapped with strategies of place making and new forms of land control, and how such radical mapping techniques emerge from within Indigenous communities to point the way toward innovative strategies of land and resource management.

Further south, the Mapuche scholars Pablo Mansilla Quiñones and Miguel Melin Pehuen situate a case study of participatory mapping in Kurakautin, Chile, within the broader context of multiple forms of colonialism and violent resource extraction in Wallmapu (Mapuche Territory). Kurakautin is a pristine natural area whose rivers are now threatened by hydroelectric development and pisciculture firms. Faced with these pressures, the Mapuche communities in Kurakautin, together with the Mapuche Territorial Alliance, mobilized to stop these projects, drawing on participatory mapping to document the threats faced by traditional communities in the area, including the threats to traditional conceptualizations of the relationship between people and their environment, while turning to web-based methodologies to give further visibility to their claims.

In Ecuador, meanwhile, Alfredo Vitery and Alexandra Lamiña describe the creative uses of participatory mapping for management of community lands and resources developed by and for Indigenous community members among the Kichwa de Pastaza. Alfredo Vitery is an Indigenous leader of international renown of the Kichwa de Pastaza people who has worked for decades in the struggle for Indigenous territoriality in Ecuador, and Alexandra Lamiña is currently a doctoral student in LLILAS at UT-Austin and an active participant in the Indigenous autonomy struggles in Pastaza, Ecuador. In their chapter, they examine how Western techniques and strategies can be adopted and modified in the context of *sumak allpa,* a concept that describes fundamentally alternative relations between time and space, the human and spiritual, and the material and nonmaterial.

Similarly, Carlos González examines the use of participatory mapping to document traditional Afro-Colombian land-use practices, including understandings of nature and society submerged under state-driven resource management systems. González, originally from the Afro-Colombian communities of the Cauca Valley in Colombia, is an ethnobotanist with a degree from the Universidad del Valle, Cali, Colombia. In his chapter, he presents a critical perspective on the role of intercommunity mapmaking strategies in forging new relationships with state actors and commercial industries centered on natural resource extraction. He examines how social cartography may serve to develop new and effective strategies to protect traditional relationships to natural resources for both cultural and material survival.

In the final section, we examine the ways in which such participatory mapping projects articulate with processes of identity formation, particularly considering the rapid social changes facing traditional communities in light of the extractivist and other state-building projects described in the previous section. We discuss how the collective productions of cartographic representations foster creative and critical thinking and deliberations about the meanings of tradition and history.

We begin with Alfredo Wagner, an anthropologist and director of the New Social Cartography Project of the Amazon (PNCSA) in Manaus, Brazil. He has oriented the work of the research center toward developing new forms of social cartography with traditional and marginalized groups, including Afro-Brazilian and urban social movements. In his chapter, he interrogates the conceptual and political relationships between mapmaking and ethnography, examining how mapping can serve as a metaphor for new forms of engagement that break Western-dominated perspectives in research. His chapter illuminates new ways to conceptualize identities in the context of land, space, and rights.

Next, Emmanuel de Almeida Farias Júnior, associate professor of the

Department of Social Sciences at the State University of Maranhão, Brazil, describes a participatory mapping project facilitated by the PNCSA in Manaus. He bases his chapter on his work over many years with Indigenous migrants to Manaus, who settle public lands and form new communities consisting of members of many different Indigenous groups, with different languages, conceptions of land and nature, and spiritual heritage. He examines a mapping process in such a settlement composed of members of a dozen different Indigenous communities that facilitated new understandings of Indigenous identities and agreements on depiction, description, and naming that served to present pan-Indigenous identities.

María Laura Nahuel, a resident of the Mapuce Lof (Community) Newen Mapu, Neuquén, Argentina, and *werken* ("messenger"; spokesperson) of the Confederación Mapuce Neuquina, also describes a participatory mapping project conducted in an urban area with significant implications for Indigenous Mapuche identities. In her chapter, she discusses the role of Western technologies for the documentation of Mapuche memories of Indigenous places within the developed urban area of Neuquén. She problematizes the struggle to capture historical memory in a context characterized by rapid social change and severe, often violent economic and political struggle. By thinking about her own research in these areas, she also reflects on her and her colleagues' relationship to Indigenous landscapes and memories as young Mapuche activists, struggling to deploy new forms of representation, including GIS and web-based technologies, in ways that do not conflict with traditional perspectives on land, space, and time.

The next chapter also emerges from personal experiences with participatory mapping in the author's home region. Davi Pereira Júnior, who was born in the Quilombola community of Itamatatiua in the southern area of the municipality of Alcântara, Brazil, is currently a PhD candidate in LLILAS, UT-Austin. He provides a unique perspective on struggles to defend Quilombola lands in the face of state and private development of a military installation, including a rocket base through a US-Brazil defense agreement. Reflecting on his shifting between identities as a scholar and as a resident of these communities, he draws on observations of the decision-making process of Quilombola mapmakers as they critically assess representational strategies in the context of complex articulations between external political and social realities.

The book also includes reflective chapters by co-editor Joe Bryan, associate professor in geography at the University of Colorado, Boulder, and co-editor Charles Hale, dean of Social Sciences, University of California–Santa

Barbara. Joe Bryan, whose work focuses on Indigenous politics in the Americas, human rights, and critical cartography, examines what he refers to as the production of new territorialities in Central America. He critically examines the innovations of participatory mapping emerging from Indigenous communities, how these innovations shape the roles and interests of external actors, and how these radical mapping techniques influence the preservation of traditional land uses, governance, cultural relationships to land, and territorial rights in Central America. Charles Hale concludes this volume by illuminating the significance of radical social cartographies given the current decline of multicultural neoliberal governance, while assessing the contribution to decolonial praxis represented by this collaboration among positioned activist intellectuals.

NOTES

1. *Cartografía participativa y derechos al territorio y los recursos* (Austin: LLILAS, UT-Austin, 2011); available at sites.utexas.edu/participatory-mapping/files/2012/12/Foro_Cartografia-Participativa_Bogota-2011.pdf.

2. *Mapas y derechos: Experiencias y aprendizajes en América Latina*, ed. Carlos Salamanca and Rosario Espina (UNR Editora, 2012); available at sites.utexas.edu/participatory-mapping/files/2012/12/mapasyderechos.pdf.

REFERENCES

Barr, Juliana. 2011. "Geographies of Power: Mapping Indian Borders in the 'Borderlands' of the Early Southwest." *The William and Mary Quarterly* 68(1): 5–46.

Biggs, Michael. 1999. "Putting the State on the Map: Cartography, Territory, and European State Formation." *Comparative Studies in Society and History* 41(2): 374–405.

Bryan, Joe. 2011. "Walking the Line: Participatory Mapping, Indigenous Rights, and Neoliberalism." *Geoforum* 42(1): 40–50.

Caquard, Sébastien, and William Cartwright. 2014. "Narrative Cartography: From Mapping Stories to the Narrative of Maps and Mapping." *The Cartographic Journal* 51(2): 101–106.

Chapin, Mac, and Bill Threlkeld. 2001. *Indigenous Landscapes: A Study in Ethnocartography*. Washington, DC: Center for the Support of Native Lands.

Chapin, Mac, Zachary Lamb, and Bill Threlkeld. 2005. "Mapping Indigenous Lands." *Annual Review of Anthropology* 34: 619–638.

Coombes, Brad, Jay T. Johnson, and Richard Howitt. 2012a. "Indigenous Geographies I: Mere Resource Conflicts? The Complexities in Indigenous Land and Environmental Claims." *Progress in Human Geography* 37(5): 810–821.

———. 2012b. "Indigenous Geographies II: The Aspirational Spaces in Postcolonial Politics—Reconciliation, Belonging and Social Provision." *Progress in Human Geography* 37(5): 691–700.

Craib, Raymond B. 2000. "Cartography and Power in the Conquest and Creation of New Spain." *Latin American Research Review* 35(1): 7–36.

Crampton, Jeremy W. 2001. "Maps as Social Constructions: Power, Communication and Visualization." *Progress in Human Geography* 25(2): 235–252.

———. 2010. *Mapping: A Critical Introduction to Cartography and GIS*. Malden, MA: Wiley-Blackwell.

de Leeuw, Sarah. 2017. "Writing as Righting: Truth and Reconciliation, Poetics, and New Geographing in Colonial Canada." *The Canadian Geographer/Le Géographe canadien* 61(3): 306–318.

de Leeuw, Sarah, Emile S. Cameron, and Margo Greenwood. 2012. "Participatory and Community-Based Research, Indigenous Geographies, and the Spaces of Friendship: A Critical Engagement." *The Canadian Geographer/Le Géographe canadien* 56(2): 180–194.

Della Dora, Veronica. 2009. "Performative Atlases: Memory, Materiality, and (Co-)Authorship." *Cartographica* 44(4): 240–255.

Dowling, Robyn, Andrew Gorman-Murray, Emma Power, and Karina Luzia. 2012. "Critical Reflections on Doctoral Research and Supervision in Human Geography: The 'PhD by publication.'" *Journal of Geography in Higher Education* 36(2): 293–305.

Hale, Charles R. 2006. "Activist Research v. Cultural Critique: Indigenous Land Rights and the Contradictions of Politically Engaged Anthropology." *Cultural Anthropology* 21(1): 96–120.

Harley, J. B. 1989. "Deconstructing the Map." *Cartographica* 26(2): 1–20.

Herlihy, Peter H. 2003. "Participatory Research Mapping of Indigenous Lands in Darién, Panama." *Human Organization* 62(4): 315–331.

Herlihy, Peter H., and Gregory Knapp. 2003. "Maps of, by, and for the Peoples of Latin America." *Human Organization* 62(4): 303–314.

Hirt, Irène. 2012. "Mapping Dreams/Dreaming Maps: Bridging Indigenous and Western Geographical Knowledge." *Cartographica* 47(2): 105–120.

Hodgson, Dorothy L., and Richard A. Schroeder. 2002. "Dilemmas of Counter-Mapping Community Resources in Tanzania." *Development and Change* 33(1): 79–100.

Hunt, Sarah. 2014. "Ontologies of Indigeneity: The Politics of Embodying a Concept." *Cultural Geographies* 21(1): 27–32.

Katz, Cindi. 1994. "Playing the Field: Questions of Fieldwork in Geography." *Professional Geographer* 46(1): 67–72.

Kitchin, Rob, and Martin Dodge. 2007. "Rethinking Maps." *Progress in Human Geography* 31(3): 331–344.

Kitchin, Rob, Justin Gleeson, and Martin Dodge. 2013. "Unfolding Mapping Practices: A New Epistemology for Cartography." *Transactions of the Institute of British Geographers* 38(3): 480–496.

Larsen, Soren C., and Jay T. Johnson. 2012. "In Between Worlds: Place, Experience, and Research in Indigenous Geography." *Journal of Cultural Geography* 29(1): 1–13.

Louis, Renee Pualani, Jay T. Johnson, and Albertus Hadi Pramono. 2012. "Introduction: Indigenous Cartographies and Counter-Mapping." *Cartographica* 47(2): 77–79.

Palmer, Mark. 2012. "Theorizing Indigital Geographic Information Networks." *Cartographica* 47(2): 80–91.

Parker, Brenda. 2006. "Constructing Community through Maps? Power and Praxis in Community Mapping." *Professional Geographer* 58(4): 470–484.

Parker, Rachel. 2009. "A Learning Community Approach to Doctoral Education in the Social Sciences." *Teaching in Higher Education* 14(1): 43–54.

Pearce, Margaret Wickens, and Renee Pualani Louis. 2008. "Mapping Indigenous Depth of Place." *American Indian Culture and Research Journal* 32(3): 107–126.

Peluso, Nancy Lee. 1995. "Whose Woods Are These? Counter-Mapping Forest Territories in Kalimantan, Indonesia." *Antipode* 27(4): 383–406.

Perkins, Chris. 2008. "Cultures of Map Use." *Cartographic Journal* 45(2): 150–158.

Perry, Keisha-Khan Y., and Joanne Rappaport. 2013. "Making a Case for Collaborative Research with Black and Indigenous Social Movements in Latin America." In *Otros Saberes: Collaborative Research on Indigenous and Afro-Descendant Cultural Politics*, ed. Charles R. Hale and Lynn Stephen, 30–48. Santa Fe: School for Advanced Research Press.

Pickles, John. 2004. *A History of Spaces: Cartographic Reason, Mapping and the Geo-Coded World*. New York: Routledge.

Poole, Peter. 1995. *Indigenous Peoples, Mapping, and Biodiversity Conservation: An Analysis of Current Activities and Opportunities for Applying Geomatics Technologies*. Washington, DC: Biodiversity Support Program.

Radcliffe, Sarah H. 2012. "Relating to the Land: Multiple Geographical Imaginations and Lived-In Landscapes." *Transactions of the Institute of British Geographers* 37(3): 359–364.

Rocheleau, Dianne. 2005. "Maps as Power Tools: Locating Communities in Space or Situating People and Ecologies in Place?" In *Communities and Conservation: Histories and Politics of Community-Based Natural Resource Management*, ed. J. Peter Brosius, Anna Lowenhaupt Tsing, and Charles Zerner. Walnut Creek, CA: AltaMira Press.

Rundstrom, Robert A. 1990. "A Cultural Interpretation of Inuit Map Accuracy." *Geographical Review* 80(2): 155–168.

———. 1991. "Mapping, Postmodernism, Indigenous People and the Changing Direction of North American Cartography." *Cartographica* 28(2): 1–12.

———. 1993. "The Role of Ethics, Mapping, and the Meaning of Place in Relations between Indians and Whites in the United States." *Cartographica* 30(1): 21–28.

Sletto, Bjørn. 2009a. "'Indigenous People Don't Have Boundaries': Reborderings, Fire Management, and Productions of Authenticities in Indigenous Landscapes." *Cultural Geographies* 16(2): 253–277.

———. 2009b. Introduction to special issue: "Indigenous Cartographies." *Cultural Geographies* 16(2): 147–152.

———. 2009c. "'We Drew What We Imagined': Participatory Mapping, Performance, and the Arts of Landscape Making." *Current Anthropology* 50(4): 443–476.

———. 2010. "Autogestión en representaciones espaciales indígenas y el rol de la capacitación y concientización: El caso del Proyecto Etnocartográfico Inna Kowantok, Sector 5 Pemón (Kavanayén-Mapauri), La Gran Sabana." *Antropológica* 53(113): 43–75.

———. 2014. "Cartographies of Remembrance and Becoming in the Sierra de Perijá, Venezuela." *Transactions of the Institute of British Geographers* 39(3): 360–372.

———. 2015. "Inclusions, Erasures and Emergences in an Indigenous Landscape: Participatory Cartographics and the Makings of Affective Place in the Sierra de Perijá, Venezuela." *Environment and Planning D: Society and Space* 33(5): 925–944.

Sletto, Bjørn, Joe Bryan, Marla Torrado, Charles Hale, and Deborah Barry. 2013. "Territorialidad, mapeo participativo y política sobre los recursos naturales: La experiencia de América Latina." *Cuadernos de Geografía: Revista Colombiana de Geografía* 22(2): 193–209.

Sletto, Bjørn, Marla Torrado, Jimena Crúz, and Andrés Galindo. 2012. "Memoria, resistencia y cartografía en la Sierra de Perijá, Venezuela." In *Mapas y derechos: Experiencias y aprendizajes en América Latina*, ed. Carlos Salamanca and Rosario Espina, 115–140. Rosario, Argentina: UNR Editora.

Sparke, Matthew. 1998. "A Map That Roared and an Original Atlas: Canada, Cartography, and the Narration of Nation." *Annals of the Association of American Geographers* 88(3): 463–495.

Thrift, Nigel. 2003. "Performance and . . ." *Environment and Planning A: Economy and Space* 35(11): 2019–2024.

———. 2004. "Intensities of Feeling: Towards a Spatial Politics of Affect." *Geografiska Annaler* 86 Series B (1): 57–78.

———. 2007. *Non-Representational Theory: Space, Politics, Affect*. London: Routledge.

Vermeylen, Saskia, Gemma Davies, and Dan van der Horst. 2012. "Deconstructing the Conservancy Map: *Hxaro, N!ore*, and Rhizomes in the Kalahari." *Cartographica* 47(2) 121–134.

Wainwright, Joel, and Joe Bryan. 2009. "Cartography, Territory, Property: Postcolonial Reflections on Indigenous Counter-Mapping in Nicaragua and Belize." *Cultural Geographies* 16(2): 153–178.

Walsh, Catherine. 2007. "Shifting the Geopolitics of Critical Knowledge: Decolonial Thought and Cultural Studies 'Others' in the Andes." *Cultural Studies* 21(2): 224–239.

Ward, Mary-Helen, and Sandra Helen West. 2008. "Blogging PhD Candidature: Revealing the Pedagogy." *International Journal of Emerging Technologies and Society* 6(1): 60–71.

Winichakul, Thongchai. 1994. *Siam Mapped: A History of the Geo-Body of a Nation*. Honolulu: University of Hawaii Press.

Wood, Denis. 2010. *Rethinking the Power of Maps*. New York: The Guilford Press.

Young, Jason C., and Michael P. Gilmore. 2013. "The Spatial Politics of Affect and Emotion in Participatory GIS." *Annals of the Association of American Geographers* 103(4): 808–823.

PART I

1

Oral Narratives in the Rincón Zapoteco

A Cartography of Processes

MELQUIADES (KIADO) CRUZ

Introduction

The web page for the Mexican National Institute of Statistics and Geography (INEGI) defines participatory mapping as a "process of gathering geographical information about the territory through collaboration with civil society, state institutions, and universities . . . with the goal of continuously updating geographical information for a better understanding of our setting, for the benefit of the nation." The definition confirms that the maps are instruments of power, a tool used to update knowledge of the national territory through public participation. The technical emphasis of their definition barely conceals its political implications, particularly when it comes to using public participation to facilitate or exploit community initiatives.

From 2006 to 2009, communities in the Rincón Zapoteco ("Zapotec Corner") contributed to a participatory mapping project that turned into an act of geopiracy.[1] The project began when a team of North American (US) geographers approached the Rincón communities with a proposal to map the territories of each of the communities in the zone. The communities initially welcomed the proposal. With maps of their territories, made by them, the Rincón communities could strengthen their control over land and resources necessary for their collective well-being.

It was a trap! The project was organized by the American Geographical Society (AGS) as part of their México Indígena (Indigenous Mexico) project. Prior to arriving in the Rincón, the México Indígena project had mapped communities in the Huasteca Potosina in northern Mexico. As we later discovered, the AGS's México Indígena project was funded entirely by the US Army through a program devoted to developing counterinsurgency tactics. We have no idea how much of the data gathered in the communities the project leaders turned over to their military backers. The researchers who led the project never told us. Instead, they accused us, the communities, of acting in bad faith, leaving us with thinly detailed maps and a couple of GPS units. The maps did not tell us anything new. They only showed everything that we had told the team.

I participated in the project.[2] The geographers trained me in how to use a GPS, taking advantage of my experience with digital media. Later on, in front of the assembly in my community, they accused me of looking to create conflict between communities. After everything had passed, I was left with a series of questions. What is a map? What kinds of territories do they make? Whose interests do they serve? The questions sparked a conversation in the Rincón communities. As is our custom in moments like this, we looked to the community itself to help us study the matter. That is how I learned the story that I relate here.

An Oral Map of the Rincón Zapoteco

In Yagavila, the community where I am from, we have our own way of mapping that predates Mexico and even the Spanish colony. It is an oral way of mapping that we learn by word of mouth, in a voice that speaks from the depths of what we are: a community. Our way of mapping works through a story that our elders tell about our ancestors, our *bënegulaza*, Yagaeche and his granddaughter Xhuaban, who became shining jaguars of light. Yagaeche and Xhuaban were the first to arrive in the place where the Zapotec people live today. They immersed themselves in the forest, climbing the mountains so that they could see how the rivers flow into the depths of the sea, perceiving all that makes us a people, the *bëne xhidza*. This is what the elders say.

> One day, long ago before time existed, Yagaeche said to Xhuaban, "We have to walk our territory so that we can figure out who else lives here so that we might live together with dignity in this land."
>
> "The territory is too big. I can't walk the whole thing," replied Xhuaban.
>
> "Don't worry, I have an idea for how we will manage," said the grandfather. "We will learn to speak the jaguars' language. We will count on them to guide us through the terrain. Riding on their backs, we will forge relations with the people and animals strong enough to make a community, since we all share in this space that gives us life."
>
> The grandfather went to the mountain to discuss the plan with

the guardians of the forest. After reaching an agreement with them, he returned to Xhuaban with two jaguars. Yagaeche said, "Let's ride them facing backward so we can learn the territory. When they cross the horizon, don't look forward, toward time. Look backward instead so that you can see the space we share with others. Riding on the jaguars' haunches, we will weave a mat [petate] from the lines we travel, tying the knots that hold our world together." The two mounted the jaguars the next day and set off for the horizon, losing themselves in their surroundings.

Yagaeche and Xhuaban carried satchels full of food and everything else they would need for their exploration of the place. They used rattlesnakes for reins to hold on to the jaguars as they crossed the mountains, controlling the speed and direction of their travel. As they crossed lands high and low, Yagaeche and Xhuaban learned the names of the hills, peaks, springs, rivers, caves, and everything else they saw.

At the start of their journey, the grandfather told his granddaughter, "From here, you go to the right while I trail along to the left until we meet up at the big river. From there, we'll walk the river banks together with the jaguars. When we return to the place where we started, the jaguars will turn to stone to commemorate our efforts. From that moment on, Granddaughter, you will be in charge of starting the rituals that our people [bëne waladza] will celebrate, honoring our jaguar-land at every cycle of life." That was the agreement that the first ancestors made, and that is what we continue to do to this day.

We know now that these same ancestors, the *bënegulaza*, became jaguars themselves, or at least became one with them, after they finished demarcating the Zapotec territory. Our ancestors tell us that Yagaeche rode the jaguar, tracing the limits of the territory from blue to blue, green to green, hiding in the corners of the world. The first ancestors had to cross these mountains, traverse their horizons, swim the rivers, and walk to the sea so that they could know and care for the lands that we talk about today, the ones that we traverse and live on.

My memory is not necessarily exact, but this story helps me enter into a conversation with many other narrators, writers, and cartographers, among others. The story interrupts the linear flow of time for all who listen. The story is also easily forgotten and can melt away whenever the people who tell the stories and their listeners lose interest.[3] There are as many versions of this account as there are narrators, and each telling ensures that the story does not die with the passing of time. I tell this story here as a way of showing another way to record a moment, mapping it before sharing my thoughts on another way of recording a moment. The comparison ensures that one way of mapping does not erase the other, but rather contributes to the creation of new cartographic narratives. To do this, it is imperative to analyze, if only briefly, the structure of oral traditions, appreciating how narratives, stories, songs, and poetry acquire their subversive content, which might contribute to new cartographic narratives.

Remembrances and Memories

The story that the elders tell is a history they know from memory. It is not an object that can be tucked away in a museum like any old artifact. It is an oral map that circulates by word of mouth, contrasting with textual maps that circulate from hand to hand, and eye to eye. The difference between oral and textual maps helps make sense of the sort of "participatory mapping with state goals" proposed by INEGI and the México Indígena project. What is the difference between what people in oral societies and people in textual societies do when they map? How has community life shaped and conditioned textual maps?

Our oral world represents a multiplicity of temporalities and memories that are flexible enough to fashion a collective narrative of community, a cartography of history, a map of the fabric of community. We know that oral communication, especially between friends and intimate acquaintances, tends to take liberties with grammar, playing with the multiple meanings of words when compared to the formal language used by state institutions and global markets. Both tendencies are often ignored in more formal settings, denying the tremendous presence of oral traditions that re-create and reinvent languages, even in societies dominated by texts and swamped by a sea of data.

In this regard, the Zapotec language (Didza Xhidza) is a map in which boundaries are rarely well defined, replaced instead with border zones and transitions. Language allows us to relate people and things, weaving a fabric from their relations. This space is made not only with narratives but also through perspectives and gestures that can pass from one person to another like decorations set out in a neighboring community for a fiesta. That is because an oral language, Didza Xhidza in our case, identifies new components of the world first, narrating a complex web of relationships in the territory that we circulate in, before attempting to represent the world. The Xhidza language creates maps from signs, investing them with meaning, deciding when and which coordinates to use, which elements to reveal, to create a social formation, a narrative, or identify a historical event—a community.

The circulation of knowledge by word of mouth has its peculiarities. A conversation between two people is the safest and most concise way for men and women in a community to communicate, to give their word, creating a level of security that is inversely related to the number of people who participate in the conversation. In this oral world, narrators never lose control over how their story spreads and circulates. They can define its audience along with the time and place of its telling. Control over the terrain of the oral is forever constrained. A popular story can be repeated or ignored. When repeated, it can be abbreviated or elaborated upon, modified and transmitted in multiple ways and languages according to the interests, tastes, and even fears of the one telling the story.

Orality contrasts with the textual. As the former commissioner of communal goods in Santa Cruz Yagavila put it in a 2001 interview, "Strictly speaking, written communication affords a far more effective level of anonymity than oral communication. Anonymous newsletters can be edited in secret, distributed clandestinely and without a signature, while oral communication—at least before telephones—is always an exchange between people who know each other. But from the vantage point of doing things secretly, the real disadvantage with writing is that once it is out of the hands of its author, its distribution and use can no longer be controlled."[4] The relative impunity of the spoken word derives from its low technological requirements. That is why private conversations are much harder to infiltrate, even for the most persistent police apparatus.

In oral cultures, anonymity is possible because forms and meanings are always fleeting, a quality that becomes an ideal vehicle for cultural resistance. Every update or modification is therefore specific to the moment, place, and public to which it refers. Narratives are recovered or interpreted according to the tastes of the audience, such that over time their origin is lost. It becomes impossible to recover the original once it has been modified by subsequent interpretations. In communities like ours that are organized by oral traditions, there is no orthodoxy or center since no primary text exists. Though this statement might sound heretical to some, it is what binds us together as an oral community. At the same time, orality attains a level of collective anonymity thanks to a constant process of adaptation, revision, foundation, or even omission.

Communality: Land and Territory

Before going too much further with this idea of oral cartography, it is worth spending some time on its source and strongest expression: community. The concept foregrounds questions of representation similar to those posed by cartography. The peoples of the Sierra Norte of Oaxaca, the Chinantecs, the Mixe, and the Zapotecs, have coined the term *comunalidad* (communality) to explain the complexity of our heterogeneous reality.[5] The term was created in the 1970s and 1980s when a wave of anthropologists arrived in the zone to study us. Much like maps in the present, *comunalidad* worked best when used to explain ourselves to outsiders, responding to concepts developed by academics and policy makers. *Comunalidad* was used to rebut the pervasive individualism imposed by dominant societies and their theories by forming a collective. Understood within communities, it articulated a "living knowledge that is practiced collectively, organizing the practice of living together and meeting collective needs."[6]

At the same time, the very idea of *comunalidad* carries a multiplicity of meanings that reflect its origins in multiple communities. As written down by one of its best-known advocates, Jaime Martínez Luna, *comunalidad* is a call to consciousness and reflection among all interested parties. As Martínez Luna writes,

> Collective life acquires meaning through work, transforming the environment through respectful relationships with both Mother Earth and her children. Through those relationships, they create and organize their people, building common bonds and responsibilities that allow them to nourish and realize the potential of the community.[7]

For another creator of the concept, Floriberto Díaz, a Mixe from Santa María Tlahuitepec, the use of the term is driven by an immediate sense of material urgency that demanded written elaboration. Díaz's writings on *comunalidad* present a deep analysis of basic Indigenous rights, education, and literacy, grounded in peoples' struggles to recover their dignity. Through his writings, Díaz used the concept to grasp the relationship between people and the Earth. He identified two primary ways: the first was through work done with respect to territory, and the second was through ceremonies and rites, both familial and communal, that establish in tangible, everyday forms the relationship between people and institutions in a unified fashion. This relationship is typically only grasped in a specific time and place as allowed by the norms and practices of coexistence interpreted by the assembly. Díaz identifies five elements that make up *comunalidad*: the Earth, as both Mother and territory; consensus reached through the deliberations of the assembly; voluntary services such as acting as a community authority; the regenerative power of collective labor; and the ceremonies and rites that express the character of a community.

> As territory, land contributes to our understanding of ourselves. In this territory we learn that community is a social relation. For that reason, Earth is life, a utopia that is created and invented daily. Every element of nature has a function in this totality, creating a concept of integrity that is present in every aspect of our lives. Earth is a totalizing space, a totality. It is impossible to separate the atmosphere from the soil or subsoil. In this regard, territory has a broad meaning. All beings organize the territories that they delimit and claim with regard to other inhabitants and other cosmic flows, mapping the movements and folds of the Earth itself.[8]

In this regard, communality is best understood as a means of self-representation in the face of the state and global markets.

Politicizing *comunalidad* has its time and place, establishing its importance through the everyday life that builds community. Despite its initial, outward-looking orientation, *comunalidad* has been used to mobilize communities' defense of our collective way of life. Their efforts restore the concept's term to its collective origins in communities, rejecting efforts by a narrow public or a specialist to capture and enclose its meaning. Their efforts recapture the term's importance as a form of self-representation that can be used to understand the behavior and practices of a marginal way of life. Community engagement with the term offers a reminder that it refers to an entire way of being that knows nothing of bodies. *Comunalidad* exists instead through words and discourse, through relationships that create and sustain a community rather than understand it. In this regard, *comunalidad* grounds a kind of "micropolitics" essential for "creating the small communities of affinity aligned emotionally as well as in thought."[9] Their efforts weave networks that make communities and forge alliances capable of opening up new political horizons that Silvia Rivera Cusicanqui contends are essential for surviving the current moment.

From this perspective, the common and dominant definition of territory is a synonym for appropriation. As commonly understood, territory involves subjecting oneself to a series of representations that, in turn, give birth to forms of behavior, investments, and questions imposed on the time and space of community. Territory bundles these symbolic and cultural elements by attributing a territorial identity to social groups, which functions as a form of symbolic control over the space they inhabit. At the same time, territory exists in relation to a lived space, perceived by the subjects who inhabit it, offering a resource for organizing the collective or communal. Territory therefore becomes intimately linked to the exercise of collective rights and the self-determination of our communities.

A territory is thus much more than a thing or an object. It is a process or dynamic; it is an act, an action, a relation, a recombinant movement, a rhythm, an iteration that one can repeat and control. In this regard, a community is always submerged within an immense movement, its originary territories continuously destroyed and violated. Our territory constitutes the space of communal life, understood as a kind of founding political ecology that gives space to the development of life in all its multiple expressions and forms. This communal space is the source of knowledge and understanding, of culture, identity, and norms of living together. The commons shapes the activities necessary for our collective subsistence, as well as being the source of the riches of the earth—natural resources—that factor into the economic production of the things that we consume as necessities of our current lives and that provide the basis for neoliberal capitalism.

The Fabric of Community

The semiotic relationship between textile, fabric, and text (*textil, tejido y texto*) helps us reflect on the webs of knowledge and exchange that we try to make when we weave things together through contact, collaboration, knowledge, experience, sources, production, and circulation, creating the fabric of community. That is the reason why (it is not by chance) the image of a web (*yëxhaj*) has such strong symbolic appeal as a unifying metaphor among people in the Rincón. The image is linked materially to nets and bags woven by people living along the Cajonos River in one part of the Rincón. The area has an abundance of maguey plants that people process to produce fiber (*ixtle*) to weave nets and bags used by people throughout the Rincón to carry their food when they go to work in the fields and forest. The shape of the bag changes with its cargo, expanding or contracting depending on the shape and weight of the load and its distribution. People in the Rincón make widespread use of the *ixtle* nets to explain community as a woven fabric. As the image of a net suggests, the elements it conjoins are not homogeneous, though they exist in the same plane, counterposed point by point. Their weave is infinite, expandable in any direction. There is no straight ahead or backward, much less a center. There are no fixed and mobile points, but rather a continual redistribution of elements. That is how people describe community, sketching out its geography and its territory.

Much like the weave of the *ixtle* bags, the fabric of community is based on qualities that allow it to be defined by multiple actions, as a web of relations bound by knots.[10] These knots are made up of two simultaneous elements that, at their most basic, are oriented either horizontally or vertically and invariably cross each other. Furthermore, these two elements do not have the same function. Some are fixed and others are mobile, such that the mobile elements pass over and under the fixed ones. This adds a second aspect to the weave. A third aspect involves the fact that the space furrowed by this action is limited or closed on at least one side. "The fabric can be infinite in length but not in width," Deleuze and Guattari write, "which is determined by the frame of the warp; the necessity of a back and forth motion implies a closed space."[11] Much like in a weaving, the back-and-forth motion is an essential aspect of community space, always changing its map, continuously territorializing, deterritorializing, and reterritorializing human actions.[12]

The weave of a net contrasts with the space drawn on maps. Without attempting to reconcile the differences between weaving and mapping, it is worth noting their multiple points of intersection and combination. Is it still possible to displace their opposition? Hands weave a striated or furrowed space, one hand performing the role of the warp, the other the weft, alternating between them. In contrast, GPS traces a space that is open in all directions, expandable in every sense, without ever losing its center.[13] For that reason, GPS "extends an invitation to all those who wish to actively integrate themselves into its textual network, reminding us that in the end, text, textile, and *tejer* (weaving) all share a common etymological root."[14]

Cartography should therefore be understood as a language through which discourse, intentions, and ideological positions are expressed. Based on that approach, to interpret maps it is necessary to understand that their strong ideological and cultural character introduces a level of subjectivity to what they show. Maps' claim to a faithful representation is always relative, since there are always multiple questions that arise once cartography's claim to represent reality is subjected to scrutiny. Every map redistributes blind alleys and paths, trails and roads, creating thresholds and enclosures that go from up to down and back again, reaching to the tops of mountains and the bottoms of canyons. When you get to the top of the mountain or the bottom, you arrive at that point only to see another mountain teasing you from the other side of the canyon. Walking around like this flips the senses. To reach the mountain in front of you, on the other side of the canyon, you have to first go to the bottom and climb the other side, only to face the same dilemma again. Cohabiting this shared space does not create a void or opposition between the subject of government and the world that is governed. Instead it folds them together, doubling back on themselves and giving cause for thought, organizing life collectively, into a common, into a community.

Digital Cartographies

To speak of participatory mapping is complicated from the outset, since it must interact with the digital and textural world, in particular with its visual strategies. Do maps change the world? Or are they just layers placed over the world that they describe? Where are the knots in this web of social relations?

Today we face a global process of territorial reorganization in which land is first measured and then alienated, remade according to the new wave of finance and accumulation through its documentation as property and resource extraction. Maps play an important role in this process, smoothing space through enclosing lands, transforming forests, water, and minerals into commodities. In recent years, those efforts in the Rincón have intensified to levels that have not been seen since the height of extractivism during the colonial period. They turn the commons inside out, transforming it into resources that the state controls as property and transforming knowledge of it into data. Their efforts seek to remake communities as a group of property owners organized by the state and markets rather than by their collective relationship to their surroundings. This new landscape looks disturbing to us, perplexing us with its complexity, inextricably linking disorder, ambiguity, and uncertainty. People can neither accept nor recognize this change, in part because the very ways this knowledge is encoded on maps is alien to them, estranged from communal spaces that include landscape and all that lies beyond territory in the narrative maps that tie people and landscape together in their oral worlds.[15]

The use of cartography goes beyond creating an unrecognizable landscape fashioned from community knowledge and everyday life. It also presents a new form of dispossession that works through digital means. Geographic Information Systems (GIS) recombine information, abstracting information from the conditions of its production and giving form to processes of knowledge production. The producers of information—labor—are thereby subsumed by those who arrange that information as the basis for what Franco "Bifo" Berardi calls "semio-capitalism." Digitizing information thereby becomes an essential site and logic for the production of value and accumulation of profit.[16] Communities like Yagavila have already been swept into this process. The digitalization of community knowledge integrates with new forms of knowledge that communities cannot overcome or escape. Communities have no choice but to engage these new forms of knowledge. They cannot reject maps. Instead they must find ways of appropriating cartographic tools for themselves, creating their own experts and technicians. At the same time, they must confront global power relations that use digitalization as a means of accumulating wealth and power.

Communal Cartographies (Oral Cartographies)

At first glance, the complexity of conceiving of oral forms of communitarian mapping is a matter of grasping the weave of social relations, inseparably bound to one another, that present a paradoxical relationship between the singular and the multiple. The events, actions, interactions, feedbacks, determinations, and chances that make up this fabric are what compose our world and create communities. The threads of this fabric are so bound up with one another that every effort to tie them off opens the possibility of new connections. These possible connections lead away from the origin of one weaving and into another, creating a series of displacements.

Maps do something similar. They do not present existing spaces; they create them in ways that invariably refer more to other maps than they do to the places they claim to show. Maps experiment with reality, continually producing something new. In contrast, the fabric of community woven through oral tradition is open to expansion in any direction, to alteration, to reduction—to continual modification. This kind of cartography is linked to the idea of memory as referring to people and objects, where media is nothing less than a space for identifying, guarding, and authenticating memories.

Many people are now convinced of the power of maps, using them to reaffirm their geography and history long denied or silenced by nation-states and to claim land rights. In past decades, maps have in fact helped numerous peoples and communities revitalize their identities and cultures, as well as their own social structures and politics. Their struggles take place in a political terrain already altered by maps, transforming understandings of territory, forms of resistance, and community itself. All the same, communities have used these maps to make important gains, winning financial compensation from companies and states; to demarcate their territories; and to resolve conflicts over land and natural resources.

These victories confirm the power of maps as much as they create changes within communities. Recognition of land rights, to take one example, often requires creating fixed and irreversible boundaries that correspond with hard lines on a map. These boundaries can easily become a source of conflict between communities, contrasting with Zapotec societies' historical approach to boundaries as fluid and negotiable, seeing them as transition zones or shared-use areas. For many Zapotec communities in Oaxaca, claiming and mapping their territories means assimilating them into the territorial model of the modern nation-state.

Maps allow peoples and communities to exist at the discursive margins relegated to them by colonization. It is now time to make new narratives. At the same time, this process facilitates translation from the oral traditions used by communities to produce and maintain geographical knowledge historically disregarded and ignored by better-known forms of knowledge circulated by dominant societies. This change happens through communities' appropriation of the codes and scientific standards associated with textual cartographies. At the same time, the risk persists that this new information will simply become blocks used to shore up the foundations of the structure created by existing power relations.

Nevertheless, peoples and communities have the possibility of combining oral and textual cartography, appropriating mapping for community purposes by way of presenting a different perspective. This perspective, in turn, suggests the possibility of finding other routes that move beyond the limits of cartographic representation and its claim to a single reality, conveying ideas, perspectives, and forms of inhabiting space generated by residents of communities.

The Shining Jaguar

A shining jaguar has already shown the potential for combining oral and textual cartographies in the Sierra Norte. In 2004, residents of La Selva in the Lower Rincón trapped and turned over a jaguar to the Attorney General for Environmental Protection (PROFEPA). The jaguar had killed a number of calves and sheep. In response, residents of La Selva decided to trap the jaguar rather than kill it because it glowed in the night, only to disappear when they tried to hunt it. Residents took this as a message from their ancestors. In 2005, they changed their minds about turning the jaguar over to the PROFEPA and decided to ask for the jaguar back so they could return it to the mountains it came from. In making their decision, residents of La Selva recalled that jaguars were their grandparents, the founders of their community and an important part of the community's natural and historical patrimony.

The shining jaguar was freed and returned to its people in the forest with a flourish of rituals and prayers, celebration, and flute music before the astounded eyes of environmental authorities and the handful of outsiders who had the privilege of witnessing the extraordinary event. After the ritual was complete, a helicopter ferried the jaguar to a location selected by the community for its release. In a matter of minutes, the shining jaguar of the light returned to the community and the mountains from where it came.

Returned to its home, the jaguar wore a specially fitted collar equipped with two locating devices. One tracked the jaguar by satellite, and the other transmitted a VHF signal that could be used to locate the jaguar and study its behavior. If the jaguar returned to the farmers' fields again, it would have to be captured and taken away permanently to a better destination.

Will jaguars adapt or abandon their place for new forms of resistance against societies of control? Will the zoo be replaced by an open animal park where jaguars move freely, bound only by natural obstacles and their movements recorded by a microchip? As I see it, the footprints of the jaguar leave possible paths that carry an endless number of stories. They are not open-ended events, however. Instead they are indications of the human-animal that we might become again.

Epilogue

"Language is a web of silences that captures sounds in each knot"—Xto Bako

The thoughts I presented here were forged across a range of contexts, times, and places, traversed at different speeds. Many voices contributed to this conversation—grandparents, relatives, friends inside and outside of the community, some of whom have already passed on and contribute here only through their written word. Writing, especially when it moves oral knowledge into the world of texts, tends to privatize information, binding it up in books and journals that are often out of reach of the communities where their content originated. I wrote this chapter by mixing elements, making a blend that borrows from many sources without intending to privatize their contents. Instead, I write to return knowledge from an overly privatized domain to the commons, which implies various challenges. One must recognize the contributions of many, remembering the people who contributed their ideas and texts. To live in common, through *comunalidad*, requires knowing how one is part of the many that make up a community. Writing should not steal from that effort. It should support it. This text is a creation of community.

NOTES

1. See Bryan and Wood 2015 and Wainwright 2012. See also the online repository of documents related to the controversy, Grossman, "Geographic Controversy over the Bowman Expeditions/México Indígena," bit.ly/2Rqa2cn.

2. Cruz 2010.

3. The story of a shining jaguar that attacked cattle and was captured alive is told in the documentary *Abuelo Jaguar* (Grandfather Jaguar), vimeo.com/147896261, made by Ojo de Agua Comunicación. The ancestors have told us that the light was a sign, and that we should not kill the jaguar. The story takes place in the small town of Cristo Rey La Selva, Laxchixila, in the Sierra Norte of Oaxaca.

4. Commissioner of Common Goods, Santa Cruz Yagavila; interview by the author, November 2, 2001.

5. Esteva 2016.

6. Velasco 2010, 187.

7. Díaz 2007, 10.

8. Ibid., 40–41.

9. *La Tinta*, 2016.

10. A knot is a point of intersection or connection, one that brings various elements together in the same place or territory. Its meaning has a certain similarity to that of "node," a concept that serves a similar purpose in understanding things like telecommunications and the internet. It conserves another meaning, though, one that shifts with our movements and uses of the term in different contexts. A node is a point on a curve that intersects itself. A node's meaning depends on the kind of network referred to. See Castells 1997.

11. Deleuze and Guattari 1997, 475.

12. It is important to note here the strong links between the works of Deleuze and Guattari and geography, particularly with regard to the concept of deterritorialization. Building on Deleuze and Guattari, territorialization, deterritorialization, and reterritorialization are always occurring concomitantly in a way fundamental to understanding human practices. Deleuze and Guattari 1997.

13. Illich 1998.

14. Sampedro Vizcaya 2018.

15. Walter Ong's work is relevant and useful in framing the relationships between oratory, art, print, and digital media. See Ong 2016.

16. Berardi 2007.

REFERENCES

Berardi, Franco (Bifo). 2007. *Generación post-alfa: Patologías e imaginarios en el semiocapitalismo*. Buenos Aires: Tinta Limón.

Bryan, Joe, and Denis Wood. 2015. *Weaponizing Maps: Indigenous Peoples and Counterinsurgency in the Americas*. New York: Guilford Press.

Castells, Manuel. 1997. *La era de la información: Economía, sociedad y cultura*. Vol. 1: *La sociedad red*. Madrid: Alianza Editorial.

Cruz, Melquiades. 2010. "A Living Space: The Relationship between Land and Property in the Community." *Political Geography* 29(8): 420–421.

Deleuze, Gilles, and Félix Guattari. 1997. *Mil mesetas: Capitalismo y esquizofrenia*. Valencia, Spain: Pre-Textos.

Díaz, Floriberto. 2007. *Escrito: Comunalidad, energía viva del pensamiento mixe = Ayuujktsënää'yën—ayuujkwënmää'ny—ayuujk mëkäjtën*. Mexico City: Universidad Nacional Autónoma de México.

Díaz González, Tonatiuh, and Fernando Guadarrama Olivera, production. 2010. *Abuelo jaguar*. Video. bit.ly/2G8PB1L.

Esteva, Gustavo. 2010. "La insurrección en curso." In *Crisis civilizadora y superación del capitalismo*, ed. Raúl Ornelas, 129–202. Mexico City: UNAM—Instituto de Investigaciones Económicas.

———. 2016. "Para sentipensar la comunidad." *Bajo el Volcán* 15(23): 171–186.

Grossman, Zoltán. N.d. "*Geographic Controversy over the Bowman Expeditions/México Indígena*." bit.ly/2Rqa2cn.

Illich, Ivan. 1998. "Un alegato en favor de la investigación de la cultura escrita lega." In *Cultura escrita y oralidad*, ed. Nancy Torrance and David R. Olson, 47–70. Barcelona: Gedisa.

Instituto Nacional de Estadística y Geografía (INEGI). N.d. "Cartografía Participativa." inegi.org.mx/app/geo2/cartpart.

Maldonado Alvarado, Benjamín. 2011. *Comunidad, comunalidad y colonialismo en Oaxaca: La nueva educación comunitaria y su contexto*. Oaxaca de Juárez, Oaxaca: Colegio Superior para la Educación Integral Intercultural de Oaxaca.

Martínez Luna, Jaime. 2010. *Eso que llaman comunalidad*. Colección diálogos, Pueblos originarios de Oaxaca. Oaxaca, Mexico: Culturas Populares, Consejo Nacional para la Cultura y las Artes (CONACULTA)/Secretaría de Cultura, Gobierno de Oaxaca/Fundación Alfredo Harp Helú Oaxaca, AC.

Ong, Walter J. 2016. *Oralidad y escritura: Tecnologías de la palabra*. Mexico City: Fondo de Cultura Económica.

Rendón Monzón, Juan José. 2003. *La comunalidad: Modo de vida en los pueblos indios*. Vol. 1. Mexico City: CONACULTA.

Sampedro Vizcaya, Benita. 2018. "Pocho Guimaraes, un artista guineano que trata que los tapices bailen." *Fronterad: Revista Digital*, August 3. bit.ly/35oYkHo.

La Tinta (Redacción), 2016. Interview with Silvia Rivera Cusicanqui: *Seguir mirando a Europa es apostar por un suicidio colectivo*. La Tinta (online magazine), bit.ly/2Gc7nRy.

Velasco, Andrés Miguel. 2010. "Epílogo." In *Eso que lllaman comunalidad*, ed. Jaime Martínez Luna, 185–188. Colección diálogos, Pueblos originarios de Oaxaca. Oaxaca, Mexico: Culturas Populares, Consejo Nacional para la Cultura y las Artes (CONACULTA)/Secretaría de Cultura, Gobierno de Oaxaca/Fundación Alfredo Harp Helú Oaxaca, AC.

Wainwright, Joel. 2012. *Geopiracy: Oaxaca, Militant Empiricism, and Geographical Thought.* New York: Palgrave Macmillan.

Wainwright, Joel, and Joe Bryan. 2009. "Cartography, Territory, Property: Postcolonial Reflections on Indigenous Counter-Mapping in Nicaragua and Belize." *Cultural Geographies* 16(2): 153–178.

2

Social Polygraphy

Territory as a Living Memorial to Culture and Nature

ÁLVARO CÉSAR VELASCO ÁLVAREZ

Introduction

In the 1970s, groups of peasants, Indigenous peoples, Afro-descendants, artists, students, and urban dwellers launched a social movement to organize around the struggle for land in Colombia. This early organizing helped create the conditions for the emergence of the contemporary Indigenous movement in Colombia, as it brought together the distinct peoples, languages, and forms of knowledge from the ancestral territories in the southwest region of the country. After twenty years of struggle, these organizing efforts culminated with the Colombian state's official recognition of the natural and cultural diversity of the nation during the Constituent Assembly of 1991. It was thanks to the dynamic social movements of earlier years that so many people of different backgrounds, professions, and trades ultimately showed their support for Indigenous communities fighting for their land and their rights.

In this chapter I discuss the concept of "social polygraphy," which emerged from this struggle for land that started in the 1970s. Social polygraphy was based on the assumption that participatory cartography can be a means of creating relationships of solidarity with marginalized communities. The Fundaminga Foundation spearheaded the development of social polygraphy as a tool that can be used to understand territory as a living fabric, woven together by memory, culture, and nature. As such, it became a way to coproduce the knowledge necessary to protect the diversity of life and defend the territories of Indigenous and Afro-descendant communities (Figure 02.01).

FIGURE 02.01. Participatory mapping workshop in Río Tefé, Yurutí del Vaupés Indigenous community, Colombian Amazon. Source: Fundaminga.

Territory as a Living Fabric

The communities involved in the land rights struggles of the 1970s and 1980s had a vision of territory as a living fabric of nature and culture. This vision was particularly evident during walks we took as part of several participatory mapping projects in the ancestral territory of the Gran Cumbal, an area in southern Colombia defined by the presence of a massive volcanic mountain known as Nudo de los Pastos (Knot of the Pastures). These walks through the Gran Cumbal prompted elders from the various communities to reflect on their memories of the area, since they see their own existence and history as inseparable from the land. The landscapes of the Gran Cumbal are marked by symbols engraved by ancestors in large stones that are found along sacred *páramos* (mountain plateaus), rivers, and lagoons. These places act as the anchors of traditional Indigenous knowledge, which is kept alive in legends and mythical stories reproduced through the memory of elders.

In particular, elders would often recall the mythical figure of Juan Chiles, whose spirit is known to rest in the volcano that is named after him. Stories about Juan Chiles were fascinating, full of anecdotes about his many brave feats in defense of his people. One day, during one of many conversations that set in motion the sharing of ancestral memory, an older man in our walking group slowly stated: "Juan Chiles became wise because he knew three things:

he knew how to unlock the strengths of the Quichua people, he knew the king's book, and he knew how to work with string." This statement resonated strongly with the rest of the group. Don Juan's ability to "work with string" refers to the ancestral custom of farming. Farming takes place within a network of invisible "strings" that connect the sun, the moon, and the stars with the seeds of the earth in order to spur the germination process. Plant growth is therefore dependent on these strings that run between heaven and earth, and the energy that flows to the plants from the celestial sphere varies with the time of year. With this understanding, we were able to see how "working with string" is truly an art that requires sensitivity, knowledge, and subtlety to balance the intimate relationship between people, nature, and the universe.

Moreover, Juan Chiles's familiarity with "the king's book" referred to a situation analogous to the very problem facing these communities today. Three centuries ago, Don Juan had confronted attacks on his territory, but through his intellect and his eloquence, he was able to defend the territory, culture, dignity, and identity of his people by wisely leveraging the "king's book" in support of his goals. Centuries later, the memory of Don Juan remained a relevant strategy for defending the rights of Indigenous peoples. The value of Don Juan's legacy is what it teaches about the importance of learning to use the law and other tools of power in the defense of human and nonhuman life in Indigenous lands.

The words of Don Juan helped us understand that the defense of communal rights must originate with the communities themselves. Community members need to recover and reaffirm their own memory, history, knowledge, and dignity, since these values are essential for sustaining and protecting their territories. This work of recovering memories in turn provides a compelling foundation for territorial rights claims from Indigenous communities. In the words of a memorable line from the 1981 meeting of Indigenous leaders in southwestern Colombia, this foundation is based on a greater basic human right that exists outside the law. As these leaders declared, "Our rights are born here; they are rooted in the land and in the community." Thus, the Indigenous right to exist and occupy land is and always has been maintained in the memory of the community and in the land itself, not in the legal mechanisms of the state.

Social Polygraphy as Ritual Conversation

As demonstrated by the anecdotes shared above, we understand social polygraphy as a ritual conversation intended to recover traditional knowledge that is found in natural features of the landscape, in the seeds of different species, and in traditional cultivation practices. It is a conversation that introduces a new way of "working with string" by drawing ancestral territorial maps with enlightened minds. Moreover, this ritual embraces the myths, celebrations, and meanings that Indigenous communities assign to their sacred places. Having this sort of conversation requires careful preparation with the traditional community leaders and elders who are recognized for their experience and knowledge. During the mapping workshops, traditional leaders will review maps, photographs, symbols, and figures depicting their territory, which in turn will prompt conversations about significant places and events. Inspired by these conversations, and referencing these symbols and other representations, they will gradually draw their ancestral map on a large, empty sheet of paper. These ancestral maps will then be continually discussed and reinterpreted, giving rise to further conversations that encourage new ways of interpreting the network of relationships represented on the maps.

Our workshops in the Gran Cumbal began with the elders, men, women, and children gathering around the table and reciting a short prayer in accordance with their traditions and beliefs. In these prayers, they would often meditate on the ways in which the three kingdoms of nature—mineral, animal, and vegetable—are related to the four elements: water, earth, wind, and sun. These relationships implicitly reference the periods of the agricultural or ritual year, which would prompt community members to draw a calendar. These calendars would then spark multiple stories related to social practices and knowledge. The *páramos*, rivers, waterfalls, and lagoons are considered sacred sites and are critical for the health of people, forests, flora, and fauna. The calendar of the agricultural year illustrates the relationship between all of these sites and the stars, illuminating the connections strung together in this intricate system. As this drawing activity is carried out, the network of relationships that determines weather patterns and the earth's relationship with different community practices and customs is made evident. Together, the conversations, the mapmaking, and the development of the calendars describe intricate ecological-cultural networks that inextricably link Indigenous communities to the land, forging an understanding of territory as a living tissue that sustains life and culture.

The ancestral relational maps produced in this process are essential to understanding the challenges of the present. In the workshops, the conversation would frequently turn to the subject of external interventions in the community's ancestral territory. People would discuss how the land had been occupied and fragmented by dominant economic, political, and legal powers over time. To visualize these unjust interventions in the community's territory, we would locate and symbolize each incident on a sheet of blank paper and then overlay this sheet on the ancestral map. The contrast between the two maps would quickly become evident, even though they were referencing the same geographical space.

Mapping the multiple interventions across the landscape clearly showed how the communities' traditional knowledge had been obscured by the dominance of monoculture and infrastructure projects—projects that reflect the intense exploitation and impoverishment of the land and the people. The ancestral map, on the other hand, showed fertile landscapes spreading across the territory, illustrating the reciprocal relationships woven between nature and culture. This map showed a living and dynamic territorial fabric built on traditional knowledge and memory.

Social Polygraphy and Critical Dialogue

Social polygraphy can also be thought of as critical dialogue that serves to develop both grounded theory as well as modes of radical action. The ancestral relational maps, with their unique calendars and symbols, as well as the drawings that emerged from these conversations, revealed opportunities for resistance and strategies for the revival of cultural identity. The recovery of ancestral knowledge and cultural practices also offers a way to reclaim the meaning of Indigenous languages. This reclaiming then transforms the relationships that community members have with themselves, with nature, and with other people. The process of cultural exploration that social polygraphy fosters thus takes on a complex, aesthetic-cognitive form, ultimately expressing itself as a desire to re-create culture, territoriality, and autonomy.

The community mapping of the Yucuna Amerú community on the Caquetá River exemplifies this kind of social polygraphy. The mapping process was facilitated by Rodolfo Álvarez of Fundaminga during a project that emerged from the work of the Consolidation of the Amazon Region (COAMA) and the Gaia Amazonas Foundation, a Colombian NGO, in 1998.[1] The "relational map" that the community produced during this workshop shows the network of organic and inorganic elements that are contemporary expressions of their ancestral culture. The networks represented in the map further illustrate the way in which various ancestral spatial phenomena now share and organize space with new things and new social practices. For example, the map depicts a chapel, a school, a community center, a soccer

FIGURE 02.02. Relational network map from the Yucuna Amerú community on the Caquetá River, Colombia. Source: Fundaminga.

field, and solar panels—all modern elements of the landscape—located on the banks of an ancestral river (with its particular large rocks and currents symbolized) that is sacred to the Amerú community (Figure 02.02). Together, these distinct elements form a new spatial pattern in which traditional sacred spaces intermingle with expressions of modernity. This pattern, perhaps unsurprisingly, has become typical of many present-day Amazonian Indigenous settlements. By revealing these networks and new relationships, the map serves to prompt dialogue and foster a better understanding of contemporary community life.

When ancestral maps and traditional calendars are connected, illustrating the space-time relationships that define the cyclical dynamics of Indigenous community life and cultural reproduction, the meanings and understandings that emerge from social polygraphy are most significant. For example, the ecological and cultural calendar-map of the Yurutí del Vaupés Indigenous community in the Colombian Amazon illustrates how the community understands, feels, and lives its territory through daily exchanges with nature and with the universe. Prepared during a three-day workshop with the assistance of Juan Carlos Peña Márquez of Fundaminga, the calendar-map takes the form of a multicolored, polygraphic, and polyphonic mandala (Figure 02.03).

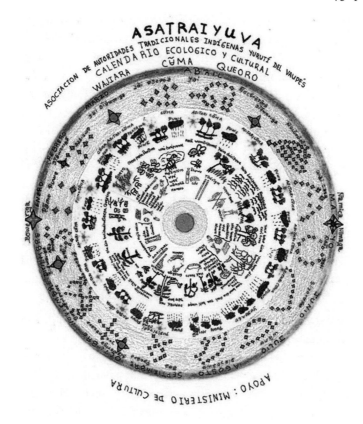

FIGURE 02.03. Calendar-map from the Yurutí del Vaupés Indigenous community in the Colombian Amazon. Source: Fundaminga.

In the Yurutí calendar, the stars relate directly to daily life. They are tied to the everyday practices of hunting, fishing, farming, and caregiving, and they thus indicate which rituals correspond to which time of year. This bold, colorful representation successfully weaves together the ancestral map and the traditional calendar. In so doing, it rekindles the profound significance of Indigenous myths and ritual ceremonies while also reasserting the value and meaning of traditional wisdom, rituals, and beliefs. Mapping projects such as this may strengthen the processes of self-organization, territorial struggle, and cultural survival of Indigenous peoples. For those of us involved in the work of social polygraphy, the process has been immensely insightful and has strengthened our resolve to press onward in the work of defending Indigenous territory.

The third and final example of the role of memory in the struggle for territoriality comes from a social polygraphy workshop conducted in the community of Chesive, located on the Paraná River in the Colombian Amazon. The workshop was initiated by a group of women community leaders, known as the *makacsis*, who had participated in the broader dialogue about territory and culture that took place among the Indigenous communities living in the Pira Paraná River basin. The methodology for this workshop was developed by Fundaminga, drawing on our previous experience in Amazonian communities, while the workshops themselves were overseen by two traditional leaders from the community, Ricardo Marín and Robertico Marín. Two representatives from Gaia Amazonas, a nonprofit organization that has supported communities in their territorial claims in the Pira Paraná River basin, were also in attendance.

On the advice of Ricardo Marín and Robertico Marín, in the first part of the workshop, participants discussed the story of Juan Chiles and the *makacsis*'s experience with the territorial rights struggle. Exploring this context helped set the stage for the development of an ancestral calendar-map. As workshop participants drew the traditional calendar to show the various significant moments they had lived and were living, imagery and symbols inspired by these moments were also added to the calendar-map (Figure 02.04). Over the course of this conversation, the workshop participants could viscerally experience the connections between memory, ancestral wisdom, time, and territory as they wove together a complex living image of their contemporary territory.

This activity had great emotional impact on both the participants and the guests. Once complete, the ancestral map represented the traditional relationship between people and their ancestors. The residents of Chesive see life as a gift that is shared with the ancestors, who still inhabit the water, the earth, the air, and all other ecosystems where both human and nonhuman ancestors reside. The workshop participants expressed excitement and joy while they were weaving together the map of the territory that sustains their traditions, but the mood changed to one of deep sadness when the map of the contemporary state of the community was overlaid on the ancestral map. The present-day map revealed a monotonous yet aggressive landscape of enclosures and monoculture, reflecting, among other harms, the expropriation of the community's territory, the erasure of their culture, and the destruction of traditional plant species. However, the mood once again shifted from sadness to hope when the workshop participants overlaid an imaginary map of their future on top of the ancestral map. As they talked about the future, people could appreciate how this process, led by the *makacsis*, had allowed them to

FIGURE 02.04. Traditional calendar-map of Indigenous communities of the Pira Paraná River, Colombia. Source: Fundaminga.

plant seeds of resurgence and begin to reaffirm their cultural heritage. These workshops ultimately revealed the potential of social polygraphy as a launching point for critical dialogue in support of territorial rights.

Conclusion

Our experiences with social polygraphy have shown us that participatory mapping must abandon the linear conception of time if it is to become a methodology that challenges dominant conceptions of life and the world. By representing time as a cyclical phenomenon, we can begin to transcend the confines of the dominant Western paradigms of time and space. For us at the Fundaminga Foundation, taking part in these processes of resurgence and re-creation of ancestral territories and cultures has been an indelible learning experience. Social polygraphy has emerged as a productive set of tools to weave together the fabric of culture, time, and space, and in so doing, it fosters emancipatory research processes and collective action to protect cultural and natural diversity. Through social polygraphy, and with a new understanding of nonlinear time, we are able to gain a glimpse of territories from the past that have been re-created on the basis of a deep-seated collective memory that recalls the very origins of human history in Colombia. The transformational power of this process is indispensable to confronting the inevitable dilemma that faces us all: the need to change in order to survive.

NOTE

1. COAMA would later earn some noteworthy acclaim for its participation in this work, receiving the Right Livelihood Award (sometimes called the "alternative Nobel Prize") from the Swedish Parliament in 1999; see rightlivelihoodaward.org/laureates/consolidation-of-the-amazon-region-coama.

3

Emulating Kuyujani

Boundary Making in the Caura River Basin, Venezuela

NALÚA ROSA SILVA MONTERREY

For Marcus Colchester

Introduction

In 1994, the Electrificación del Caroní (Caroní Electricity Company; EDELCA), a parastatal company in charge of hydroelectric development in the Guayana region of Venezuela, announced a plan to transfer water from the Caura River to the Paragua River in the Caroní River basin. The project would entail submerging a large section of the Caura River basin while leaving about 400 kilometers of the Caura River dry, significantly impacting one of the last pristine river basins in the world. The prospect of such a large-scale project led to widespread alarm in the region, not only because of the potential ecological impact but also because of the social consequences for the Ye'kwana and Sanema Indigenous populations in the area. The Ye'kwana and Sanema peoples stood to lose their settlements, hunting areas, places where they pursue shifting cultivation, sacred sites, and trails as a result of these interventions. The project would also produce great amounts of stagnant water, which would become ideal breeding grounds for mosquitoes, posing a serious public health threat in an area already plagued by malaria.

The Indigenous communities in the area and their allies spoke out against EDELCA's plans, calling attention to the ecological and social costs associated with this development. They were eventually able to stop the project, but the case alerted Indigenous communities in the area to the potential of hydroelectric development to destroy their lands. The proposed EDELCA project thus prompted Indigenous communities in the Caura River region to look for means to guarantee their futures, including exploring ways to ensure that they would have a decisive say on any future development projects that would impact the area. In particular, this crisis demonstrated to the Ye'kwana and other Indigenous groups in Venezuela that territorial recognition was of paramount importance to secure not only their rights to resources but also their right to make legally binding determinations to protect their territories.

Of the 45,336 km² that constitute the Caura River basin, approximately 38,000 km² are claimed and occupied by Indigenous groups as ancestral lands. To document their territory and pursue a successful territorial claim, the Indigenous communities in the area looked to spatial technologies and mapping strategies. I had already been working with Indigenous communities in this area for ten years, developing a relationship of mutual trust between the leaders of the Indigenous organizations and myself. My research in the area, along with my activism in support of the rights of Indigenous peoples on a national level, served as the foundation for the mapping project I describe in this chapter.

The methodology was inspired by the Kari'ña tribe of Suriname and Guyana, who had used the strategy of *auto-demarcación* (self-demarcation) of their territories when they faced similar threats to their land. The Kari'ña, in turn, connected me with the Forest Peoples Programme (FPP), which works in Guyana to help facilitate exchanges between groups advocating for Indigenous rights. The director of the FPP, Marcus Colchester, had previously worked in the Caura River basin with the Sanema and thus felt personally committed to supporting the movement for the recognition of their rights. I served as facilitator between the FPP and the Indigenous communities in the Caura River basin, trying to guide the work within a multicultural context that included specialists in cartography, FPP representatives, and Indigenous Ye'kwana community members.

These initial conversations led to a mapping approach that included data collection in the field; map design in the information lab at the Centro de Investigaciones Antropológicas de la Universidad de Guayana (Center for Anthropological Research at the University of Guayana), where I work; technical verification of information included on the maps; and finally, presentation of the map to the Indigenous authorities of the Ye'kwana-Sanema organization. The following sections describe the partnership and the project in more detail. I discuss the project's origin, the processes used to carry out capacity building and mapping, and the ways in which the project facilitated experiences of revitalizing knowledge and history. I also reflect on the anthropological lessons we learned about landscape as a social construct, in which different spatial elements serve as a repository of memory for Indigenous groups. Although I don't discuss the work following the project, including the Ye'kwana-Sanema claim for territorial recognition, which is still pending with the national government, the mapping project served to illuminate the profound importance of the relationship to land for Indigenous peoples' survival. The Ye'kwana-Sanema see land not only as a source of sustenance but also as a historical and cultural anchor that ties their identity to space.

Project Beginnings

The Ye'kwana, a group of Carib linguistic affiliation, are the largest Indigenous group in the Caura River basin. The Sanema, a subgroup of the Yanomami (of independent linguistic affiliation), are less populous and have lived in the basin for less time; their arrival dates only to the late nineteenth and early twentieth centuries (Colchester 1982; Coppens 1981; Silva M. 1996, 100–103). Members of the Hoti tribe, which is an Indigenous group of hunters, gatherers, and nascent farmers of Saliva linguistic affiliation, also occasionally live in small communities throughout the basin (Silva M. 2006). The Sanema and the Ye'kwana were mostly hostile to one another until the 1950s, when the Ye'kwana conquered the Sanema. From then on, the Sanema remained in a state of "submission" to the Ye'kwana, depending on their support while still living in their own autonomous villages. However, at the end of the 1990s, the Tujuumoto organization moved to terminate this inequitable relationship. Tujuumoto was initially established as a trading cooperative in the community of Santa María de Erebato. However, the organization gradually assumed additional functions, eventually giving rise to the interethnic Organización Interétnica e Intercomunitaria Kuyujani, which promotes inclusive and respective relations with the Sanema (Colchester, Silva M., and Tomedes 2004, 53).

A joint Ye'kwana and Sanema Indigenous organization called Kuyujani now represents the numerous communities in the Caura River basin. As part of their strategy for legal recognition in 1996, the Kuyujani Organization encouraged both internal and external stakeholder meetings: internally, they organized intercommunity and interethnic meetings in the basin, and externally, they arranged meetings with other social movements, state and national Indigenous organizations, and state institutions and political representatives responsible for environmental and Indigenous issues. One of the main concerns in the late 1990s was to improve understanding of the extent of territorial occupation and develop ways to justify why these lands were fundamental to the life of the Indigenous communities in the area. It wasn't sufficient to simply identify boundaries: it was also necessary to demonstrate how the Indigenous people used and ascribed value to their lands.

Following this initial dialogue, and building on the premise that the project should be of high technical quality, the Kuyujani Organization, in consultation with the Consejo de Ancianos de la Organización y de la Asamblea General Interétnica (Council of Ancestors of the Organization and of the Interethnic General Assembly), decided to spearhead a process of self-demarcation. The demarcation process was supported by institutions familiar to these communities, including the Center for Anthropological Research at the Universidad Nacional Experimental de Guayana (UNEG; National Experimental University of Guayana), the FPP, the Local Earth Observation (LEO), and the Centro de Investigaciones Antropológicas de Guayana (CIAG; Center for Anthropological Research of Guayana). The work received official permission from the Dirección de Asuntos Indígenas (DAI; Directorate of Indigenous Affairs) of the Ministry of Education (which was the national institution in charge of Indigenous policies at the time). The World Rainforest Movement (WRM) and FPP were the main sources of financial support.

Given the great expanse of the area to be mapped, as well as the logistical complexity of conducting such a mapping project and maintaining communication with all affected groups, the only possible way to complete the work was through direct collaboration with the Indigenous groups. Indigenous co-researchers nominated by their communities would be trained to participate in the mapping project, taking into consideration their literacy and education levels, responsibility, maturity, and commitment to the community. A team of twelve young people was formed, eight of whom were Ye'kwana and four, Sanema. The uneven numbers are due to the fact that, as mentioned before, this space was historically Ye'kwana territory before the Sanema arrived. The team of young Indigenous cartographers would be responsible for collecting field data, accompanied by three *sabios* ("sages"; holders of traditional knowledge)—two Ye'kwana and one Sanema—who would help them validate the data with members of the village.

In initial community assemblies over the course of a year and a half, community members discussed with the group which sites should be included on the map in order to demonstrate Indigenous occupation of the territory, as well as what symbology should be used. The team would use Global Positioning System (GPS) technology to georeference the exact locations of settlements, hunting areas, fishing and farming areas, sacred and historical sites, old abandoned towns, small agricultural plots, trails, creeks, rivers, rapids, mountains, and any other element of the landscape that these populations considered relevant to their culture and way of life. Ultimately, GPS points were taken at practically every location in the area.

The role of each institution involved was clearly established, which was key to ensuring productive development of the project. The Kuyujani Organization took on the executive leadership role with ultimate responsibility and authority over the project. UNEG provided academic endorsement and participated in the formation of the Indigenous teams that carried out the fieldwork and administered the project resources, performed data entry and downloads, and produced maps. For its part, the FPP participated in the capacity-building sessions, drawing on their international experience in similar projects as well as their vast knowledge of the Sanema culture. FPP also acted as a bridge between entities by leading the development of reports for the WRM.

The work formally began in November 1997 during a general assembly of communities in the area. During this assembly, the entire project scope was reviewed once again, including the organizational framework, the mapping resources, the participating staff, the general project logistics, and the content of capacity-building materials. We then moved on to the procedural phase of the mapping work as well as a review of the financial and legal aspects of the project. We discussed the anticipated results; the desired presentation of the final report to donors, partner institutions, and the communities; and the future of the Indigenous teams upon completion of the project. The self-demarcation efforts would be concluded with a proposal for future steps that should be followed to achieve legal recognition and the development of a plan for self-demarcated territorial management.

Looking at this project retrospectively, it is regrettable that this positive effort has not yet led to actual territorial recognition: despite having given its approval to the project, the government failed to grant collective titles to the Ye'kwana-Sanema before President Chávez took the position that large-scale demarcations such as this represented a threat to national sovereignty (Chávez 2005).

Capacity Building

The capacity-building process, including the training in map literacy, GPS usage, data entry, symbol usage, contour line drawing, place designation, and indication of rivers and creeks, served to refine the methodology used in the project. We also wanted to make sure the mapping team was well organized. One team member took GPS coordinates while another marked the coordinates on a spreadsheet. Later, the points were marked on sketches and maps. During the actual data collection process, before sending any information to the CIAG lab, the cartographers took a first pass at verifying their own data, which would then be reviewed again before being digitized.

During the training period, we discussed the complex issue of orthography.

A group of teachers was appointed who would reconcile different spellings and ensure the text was accurate in both the Ye'kwana and Sanema languages. Often during the capacity-building sessions, stories would be told about the origin of the place-names. One such example is the name Nichare. The story goes that many years ago, there was a group called Winkiare (Wonkiare) that led a massacre against the Ye'kwana on a site that today is called Nichare. The original Winkiare or Wonkiare was transformed into either Minchiare or Nichare, and group members use both terms today to refer to the same site.

The capacity-building sessions took place in Salto Para, a significant location that forms a natural border in the basin, and were carried out simultaneously in Ye'kwana, Sanema, Spanish, and English. The non-Indigenous technical field team was made up of an anthropologist who specializes in Sanema culture (Colchester), an anthropologist who specializes in Ye'kwana culture (myself), and a geographer with experience in Indigenous self-demarcation projects. The Indigenous team included a general coordinator who represented the Kuyujani Organization, a technical field coordinator, a group of elder advisers from the different communities, three *sabios* who traveled with the Indigenous cartographers, and the young people who had been trained to collect data. During the trips, which were primarily by river, each team member (except for the *sabios*) would be responsible for additional functions such as rowing, navigating, fishing, or preparing food.

The Ye'kwana are incredible navigators. Their knowledge of astronomy and of constellations that mark the seasons was of fundamental importance for the project. GPS technology was only an extra tool that allowed them to locate in precise detail what they already knew from navigating with traditional means. Team members would say, in jest, that some of the elders had GPS "in their heads." The technical training later proved useful in other projects developed in the river basin, such as the Plan de Manejo (Area Management Plan) developed by the communities as well as the boundary marking of reserve areas (*somajö*). GPS technology allowed these spaces to be represented on a map that everyone could see rather than landmarks on the physical terrain.

Determining what to include and what not to include on the map was a task that the *sabios* in each group would decide in accordance with their historical knowledge. The younger members of the groups would always ask their elders and the *sabios* for the correct place-names. On one occasion, one youth realized that near the northern limit of the territory, close to Kumaaka Creek, there was another small creek that didn't yet have a name. The Indigenous cartographers proposed naming the creek after me, and they consulted the *sabios* who accompanied them about this idea. The *sabios* liked the proposal, consulted with the other elders, and approved the naming later during a group assembly. In finalizing the map, a small creek was baptized with the name Nadua (which is my name in Ye'kwana orthography) in my honor and in memory of the self-demarcation project. This reveals a little about the way in which new place-names are generated in the community—in this case, the naming was inspired by a significant event and my unique presence as the sole woman technician on the team.

On one of the training days, we received a visit from the Grand Chief of the Ye'kwana, Gaetano Pérez, who told the workshop participants,

> We have a right to this land. Some may say that we possess a lot of land . . . that this is a big piece of land. But we need this land. Our medicines are here, our history is here, we have knowledge of how to care for this land, and for those reasons we should fight for it.
>
> Years ago, we were many: Piaroa, Pemón, Panare, and others. But now we Indigenous peoples are few; there are few of us left. Because of this, we have to be united. I have contacts with other Indigenous peoples who can fight with us and help us claim the land. (Chief Pérez addresses Chief Mariano, of the Sanema:) Here in this area there used to be chiefs who would say, "Let's get rid of the Sanema, we want to see them gone." I say the opposite; we live here with the Sanema, we work together, we fight together like brothers and like friends. Let's, then, move forward as brothers and as friends. Let's fight for this land, Ye'kwana and Sanema together. I already have eight years fighting for this, and now is the moment, make sure that you all continue to learn [your technical skills]. This is everything . . .

Over the course of five weeks, the Indigenous people learned just as much about their own culture from the elders as they learned and practiced technical mapping skills. For me as an anthropologist, this time was extremely rich. It facilitated in situ observance of many instances of cultural conceptions of space, which are described in the following section.[1]

From Geographical Landscapes to Cultural Landscapes

Early on in the project we traveled to the upper part of Salto Para, to the abandoned facilities from a hydroelectric dam that had been built in the area in the 1970s. These abandoned structures now serve as spaces where the Indigenous communities carry out diverse activities and events, including the training workshops for the mapping project.

The Caura River extends 730 kilometers from its source to where it meets the Orinoco River (Peña M. 1996, 29). Our trips on the river were launched from its northern end, near the Maripa village. From there, we would travel against the current, spending up to two weeks to reach the training site if we only traveled during the day with an outboard-motor-powered vessel and with heavy passenger and cargo weight.

The biggest obstacle in navigating the Caura is the Salto Para, a large waterfall that reaches 60 meters in height and is more than 2 kilometers wide. When you arrive at the lower end of the waterfall, you must leave your boat on a beach called El Playón. To access the upper part of the Salto Para, you have to climb the mountain along an old road on which all kinds of merchandise are transported by hand, since there is no other way to do it. This means that the Salto Para is not only a natural wonder but that it also forms a physical border between what is accessible and what is clearly Indigenous. It is the door to another world and another culture.

During the trip from Maripa to Salto Para, you pass through a long stretch of mestizo communities before arriving in the Ye'kwana community of Boca de Nichare. One of the main challenges during the self-demarcation process was deciding precisely where the northern border would be located. Since the original limits of the ancestral territory ranged from Kumaaka-Mäkädädi Creek to the head of the Aro River, some felt this relatively young community should not be included in the territorial claim. For their part, however, the inhabitants of Boca de Nichare argued that they were just as much a part of the Ye'kwana heritage and that they deserved to be included in the demarcation. They were eventually granted this recognition.

The trip from Boca de Nichare to Salto Para follows a route where many of the geographical features are not named. From "stream 5000" onward, however, the streams begin to be named, and as you approach what is considered Indigenous territory, the toponyms and their associated origin stories begin to proliferate. Streams, rocks, and hills all have their own names associated with myths and stories. As you get to the center of the Ye'kwana territory, there is practically not a single rock, mountain, or stream without a name and a history.

As you approach El Playón at the lower end of Salto Para, you encounter many sacred sites that should not be looked upon directly, such as the rock where the mythic hero Kuyujani's sister experienced her first menstrual period. By staring at the rock, the onlooker will experience an endless hunger that will never be satisfied and that will cause gradual and unending weight loss—a disappearance of sorts. And so it goes in this way, with many other rocks, mountains, and other natural features linked to histories of Kuyujani or other mythical figures. Additionally, there are origin stories and creation myths that explain natural wonders, such as the following account detailing the origin of Salto Para:

> At the head of the river (Ijudunña) near the Wanadi Enadinña, there once lived a snail. This snail bathed every day in a small pool where villagers retrieved water. The villagers were annoyed whenever they saw the snail in the water, because it made the water dirty and undesirable. So the villagers agreed that it was best to get rid of the snail— they decided they didn't want it there any longer. But the snail had friends that wanted him to stay where he was because of the beautiful music he produced. So as he left his small pool, the friends went running ahead of the snail in order to cut off his path as he went toward Kawadi Matasodi (the Erebato current). This created the Salto Para, so the snail couldn't leave the waters where his friends wanted him to stay. Effectively, when the snail finally arrived at the Salto, he saw that he could not pass and decided to turn around. But instead of following the way he had come by the Erebato, he left along the Caura. When he arrived at the headwaters, since the passage was very narrow, he started spreading slime from the Aikeni point. From there, he went along the Auaris and never again returned. This is how the Salto Para came to be.

Another story explains why the soil near the Salto Para is yellow: A man named Yaijudumö once moved from the river's headwaters to the area by the Salto. His sister traveled with him, and upon arrival she refused to eat because she did not like the food. To make his sister eat, Yaijudumö prepared an arepa with soil from Ijuduña (the homeland by the river's headwaters) and left it out for his sister, since she only liked the food of her native land. It is because of this that the soil near the Salto is the same as the soil around the river's headwaters.

Ultimately, as I have argued in other work (Silva Monterrey 2010, 217–219), places are not merely geographic reference points but also constitute a cultural landscape—that is to say, a geographic space with social significance. In this sense, the concentration of toponyms is a clear indicator of symbolic appropriation, which results in landscapes becoming readable texts, as Santos-Granero (2002, 47) argues. History is written through origin myths, the sagas of the creators, and sacred experiences of the ancestors. According to the stories of the Ye'kwana, the mythical hero Kuyujani demarcated Ye'kwana territory during a trip he made with his sister (Silva Monterrey 2010, 240–243). The Sanema concur that this trip included their ancestors as well, and the Ye'kwana voice no disagreement with this belief.

Other Lessons from the Training Period

All of these experiences—the actual trip to the training site at Salto Para as well as the time spent living with the cartographers, elders, and others—together facilitated incredible coproduction of knowledge. During the workshop, a parallel learning process took place as "lessons" on Indigenous cultural history were given after we had finished formal instruction, when we would sit and talk with one another and contemplate the landscape. On one occasion, sitting on the bank of the river, we saw an isolated stone shining iridescently underwater. Community members explained that indeed this was not a stone, but rather it was the eye of the *dueño* ("owner" or "master") of this part of the river, who was watching us. They told us not to make eye contact and, more importantly, not to touch the stone, because if someone touches this type of stone, they can fall gravely ill.

Community members also told us about the necessary precautions to take while crossing through rapids during our boat trips, as each rapid also has a *dueño*. *Dueños* appear at first glance to simply be isolated luminous stones or other unassuming natural features. Normal people cannot see the *dueños*, but shamans are able to see them, despite their disguise. The shamans told us that there were many smaller iridescent stones that are actually children playing, but they are invisible to all people except shamans.

On one occasion, they pointed out that within the Salto Para lies the great city of Wiyu (the giant serpent that inhabits the rivers, according to myths), including an airport, restaurants, and highways. As they were telling the story, the shamans indicated where in the landscape each feature was located. Several adult men, as well as some young men with the group, tried to specifically locate each of the sites mentioned in the tale. For them, it was a matter of identifying real places rather than discussing myths.

Sometimes during the fieldwork, we would stop the boat for a while if a rainbow appeared in the middle of the river. Navigation was prohibited until the rainbow disappeared, as rainbows form the crown of Wiyu (the feathered serpent), and if you cross through the crown, it will make you sick. The area in front of the Salto has many Wiyu, which is the reason people abstain from entering the water there. Wiyu are upset by people bathing, playing, or making any kind of disrupting noise near them. For this reason, right in front of the Salto, where the great city lies, fishing, bathing, and all other activities in the water are entirely prohibited.

On another occasion, navigating up to Dedejuimö Creek, some of the youth carefully moved the boat to the side of a series of submerged rocks that were aligned in a row. For the Ye'kwana, aligned rocks are considered an indication of the bridge of the Mawaris, other beings that are found in nature (see Silva Monterrey 1997, 71; and 2010, 224). Anyone who touches these rocks or disrupts the alignment of the bridge will immediately fall ill. When we came across such a rock alignment, I asked if this Mawaris bridge was going to be included on the map or if they wanted to take GPS coordinates to mark the spot, but no one responded.

On another occasion, someone in the group mentioned that a hidden paradise was supposed to be located nearby, with delicious fruits and a large garden of banana and plantain trees. As the site in question was relatively close to the Salto Para, the group decided to go to this place so that we could mark the location with GPS and include it on the map.

For the Ye'kwana, the story of this hidden paradise was a *watunna*, that is to say, a narrative of successive stories and myths that blend together and become indistinguishable, as I have argued in other works (Silva Monterrey 2010, 36–38). So with this understanding, and following nothing but the clues left in the *watunna* about the garden's location, a group of cartographers, a *sabio*, and I searched for this paradise in the dense jungle for more than seven hours. Every so often, the Indigenous leaders thought we were getting closer to the site based on wayfinding markers mentioned in the story. But for as much as we searched, we never found the hidden paradise. After making several circles around the location where it was assumed the garden should be, we had to accept that the site would not be found. The team was disappointed after having gotten so close to where the paradise should have been. Yet they were all assured it was there—so close yet so far.

Surely we know that Indigenous narratives such as the *watunna* are stories that correspond to historical events as much as they do to myths, but traveling through the circular timeline of a myth is something that I had never experienced before. In this case, the myth was more contemporary: the place existed, but it was simply not visible to those of us who were not shamans. It was something so real that anyone in the world should have been able to see it. I am not talking about the distinction between myth and story—this is something different—rather, I am talking about how the Indigenous people truly believed that this paradise was accessible and tangible to them.

This certainty about the reality of myths is not rare. In the natural wonders of the area, the Ye'kwana distinguish between different types of mountains: those called *jüdü* and those called *ewütü*. The latter are mountains that are occupied by the mythical figure that they reference. For example, near the Salto Para, there is a small mountain called Kusawedu Ewütü, which is where, according to the Ye'kwana, the sister of Kuyujani lives. The sanctity tied to these spaces is what keeps people from looking for or visiting Kuyujani's sister. Even without proof of her occupation of this space, they are convinced beyond the shadow of a doubt that she can be found there.

These events made it clear that the process of demarcation was not only a process of marking points on a map but also a process of reviving Indigenous culture, particularly the *watunna*. The strengthening and celebration of culture through experiences such as these is an intangible value of Indigenous cartography and self-demarcation.

Beyond Self-Demarcation

After one year of intense fieldwork and lab work, the self-demarcation process culminated in the production of a map that was firmly and strongly validated by the Ye'kwana-Sanema communities (Figures 03.01a and 03.01b). In 1998, the Kuyujani Organization presented the map, along with a request for land title, to the office of the attorney general. Later on, in light of the new constitution, they registered the map in the Servicio Autónomo de Propiedad Intelectual (SAPI; Venezuelan Office of Intellectual Property) as the collective property of the Ye'kwana and Sanema tribes of the Caura River basin. This event was of national significance.

The Indigenous mapping experience in the Caura River basin inspired both the 1999 Venezuelan constitution (RBV 2000) and the development of the Law of Demarcation of Indigenous Habitats of Venezuela (RBV 2001). Moreover, in 2002, it became the first case since these legislative changes were made to be brought before the National Commission of Demarcation. In October 2006, the Ye'kwana case was finally approved and celebrated with applause. The government then ordered the development of a title document, which ended up in a notary book in Caracas where it still lies, awaiting the president's signature. The reasons why the land title was never officially granted to the Indigenous peoples of the Caura River basin remain unexplained to this day. The process appears to be paralyzed.

Toward the end of 2006, a mining project began in the Caura region. At the beginning, the Ye'kwana and the Sanema were strongly opposed to mining in the area, but today, mining has become common in both communities. As a result, ecological damage and public health hazards have also become more prevalent. The elders and a fairly large group of older men still resist the practice, but, alas, they remain in the minority. Yet despite these setbacks, the Kuyujani Organization has not ceased its work. The organization took the initiative to come up with land development guidelines so they will be prepared for the day when their territorial rights are finally and officially granted to them (Organización Indígena de la Cuenca del Caura "Kuyujani," UNEG, and Forest Peoples Programme 2012).

In other words, there is still hope. And perhaps, when the moment arrives and the great demarcation effort by the communities is finally recognized, the situation could change. The elders may yet win the battle against mining, and some of the damage to the land could be reversed. Nevertheless, as of this moment, the situation looks bleak. To add to the challenges, a group of ecologists with no connection to the region recently managed to have the Caura River basin deemed a national park (RBV 2017) without the communities' knowledge. Moreover, the government recently imposed a new mining project in part of the river basin (RBV 2016) with the goal of promoting large-scale extraction activities in the region.

Representatives of the Kuyujani Organization today use the map from the self-demarcation project as a tool to legitimize their land rights in the face of the government, mining, and those who would call their territory the "Caura National Park." The map shows that they have been, and continue to be, the original inhabitants of this space. Generations of oral tradition are preserved in this map, but at the same time, the map symbolizes the beginning of a new chapter of Ye'kwana and Sanema history.

Conclusion

From its inception, this mapping project was intimately involved in a process of cultural recovery and identity formation. The mapping process facilitated the transmission of community knowledge from the elders to the new Indigenous organization and to community members who watched meetings from the sidelines, attentively listening to everything that was said. It also fostered the coproduction of knowledge about the complex links between cultural identity and territory.

In particular, the mapping process illuminated how lived experiences and

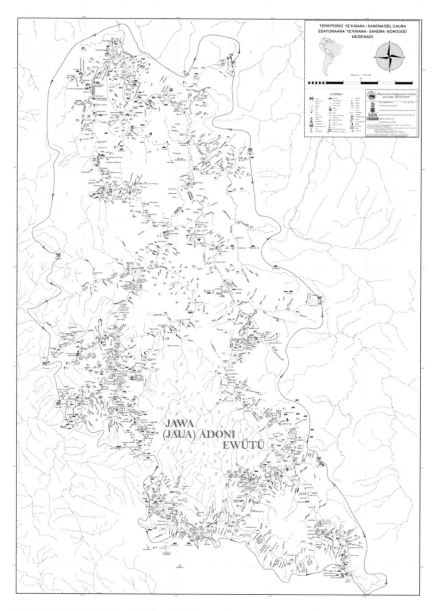

FIGURES 03.01A & 03.01B. Map of Ye'kwana-Sanema territory in the Caura River basin, Venezuela. Source: Nalúa Rosa Silva Monterrey

FIGURE 03.01B

important events live on in the toponyms of natural places such as rivers and waterfalls. The Ye'kwana and the Sanema conceive of landscape as a tangible medium of historical memory, challenging conventional classification and fostering a mapping process that was reflective, critical, and led by the communities themselves. Learning that territory is not an empty space but rather a landscape full of significance, of history, of culture, of memories, is perhaps the most important lesson from this project.

NOTE

1. See Colchester, Silva Monterrey, and Tomedes 2004 for additional details about the project.

REFERENCES

Chávez, Hugo. 2005. "Discurso de entrega de tierras a los indígenas." Santa Rosa de Tácata, Estado Anzoátegui, Venezuela (unpublished).

Colchester, Marcus. 1982. *The Economy, Ecology and Ethnobiology of the Sanema Indians of South Venezuela*. 2 vols. PhD diss., University of Oxford, Oxford, England.

Colchester Marcus, Nalúa Silva Monterrey, and Ramón Tomedes. 2004. *Protegiendo y fomentando el uso consuetudinario de los recursos biológicos en el Alto Caura*. United Kingdom: Forest Peoples Programme. Available at https://www.forestpeoples.org/es/topics/convenio-sobre-la-diversidad-biologica-cdb/publication/2010/protegiendo-y-fomentando-el-uso-c.

Coppens, Walter. 1981. *Del canalete al motor fuera de borda: Misión en Jiwitiña y otras áreas de aculturación en tres pueblos ye'kuana del Caura-Paragua*. Caracas: Fundación La Salle de Ciencias Naturales, Instituto Caribe de Antropología y Sociología, Monografía No. 28.

Organización Indígena de la Cuenca del Caura "Kuyujani," UNEG, and Forest Peoples Programme. 2012. *Pautas para el manejo de los hábitats ye'kwana y sanema en la cuenca del Caura. Elaborado a partir de las reflexiones de las comunidades indígenas ye'kwana y sanema de la cuenca del Caura*. Moreton-in-Marsh, UK: FPP.

Peña M., Orlando. 1996. "Hidrografía." *Scientia Guianae* 6. *Ecología de la cuenca del Río Caura, Venezuela*. Vol. 1, *Caracterización general*, ed. Judith Rosales and Otto Huber, 29–33. Caracas: Universidad Nacional Experimental de Guayana (UNEG); Fundación Instituto Botánico de Venezuela (FIBV).

Peña M., Orlando, and Otto Huber. 1996. "Características geográficas generales." *Scientia Guianae* 6. *Ecología de la cuenca del Río Caura, Venezuela*. Vol. 1, *Caracterización general*, 4–19. Caracas: UNEG; FIBV.

República Bolivariana de Venezuela (RBV). 2000. *Constitución de la República Bolivariana de Venezuela*. Gaceta Oficial No. 5.453 Extraordinario, March 24, 2000. Ministerio de la Secretaría. Caracas: Imprenta Nacional.

———. 2001. *Ley de demarcación y garantía del hábitat y tierras de los pueblos indígenas*. Gaceta Oficial de la República Bolivariana de Venezuela 37.118, January 12, 2001. Caracas: Imprenta Nacional.

———. 2016. *Decreto 2.248 de creación de la zona de desarrollo estratégico nacional "Arco Minero del Orinoco."* Gaceta Oficial de la RBV. Año CXLIII, Mes V, No. 40855. Caracas: Imprenta Nacional.

———. 2017. *Creación Parque Nacional Caura.* Gaceta Oficial de la RBV. Año CXLIV, Mes VI, No. 41.118. Caracas: Imprenta Nacional.

Santos-Granero, Fernando. 2002. "The Arawakan Matrix." In *Comparative Arawakan Histories: Rethinking Language, Family and Cultural Area in Amazonia,* ed. Jonathan D. Hill and Fernando Santos-Granero, 25–50. Urbana: University of Illinois Press.

Silva Monterrey, Nalúa. 1996. "Etnografía." *Scientia Guianae* 6. *Ecología de la cuenca del Río Caura, Venezuela.* Vol. 1, *Caracterización general,* ed. Judith Rosales and Otto Huber, 98–105. Caracas: UNEG; FIBV.

———. 1997. "La percepción ye'kwana del entorno natural." *Scientia Guianae* 7. *Ecología de la cuenca del Río Caura, Venezuela.* Vol. 2, *Estudios especiales,* ed. Otto Huber and Judith Rosales, 65–84. Caracas: Bioguayana.

———. 2006. *Introducción a la Etnografía de los Pueblos Indígenas de Guayana.* Puerto Ordaz, Venezuela: Fondo Editorial UNEG.

———. 2010. *Pouvoir, parenté et société chez les Ye'kwana du Caura, Vénézuela: De la diversité a la synthèse.* Sarrebruck, Germany: Editions universitaires europeennes.

PART II

4

Revealing Territorial Illusions and Political Fictions through Participatory Cartography

WENDY PINEDA

Introduction

The state of Loreto is home to more than 60 percent of the Indigenous population in the Peruvian Amazon. Yet despite the prevalence of these communities, the prevailing "identity" of the region is increasingly centered on its status as an oil producer. Petroleum production has truly become central to the regional imaginary, undergirding development models that are incompatible with Indigenous environmental visions. A historical perspective reveals that this is nothing new—Indigenous people in the Peruvian Amazon have long had their rights violated, first through the extraction of rubber and wood, then later through practices looking to exploit the petroleum and precious metals found in Indigenous lands. Cartography has consistently played a central role in the imposition of such extractivist regimes of regional development. As in other parts of the world, cartography has been used as a tool of epistemic violence that negates and erases Indigenous peoples in Peru, thus maintaining state dominance over Indigenous territories.

Yet in Loreto, petroleum production in particular is spurring collective resistance against the normative ordering of Indigenous territory. Through a process of social cartography, communities use local knowledge to harness the power of maps and confront dominant spatial narratives that fail to reflect Indigenous peoples' territoriality. Indigenous peoples in the Peruvian Amazon have thus turned to mapping to challenge the state, to document and defend their territories, and to reflect critically on their own everyday territorial practices. As I will discuss here, social participatory cartography has proven to be an effective strategy for confronting extractivist policies in the Peruvian Amazon. This process serves as a canvas for the articulation of collective rights and reinforces social cohesion while facilitating what I refer to as "confrontations" with official maps.

Such confrontations between official cartography and community-based maps bring to light the profound differences in how Indigenous peoples and the state conceive of land and natural resources. This analysis helps Indigenous communities see and represent how dominant forms of development have impacted their livelihood. Moreover, it presents an opportunity to articulate Indigenous peoples' own socio-spatial conceptions. Confrontations allow for information found on official maps to be validated or challenged based on its correlation with actual spatial phenomena, local practices, and histories—all of which are revealed through social cartography. By creating opportunities to challenge official maps, especially in areas contaminated by petroleum extraction, Indigenous people in Loreto have been able to validate their claims, thus subverting the authority of the very institutions that have historically asserted power through maps.

However, although such cartographic confrontations allow communities to make their voices heard and press their claims, important contradictions may also arise in this process. First, in order to be most effective, community maps must be continually updated, putting pressure on limited resources for social cartography. And second, cartographic confrontations may incite internal conflicts between populations that co-manage resources within the same territory, perhaps unintentionally revealing sensitive geospatial information about natural resources.

In this chapter, I describe how Indigenous peoples affected by oil development in the Peruvian Amazon have deployed participatory mapping to protect their territories and self-determination through cartographic confrontations. Prompted by the impending expiration of earlier petroleum contracts and a new round of petroleum bidding in the Amazon, the Indigenous Achuar people of the Corrientes River basin initiated a social cartography project to challenge oil development in their region. Between 2005 and 2011, I was part of an Achuar mapping team that visited thirty-two communities in the basin. Our effort was built on a platform, approved by the Achuar Assembly in 2006, which called for environmental rehabilitation, health interventions, and the development of life plans (*planes de vida*) for Achuar communities. The assembly intended the mapping project to serve as a means of documenting and monitoring life in the basin by "promoting recognition of Indigenous territory and oil development's effects on it, with the goal of guaranteeing control over their territory and ensuring subsistence." Indigenous Quechua peoples in the Pastaza River basin, Kichwas from the Tigre River basin, and Kokamas-Kukamirias from the Marañón River basin also carried out similar initiatives in 2009, 2011, and 2013, respectively.

In June 2011, all five ethnic groups formed a common platform, Indigenous People United in Defense of Their Territories, known as PUINAMUDT. The platform emerged out of the communities' shared experience of four decades of resistance to oil development, in the years before then president Ollanta Humala signed Peru's law of "consulta previa" (securing the right of Indigenous communities to have prior consultation on development projects that could affect their land) into action. The PUINAMUDT platform made a series of nonnegotiable demands, including (1) evaluation of the social and environmental impacts of oil development, (2) environmental remediation to address those impacts, (3) full titling of Indigenous territories, (4) compensation from oil companies for use of Indigenous land, and (5) payment for damages and losses. In 2013, the group held meetings to call for prior consultation with regard to oil drilling projects and to evaluate damages that had already occurred, an assessment that prompted them to declare an environmental emergency in the river basins where PUINAMUDT communities live.

Company Interventions and the Consequences of Indigenous Policies

As noted above, the advance of the petroleum frontier into Amazonian territories has posed a severe threat to Indigenous rights over many decades, provoking a number of serious social conflicts. In the late 1940s, Mobil Oil became the first company to conduct geological studies in the hydrocarbon basins in the northern Amazon. Later on, in the 1960s, explorations by Mobil Oil–UNOCAL involved creating 625 kilometers of conventional seismic lines,[1] followed by exploratory drilling at three oil wells. Based on the seismic surveys, the Peruvian government drew up official state maps that depicted two drilling lots in the area, labeled 1AB and 8, respectively. These lots were auctioned off in 1971, awarding oil companies drilling concessions to an area that included the territories and natural resources of the Achuar, Quechua, Kichwa, Kokama-Kukamiria, and Urarina people. Currently operated by Pluspetrol Norte, Lots 1AB and 8 remain the principal crude oil and royalty producers in the northern Amazon, and state agents and private companies maintain that oil drilling in these locations is in the "national interest" and is thus a "public necessity." These arguments have been used to justify the development of several other oil reserves in the northern Amazon.

Petróleos del Perú also conducted exploratory geophysical studies in the same region between 1980 and 1982, followed by intensive geological field sampling in 1984. The latter was done with the purpose of conducting geochemical and geophysical studies and reinterpreting results from seismic testing. Then in 2001, the PARSEP Group[2]—a partnership between PERUPETRO, the Canadian International Development Agency (CIDA), the Canadian Petroleum Institute (CPI), and Tecknica Overseas, Ltd. (TOL)—conducted a review of results from exploration activities in the region. Their final report, "The Hydrocarbon Potential of the Santiago Basin," is indicative of the group's interest in exploiting the natural resources of the land. While loaded with detailed geological maps of the region, this report fails to make a single mention of Indigenous peoples living there.

All of these petroleum companies have operated irresponsibly in the region, ignoring Indigenous territories and severely polluting the environment through their activities. The toxic substances involved in extraction have a particularly strong impact on vulnerable populations, as levels of contamination are well above any standards of what is considered "safe." And all of this pollution has occurred despite a 1984 declaration from the National Office of Natural Resource Evaluation that the Santiago basin was one of the most critically endangered environmental zones in the country. It was not until the twenty-first century, in the year 2000, that the Peruvian state called for improved management of environmental risks and remediation of damages caused by oil exploration. Those calls are still unanswered, condemning Indigenous peoples to live in a permanent state of emergency.

Significant endemic biodiversity characterizes the Napo tropical forest eco-region, providing the necessary resources to allow Indigenous inhabitants to enjoy a self-sufficient existence. Prior to oil development, Indigenous communities and their ancestors lived freely in these forests, disconnected from large urban centers in relative geographic isolation. They obtained territorial autonomy by dominating other groups and collectively developing their own laws governing social relations. Although the arrival of oil industries in this area suppressed many of these practices, it did not eliminate them completely. Because of this lingering resistance, the oil companies developed strategies to deliberately render Indigenous peoples invisible and obscure the environmental damages caused by extraction processes, attempting to absolve themselves of any responsibility for rights violations.

In this context, state policies facilitating massive investments in oil production, reinforced by the streamlining of permitting procedures that allow expedited review of environmental impacts and fewer obligations for mitigation, have helped further the agenda of the oil companies. This reality puts the Peruvian state in a retrograde political position with respect to the environment, as these practices systematically violate collective rights and

FIGURE 04.01. Mapping workshop in the Cuenca del Corrientes. Source: Wendy Pineda.

erode public trust. Ultimately, these policies have paved the way for an oil exploration–based enclave economy to effectively replace Indigenous subsistence economies in the Peruvian Amazon. Communal forest use has given way to indiscriminate exploitation of forest resources that puts the future of Indigenous communities at risk.

Mapping and Visibilization: Creating the Base Maps

Faced with the destruction of their territories, Indigenous communities decided to use social cartography to most effectively represent the full spectrum of challenges they face. Through mapping, they would be able to show the impacts of development policies imposed in their territories, while also developing their own strategies to rescue their territories and manage the impacts of extractive industries (Figures 04.01, 04.02, and 04.03).

Before the Achuar mapping project, Indigenous communities in the Peruvian Amazon had limited opportunity to participate in assessments of the social and environmental impacts of oil exploration. Oil company

FIGURE 04.02. Mapping workshop in the Cuenca del Corrientes. Source: Wendy Pineda.

FIGURE 04.03. Mapping workshop in the Cuenca del Corrientes. Source: Wendy Pineda.

representatives would simply guide state inspectors to sites with low levels of contamination without the participation of the local communities, and any investigation of environmental harm was consigned to standard, industry-determined environmental management indicators. The result was an incomplete evaluation that did not account for multiple environmental impacts that the Indigenous communities directly experienced. In this context, the Indigenous communities understood that it was not enough to make themselves visible through mobilization. If state officials were to understand their claims, affected Indigenous communities would have to become their own experts and produce their own environmental impact assessments to challenge the narrative promoted by interests.

In 2005, the Indigenous peoples organized in the Federation of Native Communities of the Corrientes River (FECONACO)[3] demanded technical training in GPS data collection and georeferencing methods so they could better engage with specialists hired by the oil companies. A few months later, and as a result of this training, the FECONACO communities decided to produce their own maps of their territories. Several academic institutions and nongovernmental organizations provided technical and financial support for the project, helping develop an Indigenous method for both mapping and monitoring the impacts of oil development (Figures 04.04 and 04.05). I participated in this project as a cartographic technician, developing and training Indigenous monitoring teams in ethnocartography.

The FECONACO mapping project revealed that state maps ignored the existence of Indigenous communities in the four river basins, denying their claims of environmental impacts. In a move designed to erase the existence of traditional communities, these maps depicted the four river basins simply as unproductive lands with no existing uses and, therefore, freely available to the state. On top of this, state-issued property titles belonging to a few native communities in the region similarly excluded any reference to oil fields and land concessions to oil companies. Environmental monitoring institutions also had incomplete records regarding polluted sites and often lacked geographic coordinates of the exact location of the environmental hazards. Furthermore, because the region was construed on official maps as forested and without human presence, the state was able to categorize Indigenous areas as industrial zones, a zoning category that permitted oil companies to pollute each kilo of soil with up to 30 grams of petroleum.

Despite their shared interest in claiming territorial rights, Indigenous families who participated in the mapping workshops nonetheless had different interests and expectations for the project. Community members were

FIGURE 04.04. Indigenous monitoring team. Source: Wendy Pineda.

FIGURE 04.05. Oil contamination in the Cuenca del Corrientes. Source: Wendy Pineda.

the first to begin tracing the initial lines on the map, orienting themselves by following the rivers and streams. Next, men and women would map sites that were particularly important to them as individuals, as families, as a community, and as a people, recording the place-name for each significant site. In cases where an area or place did not have a name, community participants created one through consensus.

As the map became more complex, community members would recount stories and legends of the formation of the region as told to them by their elders. These moments were critically important, especially for communities undergoing sociocultural changes that meant elders were no longer effectively transmitting their knowledge to the next generation. If acculturation meant that people were no longer listening to their elders, the mapping project afforded a chance for elders to reconstruct and fortify communal historic memory, often bringing tears to people's eyes.

Alongside this recovery of oral traditions, our mapping team also developed methods for self-demarcating intercommunal boundaries. This effort turned out to be the most effective way to recover and document Indigenous concepts of territory as well as the rules regulating land-use practices. In the Peruvian Amazon, boundaries are not simply lines separating communities; instead, they function as common spaces through which Indigenous territories are made. Within such boundary zones, several distinct communities can simultaneously exercise territorial autonomy. This is particularly true of river basin boundaries. Given the coincidence of territories in these areas, boundaries along river basins were among the most strictly ordered by internal self-regulation as dictated by communal norms.

Once the maps were drawn, GPS teams used them to locate the most important spatial features and sites. Community members recently trained in GPS developed the data collection methods, using cameras and GPS units to develop a georeferenced registry of resources and environmental incidents along routes identified by the Achuar Assembly.

The first of several challenges in the project occurred when we asked the assembly for permission to take the map outside the territory so its features could be digitized. Community members preferred to use only the original sketched maps for their territorial claims and internal management, but in order to use these maps in dialogue with the state, they had to be digitized and turned into more conventional, technical maps. Using Geographic Information System (GIS) software inevitably requires the map to be taken away from the community; even with GIS stations in the communities, only a handful of community members would be able to use them. Because of the problematic and even traumatic implications of digitization, we decided to proceed in stages. First we would make a draft digital version of the map, and then we would return that draft to the community a few weeks later so that community members could check the maps for accuracy and correct them in "validation" workshops.

Mapping and Visibilization: Validating the Maps

The challenges continued during the validation workshops, beginning with our effort to explain how the original communal sketched maps had been converted into digital versions and how community members could read these redesigned maps. The connections between the original and digital maps were not always obvious, but community members eventually began to identify areas that needed to be corrected in both map versions. The corrections reflected their understanding that digitization went beyond just changing individual feature symbology to actually change the entire space being mapped.

That is to say, in some places, it became necessary to fill in areas that appeared blank on the digital maps. This was not because the original maps were wrong, but rather because their features were distinct and dispersed. In the original map, one point would represent a number of similar features, leaving the impression of an empty space. Also, community members had drawn many points on the original maps that could not be georeferenced using GPS. For example, zones such as hunting areas could not be correctly digitized from the perspective of Western cartography, given that they contained no explicit georeferenced points. Instead, a series of points indicating a hunting area would have to be transformed into polygons (area features) to more accurately reflect how Indigenous peoples perceived that space.

Furthermore, the original community maps included "micro-zones" based on the communities' spatial understanding of their cosmovision. The maps reflected integrated environmental and social orders that allowed for territorial uses to be differentiated without being separated or compartmentalized, thus resisting the typical cartographic process of dividing uses with strict lines on a map. The use of Indigenous concepts to autonomously organize, zone, and regulate Indigenous territories conflicts with Western and imperialist zoning maps that only serve to fragment community spaces. In light of this, the validation workshops also offered a second key moment to rescue and document traditional strategies of territorial organizing particular to these communities.

Since the mapping was a collective and participatory process involving various communities, disagreements occasionally arose. While the maps were still in the process of being developed, some communities decided to go ahead and use them in defense of their own interests. For example, in 2007 and 2008, the Achuar community of Belén on the Plantanoyacu River and the Quechua community of Santa Isabel on the Copalyacu River both used draft maps to claim their territorial rights despite lacking legal titles from the Peruvian state. The community of Santa Isabel had already granted the concession of Lot 101 to Talisman Energy, a Canadian oil and gas company, but now the communities wanted to use the maps to expel the oil company from their territories. Given that the lands had not been titled, however, the maps had no legal standing. Without legal proof of ownership, the communities were forced to allow the company to operate within their lands.

On another occasion, after boundary lines had been drawn up between two communities, one of the communities invaded hunting camps established by the other community within the boundary space shown on the map. Hunters also invaded so-called alliance camps convened by the two communities for the purposes of clearing boundary lines. In the end, the community that aggressively invaded the boundary was allowed to permanently occupy it, illustrating the paradoxes and contradictions of mapping projects, even those organized by Indigenous federations themselves.

Internal Uses and Consequences of the Maps

In 2010, we returned the final maps to the communities in both their handcrafted and digital forms. We hoped that the maps could be used to resolve the various conflicts that had arisen during the mapping process, since boundary consensus documents between communities are indispensable requirements for land titling in Peru. In a series of assemblies and meetings, several of the communities were able to reconcile their boundaries, but others still remained in conflict over how and where to demarcate one another's territory. Given that FECONACO had opted to pursue a claim for a single contiguous Indigenous territory in Cuenca del Corrientes, without internal boundaries, the assembly had to wait until all disputes between communities were reconciled before presenting their claim to the Peruvian state. Also, FECONACO decided to wait until President Alan García Pérez's term had ended, since not a single native community had received land title during his administration.

Ultimately, FECONACO was able to use the community-based maps to demand infrastructure improvements to prevent further oil spills, environmental remediation for damages caused by oil production in Lots 1AB and 8, and the provision of environmental monitors to continue geo-referencing important sites within the communities. Moreover, the social cartography process allowed Indigenous people to make visible their own strategies of territorial ordering, their traditional governance structures, and their cultural norms governing natural resource management. Through the mapping process, they were able to identify important areas of resource use and spiritual sites that were impacted by contamination from the oil industry, as well as areas governed by complex common-use agreements.

These areas included ecosystems with a variety of uses, such as *palmichales* (areas for collection of palm leaves); areas for wood collection known as *manchales*; *cochas* ecosystems, or lakes and ponds for fishing; and hunting areas known as *colpas*. Uses of these areas are typically governed by oral agreements made in accordance with the purpose of the resource being used. For example, in a lagoon or *cocha*, only family subsistence fishing will be permitted unless there is a preestablished fishing quota for selling or trading fish with nearby communities. Often, the agreements stipulate the sanctions for failing to abide by internal regulations.

Community members also mapped so-called reserve zones, areas with an abundance of resources that are reserved for food shortages and other emergencies, as well as spiritual areas important for vision-quest practices. These isolated sites are the homes of spirits, such as the "Mothers of the Mountain," that guarantee an abundance of resources and productivity. The reserve sites are ruled by the *supay*, demons that punish those who enter these untouchable sites without permission. In the mapping project, community members were able to map areas contaminated by the oil industry that encroach on these reserve zones. As the community members explained, activity from the industries was so disturbing to the mountains spirits that it prompted them to flee, taking the productivity of the ecosystem with them. The social cartography project thus allowed the communities to recover their territorial autonomy while also critically considering new resource management strategies in light of the pressures wrought by extractivism.

Countermapping and Making Dominant Policies and Imaginaries Visible

Participatory mapping projects tend to focus on the map production process without considering the potential for participatory dialogue and empowerment *after* the maps are completed. To change this pattern, we intended that our mapping process would move beyond cartographic production to social mobilization, seeking to make political power structures visible by analyzing how the imaginaries produced by the petroleum industry contrasted with Indigenous peoples' lived experiences. The community members who participated in the mapping project had already questioned both the failure of the state to pursue the development projects that had been promised as well as the lack of concern over environmental contamination evinced by state agencies. Now, we sought to analyze the spatial and social impacts of state policies in more depth.

We pursued this cartographic confrontation by analyzing state maps showing public services and infrastructure development in communities within petroleum exploitation zones, allowing community members to see the truth and thus demystify the extractive development model. The state maps showed that many of these territories, whose natural resources generate millions of dollars for the Peruvian state, do not even have access to natural water sources or potable water. The basic service networks in the Quechuas del Alto Pastaza communities are deficient in comparison to those of the petroleum enclave communities in Lot 1AB. In fact, our analysis of official maps showed that only people working in the oil fields have access to water not contaminated by heavy minerals and hydrocarbons in Lot 1AB.

The cartographic analysis following the mapping project also allowed community members to better understand the public policies and legal principles supporting the oil industry, particularly the concepts of "land" as defined in Peruvian law. For the Peruvian state, Indigenous "land" rights do not apply to the control of natural resources, archaeological remains, or any other goods regulated through special laws. Instead, these "rights" are merely rights to use forested lands. In this political imaginary, since Indigenous people did not have "property" rights or other evidence of possession of their lands, the lands in the Corrientes River basin could therefore be deemed "freely available" by the state.

However, the social cartography process demonstrated that Indigenous people in fact *did* exercise their territorial rights by traditionally occupying all of the territory in the Corrientes basin, leaving no lands available for expropriation. While FECONACO's map proved that thirty-five native communities occupy the entire Cuenca del Corrientes, official maps showed that the state had only recognized some form of collective land title to 10 percent of the basin. Thus, the community-based maps showed that the laws used to facilitate subsurface resource use run counter to Indigenous territorial conceptions as well as Indigenous rights. Unfortunately, this disconnect was further embodied in a land titling case from November 2012 in which the court ruled that none of the sites under oil company easement were eligible for Indigenous titling.

Although land titling has proved legally difficult in the face of encroachment by the oil industry, our documentation of contamination has also presented technical and logistical difficulties. Oil production is confined to closed-off "petroleum enclaves" that are difficult to access, but damages wrought by the industry might have occurred in other areas that are not under current production. In the case of these challenges, in our social cartography we decided to map not only those sites that are currently contaminated but also the historical memory of contamination, including its origin, its nature, and its migration.

In doing so, we were able to produce participatory maps that show that contamination doesn't just exist on the surface but rather moves through entire ecosystems that make up the territory, in stark contrast to state and industry maps that merely symbolize contamination with small sampling "points." The various maps elaborated by FECONACO demonstrate that the pollution seeps from the petroleum fields and, given the dynamics of the subsurface water flows, concentrates in areas close to the communities. To date, historical documentation conducted as part of the mapping project has shown that the Pluspetrol Norte company destroyed seven *cochas*, or lagoons, between 2006 and 2013. The maps, along with photos and videos taken by Indigenous environmental monitors, are continually being handed over to the state's Environmental Evaluation Offices to help precisely date the contamination events.

In typical environmental impact studies carried out by the Peruvian state, petroleum companies have been able to minimize the extent of their contamination and ignore information provided by Indigenous people. Furthermore, state evaluators and monitors are only required to work within the petroleum enclaves and do not monitor extended contamination zones within Indigenous territories. The participatory maps, therefore, have helped reveal the migration routes and flow patterns of oil industry contaminants, challenging official environmental data and extending the space of environmental evaluation and oversight.

Discussion

The democratization of cartography through practices of countermapping has helped Indigenous peoples in Peru's northern Amazon realize a number of objectives. Mapping processes have reinforced juridical and administrative efforts to win recognition and titling of collective territorial land rights, while also serving to document Indigenous peoples' historical memory of their intangible territorial patrimony. In particular, placing official cartography side by side with participatory cartography has helped expose and challenge state policies that affect Indigenous territories. Visibilizing the impact of state policies in Indigenous communities is absolutely necessary in order to learn from history, as well as to transform it.

Our participatory maps can thus be understood as "maps of political impunity" that reconstruct the political history of invisibilization in the northern frontier of the Peruvian Amazon, demonstrating how Indigenous territories and peoples have been divided by extractivist polices. With the state's permission, oil companies have become the new territorial hegemons in this area. To protect the oil companies, the state has decreed that Indigenous lands be freely available, granting free easements to the companies while denying land titles to the Indigenous communities who live above the oil deposits. In doing so, the Peruvian state has made itself invisible behind the screen of the oil industry, making it easier to take away juridical protection for Indigenous communities.

However, the cartographic confrontation we developed in the Cuenca del Corrientes made these state policies visible. As this case shows, social cartography has the potential to return decision-making power to communities, providing them with the power to demonstrate and critically analyze how four decades of state policies have reconfigured their territory. Through social cartography, Indigenous people have been able to mount a cohesive and effective response to the oil industry and to the Peruvian state that supports it, allowing them to pursue their ancestral territorial autonomy and seek necessary reform in the face of destructive extractivism.

NOTES

1. Seismic surveys are a common technique used to map subsurface oil. It uses explosives distributed at regular intervals over a large area to create a seismic (shock) wave that travels through the subsurface. The movement of the waves is recorded, measuring the time they take to reflect or "bounce" off subsurface formations. In tropical forests, this requires cutting "seismic lines" in a grid pattern to position explosives and recording equipment.

2. Program of Technical Assistance for Energy Sector Regulation in Peru.

3. See feconaco.org.

Mapuche Cartography

Defending *Ixofillmogen*

PABLO MANSILLA QUIÑONES AND MIGUEL MELIN PEHUEN

"We have faith and confidence in the men who direct the destinies of the Frontier, and we appeal to their patriotic zeal to reduce at once a territory that until now is only an anomaly in our map." *El Meteoro*, August 17, 1867[1]

Wallmapu, the territory of the Mapuche Nation, extends from the Andean cordillera to both the Atlantic and Pacific Oceans.[2] Since the 1800s, Chile and Argentina have launched campaigns aimed at reducing and fragmenting Wallmapu through military conquest and settlement. In Argentina, this effort began with the "Conquest of the Desert," which aimed to settle a region regarded as devoid of inhabitants (Serje 2011). The Chilean state took a different approach with their "Pacification of the Araucanía," relying on military force to subjugate a territory that neither the Inca nor the Spanish Crown had been able to control (Bengoa 2000). Both countries treated the area as a frontier, a cartographic "anomaly" that challenged their sovereign claims to territory.

Grounded in military conquest, Argentina and Chile have since extended their colonization of Wallmapu through policies of economic and political integration that continue in the present. These policies effect a kind of structural violence reinforced by national maps that have had profound effects on the materiality of Mapuche life and landscape, deterritorializing the very idea of Wallmapu itself. This process has affected Mapuche "territorial knowledges" (Castro-Gómez 2000; Mansilla, Quintero, and Moreira Muñoz 2019), grasped in part through the loss of the Mapuche language, Mapuchezugun. Language is vital to the Mapuche people's ability to practice their culture through activities like knowing place-names and understanding nature, both of which have been steadily replaced by Spanish concepts and words. These same efforts carry over into cartography. Argentina and Chile have used maps strategically to advance a particular knowledge of territory that reinforces and consolidates their efforts to control Mapuche territory. Their efforts express a coloniality of power that the Mapuche people have challenged, rejecting the idea of their territory as a frontier or cartographic anomaly. In response, the Mapuche people have engaged in multiple forms of territorial resistance and struggles, including efforts to map Wallmapu (Mansilla and Melin 2019). Their struggle raises an important question. Can maps made by the Mapuche people adequately challenge the material and discursive practices used by the Chilean and Argentine states to assert their territorial power over Wallmapu?

The authors of this paper have worked together with Mapuche Lofs and the Alianza Territorial Mapuche (ATM; Mapuche Territorial Alliance) since 2013 to explore the potential of maps for restoring Mapuche territorial power. To that end, we have adopted methods and techniques from social cartography to map Wallmapu and develop a Mapuche cartographic language. Our discussion in this chapter focuses on a portion of that work in the Kurakautin region in the foothills of the Andean cordillera, conducted over a five-year period from 2013 to 2018. We worked with four Mapuche Lofs, or territories, in the Kurakautin region: Kontué, Radalko, Kolliko-Folilko, and Hueñivales. Along with the Kurakautin region, all four Lofs are located in the region of Wallmapu they know as Gvlümapu. Extending from the Andes to the Pacific Ocean, Gvlümapu often appears on Chilean map as the Araucanía. In recent years, Chilean officials and private companies have targeted the region for hydroelectric projects, constructing a system of dams and electricity-generating facilities in mountainous river valleys of the Andes like those found in the Kurakautin region. The four Lofs in this project worked with the ATM to challenge these projects. This chapter discusses our efforts to challenge one project in particular, the Doña Alicia hydroelectric project.

Building on the approach taken by the Lofs, our method focused on using Mapuche concepts to organize understandings of geographical space. Others have pursued similar approaches to document Mapuche territoriality, particularly in Chile (Hirt 2013; Huiliñir-Curío 2015). Our work differs in its emphasis on *rakizuam*, Mapuche knowledge, as the basis for mapping. Part of our concern is methodological. The ATM and Lofs in the Kurakautin region have organized their opposition to the Doña Alicia project in terms of defending *ixofillmogen*, a Mapuche concept that refers to all forms of life. Our mapping efforts followed this lead, using Mapuche knowledge and concepts to answer the question of what we were mapping as well as how we were using maps to communicate that knowledge. Our goal was to use these concepts to further guide our use of technologies like Geographical Information Systems (GIS) and drones, rather than having mapping technologies drive the process.

Another reason for our emphasis on Mapuche knowledge is political, and it concerns how cartography is used to discipline understandings of space. That approach shapes dominant approaches to cartography, accelerating processes of deterritorialization. The effects of deterritorialization are as much material as they are ontological (Blaser 2009; De la Cadena 2010; Escobar 2014), attacking the material and symbolic basis for Mapuche existence along with all other forms of life that make Wallmapu (Mansilla 2019). Among these other forms of life are flora and fauna, as well as forests, mountains, and rivers. Through our mapping work, we have sought to expand and deepen Mapuche territorial knowledge of the Kurakautin region through cartography. Our use of cartography is intended to reinforce the reconstruction of Mapuche territory through intercultural practices that involve youth and adults, men and women, across different communities. Historically this work has been done through *xawün*, or gatherings, that inform social mobilization in defense of territory. As discussed here, this approach goes beyond recognition of territorial rights to efforts to transform understandings of territory itself.

Our mapping work has met with modest success. The Lofs successfully stopped the Doña Alicia project in 2018. In 2019, the *logko* of Lof Radalko, Alberto Curamil Millanao, received a Goldman Prize on behalf of the Lof for its successful effort to stop two of the hydroelectric projects in the Kurakautin region. However, Curamil was unable to accept the award in person. Shortly after the dam project was halted in 2018, Chilean police arrested Curamil in what appears to be an attempt to silence opposition to hydroelectric projects. He has been in jail ever since, where he awaits a trial in Chilean courts. Curamil's arrest has not deterred other Lofs in the Kurakautin region, which have gone on to stop the Pintoresco and Río Blanco hydroelectric projects. In each case, the Lofs have used mapping to rebuild Mapuche concepts of space and territory and to formulate legal challenges using Chilean and international law. The result has been the fashioning of a series of geographical-territorial and sociocultural-anthropological arguments that helped stop the dams through the use of Mapuche knowledge.

Extractivism in Wallmapu

The military campaigns launched by Chile and Argentina in the mid-1800s sought to annex Wallmapu by military force, propelled in both cases by desires to use "empty" land and "free" resources to increase exports of basic agricultural commodities. This same approach continues to this day through neoliberal policies adopted by both countries. Neoliberal policies enacted during the past four decades continue to put forth development projects focused on extractivism and the commodification of nature. Both rely on the continued deterritorialization of the Mapuche people, accentuating the fragmentation of Wallmapu set in motion by military campaigns in the mid-1800s. One aspect of their efforts aimed to dismantle Mapuche Lofs, the basic unit for socio-spatial organization of the Mapuche people, by dividing them into family groups that were resettled on land grants made by the Chilean and Argentine governments (Bengoa 2000; CEPAL/ATM 2012). Chile developed this approach by issuing land grants (*títulos de merced*) to the Mapuche people to encourage them to settle on lands set aside for them. While many Mapuche were thereby "reduced" to occupying a fraction of Wallmapu, many others were left without land and forced to migrate to cities in search of work. Over the course of the twentieth century, loss of land and economic pressures worked in concert with the political efforts to displace the Mapuche people, enacting a form of structural violence that condemned them to living in poverty in cities or on an ever-dwindling land base. By way of illustration, the 2008 Historical Truth and New Deal for Indigenous Peoples (Comisión Verdad Histórica y Nuevo Trato con los Pueblos Indígenas) convened by the Chilean government surveyed 413 land titles issued to the Mapuche people between 1884 and 1923. The Commission found that the Mapuche people had lost title to 31.6 percent of the land granted to them after the "Pacification of the Araucanía," or an area totaling 26,459.3 hectares.

The military dictatorship that took control of Chile in the 1970s accelerated the dispossession of the Mapuche people as a means of accumulating wealth (Calbucura 2015). At first this was done by military force, rolling back agrarian reforms, and expropriating Mapuche communities. Neoliberal policies helped extend their efforts beyond land to include other resources such as water. The water code established by the dictatorship in 1981 eliminated the concept of water as a common good, separating the ownership of water from the ownership of land to create a new system of private water rights. These changes created a "water market" based on the sale and purchase of water rights (Panez Pinto 2018). Extractive industries benefited from this new market, using it to acquire water rights needed to expand forestry, aquaculture, mining, and energy production. In each case, water rights helped subsidize the expansion of extractive industries that, in turn, increased the demand for more water rights. The forestry policies promoted by the dictatorship stand out in this regard, as water rights were purchased to expand plantations and drove demand in such a way that they have made water a scarce resource in areas known for their abundance of rivers and precipitation.

After the end of the military dictatorship in 1990, democratically elected governments did not end the implementation of neoliberal policies so much as perfect their implementation. The results are visible across Mapuche communities. Water shortages are now common in these communities, forcing Mapuche people to purchase potable water from private providers who haul it in by truck. This marks the profound transformation in access to water wrought by neoliberal policies, disrupting the Mapuche peoples' relationship to water, denying an important element of their spirituality and lives, and transforming their relationship to nature. Mapuche communities have responded through mobilization in defense of territory, expanding their struggle beyond land to include other "resources" such as water. While much of the focus has been on mobilizations in Chile, similar mobilizations have occurred in Pvelmapu, the region of Wallmapu that extends east from the Andean Cordillera to the Atlantic into lands claimed by Argentina. Both countries have accused Mapuche activists of terrorism, threatening private property rights fundamental to Argentine and Chilean national societies. The ensuing criminalization of protest has resulted in the jailing of community leaders and widespread human rights violations.

The Kurakautin region demonstrates the merging of struggles for land and water. Located in the Andean foothills, the region has numerous streams and rivers. Privatization initially targeted so-called nonconsumptive uses of water, such as hydroelectric projects and pisciculture, that return water to in-stream flow after using it. These uses now affect a large portion of surface water in the region and are creating a scarcity of potable water. As a result, communities throughout the Kurakautin have been forced to purchase potable water from privately run trucks. The proposed Doña Alicia hydroelectric project threatened to exacerbate this situation. Capable of generating 6.3 megawatts of power, the US$20.3 million project was designed to link into power grids in central and northern Chile. The project would have created a 1.3 hectare reservoir, affecting 2.9 kilometers of river and 12.9 hectares of land. A 2013 environmental impact assessment of the project determined that it would have no impact on Mapuche communities and cultural sites in the area—despite never consulting with the communities themselves. The assessment justified its conclusion based on its determination that the nearest Mapuche communities were located outside the affected area. The report claimed that the nearest Mapuche communities, Benancio Huenchupán, Quilape López, and Carmen Paillao Vda. de Liempi[3] were located 13, 17, and 21 kilometers outside of the area affected by the project.[4] The authors of the report used this reasoning to dismiss Mapuche concerns about the project and exclude them from the consultation process.

Mapping the *Xawümen* of the Mapuche Lofs

Countering the determination of the anthropological report, two of the communities, Quilape López and Benancio Huenchupán, mobilized in opposition to the Doña Alicia project. They were joined by two other Mapuche communities not named in the report, Liempi Colipi and Pancho Curamil. All four Mapuche communities contended that the project would have significant impacts on the environment, threatening their way of life and relationships to the Cautín River and surrounding area. The four communities argued that the project would destroy important Mapuche cultural sites used for religious ceremonies, impede access to land and resources essential to communities, and damage areas used for collecting medicinal plants (*lawen*). They used the Mapuche concept of *ixofillmogen*, "all forms of life," to mobilize their opposition to the hydroelectric project.

Ixofillmogen guided the communities' legal opposition to the project. The International Labour Organization's Convention 169 on Indigenous and Tribal Peoples specifically establishes Indigenous peoples' rights to territory and consultation on projects affecting them. Chile ratified ILO 169 in 2008, binding the country to the terms of the convention in its entirety, without exception. The communities further argued that the Doña Alicia project violated at least three clauses of Chile's General Environment Law 19.300, requiring environmental impact assessments to address cultural and economic impacts, including displacement, loss of access, impacts on mobility, and irreversible harm to religious and cultural practices.[5] The rules for conducting an assessment further require evaluation of any cultural impacts generated by proposed projects, including disruption of indigenous economic and cultural activities, impediments to free movement and travel, and impediments to any and all practices fundamental to the social cohesion of the affected group or community.[6]

In support of the communities' opposition to the Doña Alicia project, we used a combination of participatory action research and social cartography aimed at presenting Mapuche knowledge of the area and identifying the project's effects. Our results are published in the atlas *Cartografía cultural del Wallmapu: Elementos para descolonizar el mapa en territorio Mapuche* (Cultural Cartography of Wallmapu: Elements for Decolonizing the Map of Mapuche Territory; Melin, Mansilla, and Royo 2019). The mapping work was organized in three stages. The first stage involved meeting with Mapuche communities in *xawün* gatherings organized around *nguellipun*, traditional prayers. Each *xawün* gathered Mapuche from different Lofs spread out across the Kurakautin region to plan and discuss mapping work according to Mapuche territorial knowledge. The second stage involved meetings with individual Lofs, convened by them, to initiate the mapping work. This stage of the work was based on the concept of *nüxamkawün zugu*, a process for organizing collective discussion among the Lofs following community protocols about timing, location, and participation. This approach dictates that community elders are always the first to speak, followed by adults. Youth and children drew maps illustrating the presentations, making the meetings into a space for intergenerational transmission of knowledge. During these meetings, our team also supplied drones that were used to take pictures with a bird's-eye view of the area and assist with documenting Mapuche territorial knowledge. Finally, the third stage consisted of meetings among neighboring Lofs aimed at facilitating discussion and identification of historical boundaries between them. This phase of the project considered a multiplicity of ways of knowing and identifying boundaries, which aimed to ensure that any new boundaries created by the project would not create conflicts among the Lofs. The meetings also included discussion and review of the maps produced by the project, with the goal of creating a unified political position with respect to the hydroelectric project.

The mapping project began by drawing the historical boundaries of the Lofs in the Kurakautin region. This step was important for grounding the mapping work in Mapuche forms of organizing territory that had been dismantled by the Chilean military's annexation of the Araucanía. Under Chilean rule, the Lofs were replaced by land grants named for the *logko*, or chief, who was assigned the title, as occurred in Benancio Huenchupán. To this day, the Chilean state regards Mapuche territorial claims as limited to the area covered by the land grant system, confining Mapuche rights and denying the social and spatial importance of the Lofs. Mapuche people refute the emphasis on land grants, insisting on the central importance of the Lofs in identifying the location and extent of their territorial claims. Accordingly, the maps produced by our project replaced the names of the four Mapuche communities affected by the hydroelectric project with the names of the Lofs. The communities of Liempi Colipi, Quilape López, Benancio Huenchupán, and Pancho Curamil—all names of *logkos* given the land titles—were replaced with the names of their respective Lofs: Lof Kontué, Lof Kolliko-Folilko, Lof Hueñivales, and Lof Radalko. Working with elders from each of the Lofs, we documented the historical practice of delimiting Lofs by rivers and watershed divides, replacing the land grant boundaries previously used to identify Mapuche communities. From a Mapuche perspective, these boundaries,

FIGURE 05.01. Social map of the original territorial extension of Lof Hueñivales and the Benancio Huenchupán land grant, Chile. Source: Pablo Mansilla.

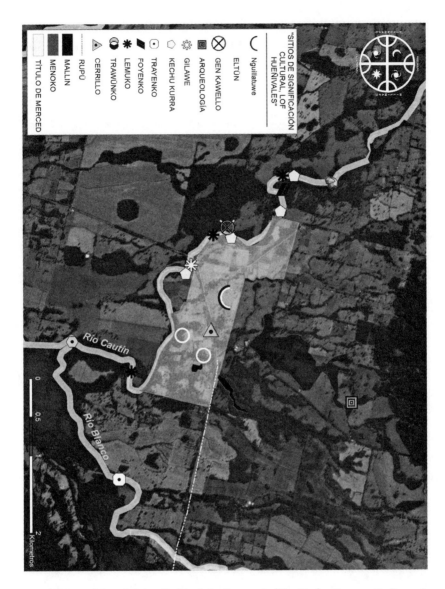

FIGURE 05.02. Map of places of cultural significance, Lof Hueñivales, Community Benancio Huenchupán, Chile. Source: Pablo Mansilla.

or *xawümen*, unite and link different parts of the territory as opposed to dividing it, since each is the product of discussions and agreements between Lofs developed over generations. This approach contrasts with the dominant uses of boundaries to delimit individual property rights, distinguish between different forms of land use, or define particular places (Mansilla and Melin 2019). Instead, the use of *xawün* emphasizes the existence of Lofs within a continuous space, structuring the broader space of Wallmapu.

These points are all apparent in the map of Lof Hueñivales that covers 32,350 hectares of land and includes the Mapuche land grant community of Benancio Huenchupán. In contrast, the Benancio Huenchupán land grant is only 190 hectares, or less than 0.6 percent of the Lof. Even that number represents a reduction from the 260 hectares initially granted by Chilean officials to the community due to usurpation by private, non-Mapuche owners. Replacing the land grant boundaries with the *xawümen* of the Lof registers the extent of their territory in the region, including an important area used for summer pasture (*veraneada*).

Mapping *Ixofillmogen*: Rivers, Rocks, and Mapuche Spirituality

As previously mentioned, the Lof is the social and spatial basis for organizing Mapuche life, including collective memory, giving form to an identity as a people belonging to a particular place. The importance of the Lof underscores the destructiveness of the deterritorialization carried out by the Chilean state, which replaced Mapuche concepts with property rights by way of assimilating them into the dominant social and spatial values of national society. Our emphasis on mapping Lofs grounded our approach in Mapuche understandings and knowledge, and was reinforced by mapping place-names in Mapuchezugun, the Mapuche language, as remembered by elders. These place-names, in turn, provided a wealth of information about the territory that state maps continually threaten to erase.

Lewfü, or rivers, like the Cautín, hold particular importance in Mapuche life, organizing religious practices and relationships among Lofs. Through them, a different concept of territory materializes. One of the more important aspects of the rivers are *guillatun feyentun*, or river prayers, which bring together Lofs throughout the region. Just as in other Lofs, residents of the community of Benancio Huenchupán regularly travel the river that bounds their Lof, wading into its currents to say prayers and perform ceremonies that give them strength and energy in their daily lives. One of the more important ceremonies involves using the force of the river's own sound (*traitraiko*) to summon rain by crossing the river with animals and to heal children who have difficulties with language and communication. Each of these activities appeals to the Gen, or spiritual forces, that inhabit the river and can help people overcome difficulties. That importance was recorded on many of the maps produced by the project that refer to the Gen Kawello, or Spirit Horse, that cares for a particular place and ensures the persistence of *ixofillmogen*. Each of these activities demonstrates the relationship between the Mapuche Lofs and the river. Hydroelectric projects like Doña Alicia cannot help but alter this relationship, forcing the Gen to flee and threatening the equilibrium of *ixofillmogen*, bringing death and disease as well as preventing Mapuche people from holding ceremonies like the *nguillatun* and *llellipun* that require the presence of the Gen who inhabit the rivers, mountains, and hills. Gen also live in the forests, rivers, and oceans, together forming the equilibrium vital for human existence. For Mapuche people, maintaining their relationships with the Gen is essential to their coexistence with other people and life-forms that surround them. Their collective force forms their world. If the rivers are dammed or the forests flooded, the Gens will not hear the people's calls and risk being lost forever.

These relationships extend to plants, particularly those used by Mapuche people for medicine. Mapuche plant medicine combines techniques, practices, and concepts that together shape Mapuche health and well-being (Citarella 2000). Through the mapping project, we documented an important class of medicinal plants, *lawentuwün lewfü*, associated with the flow of water in rivers (*lewfü*), swamps (*mallín*), and springs (*menoko*). These latter two water sites are particularly important for the concentration of medicinal plants found there, many of which are used by *machi* and *lawentuchefe* (healers) to cure the sick in *guillatun* ceremonies at key sites along the banks of rivers. These ceremonies require that the sick person bathe using only certain herbs, combining them with the water in a particular place to clean their body and spirit of bad energy and causes of illness.

The proposed Doña Alicia project would have affected a particularly important area of riverbed where three classes of plants, shrubs, and trees used for Mapuche medicine are found. In particular, the project would have affected groundcover plants (*kachu lawen*), such as *chelún, limpia plata, berro, perilla, menta negra, menta blanca, frutilla, nalca*, and *yerba de vaca*. It would also affect medicinal shrubs, including *corcolén, traiga, canela, foye, pitra, matico*, and *weya*, along with trees used for medicine such as *radal, tepa, laurel*, *triage*, *maqui*, and *maiten*. By identifying these plants with the Lofs, the project also documented their regional importance to *machis* that come from the central valleys and Biobío River basin to harvest *lawen*.

The mapping project extended into other aspects of the river. *Kurantu*, or rocks, serve a variety of important purposes. The Kurakautin region is particularly known for its *kaxün kura*, a kind of rock historically used by Mapuche people for a variety of household and spiritual purposes, ranging from spearheads to *pimuntuwe* used for rituals. Benancio Huenchupán is also well known for a series of rocks that make particular sounds, speaking for nature and making seasonal weather forecasts.

As the mapping project gained momentum, it deepened our collective understanding of *ixofillmogen*. Since the time of the Chilean military campaigns, Lofs have coordinated collective work efforts aimed at helping Mapuche people sustain themselves and maintaining their relationships with one another. Examples of this collective labor include *mingako*, community labor performed to meet subsistence needs. Communal efforts known as *rukan* organize the construction of houses in the Lofs. Funeral ceremonies known as *eluwen* organize and maintain *eltün*, cemeteries, that anchor Lofs, while *guillatun* ceremonies convene Lofs at particular sites mapped as *nguillatuwe*. Collective labor is also used to mobilize against state programs through *wigkakezugu*, while *igkamapu* are used to reclaim and recover lands stolen by third parties in violation of Mapuche rights. Finally, communities have their own ways of organizing economic activities, *moñewe zugu*. Mapuche Lofs throughout the Gvlümapu rely on livestock and agricultural production to meet immediate cash needs. Both activities are founded upon collective control over territory. Rivers and streams are vital sources of water, while common summer pasture areas are essential for grazing. The latter activity further gives importance to *gilawe*, herding trails, used to move stock from winter to summer ranges.

Each of these concepts and practices helps us understand *ixofillmogen*. They also pose a unique set of challenges when it comes to cartography. Rather than using conventional cartographic techniques to map them, at each stage in the process we used our understanding of *ixofillmogen* to guide our efforts and develop a Mapuche cartographic language. Some of these elements like the *xawümen* were relatively easy to map, despite the challenge they present to the idea of boundaries as they are typically mapped. Other elements required challenging cartographic conventions directly. In this project, the Lofs took the initiative to align the maps with the rising sun in the Pvelmapu. Putting Pvelmapu at the "top" of the map helped align it with a Mapuche cosmovision. So did the replacement of the traditional compass rose with a *kultrün*, the Mapuche drum used for ceremonies. This element is incorporated into the upper left-hand corner of each of the maps presented in this chapter. The *kultrün* is used to further identify the four cardinal directions in Mapuche, each of which corresponds to a different territorial identity within Wallmapu: Pvelmapu to the east, Pikunmapu to the north, Gvlümapu to the west, and Willimapu to the south.

Conclusions

By mapping these relationships, the project provided the basis for recognizing the broad range of *welulkawün wirin zugu*, or cultural sites, in the area affected by the Doña Alicia hydroelectric project. The mapping work directly contradicted the conclusion in the anthropological report appended to the environmental impact statement, which claimed that "there are no indigenous cemeteries, modern or historical, located in the affected area, nor is there evidence of any other cultural sites, including recently used *nguillatúe* and *palihue* sites, that any of the people interviewed by this study could identify."[7] Moreover, our mapping project demonstrates how even the idea of "cultural sites" oversimplifies Mapuche knowledge, reducing their extent, number, and location in ways that continue to destroy Wallmapu by assimilating it into dominant spatial categories. The problem is not one of ethics or even method. It is a violation of Mapuche peoples' rights. Denying the importance of, for instance, *menoko* (springs) and *ngenko* (water spirits), becomes just another aspect of the cultural genocide that began with the military annexation of Wallmapu and the dismissal of Mapuche territorial practices and knowledge. Environmental impact assessments that respond to needs and concerns arbitrarily identified by external (non-Mapuche) interests only extend colonial power further. The mapping work discussed in this chapter therefore goes well beyond limited notions of cultural and environmental impacts to identify the tremendous threat that the dam poses to Mapuche life and culture. It also underscores the real importance of having the people who live in the area affected, the Lofs, be in charge of assessing impacts.

All of these points make clear that the Mapuche peoples' struggle against deterritorialization by the Chilean state goes well beyond reconstituting an ancestral territory and recovering control over water. The struggle for *ixofillmogen* poses a fundamental challenge to dominant ideas of the environment, water, and territory itself. In their current form, each of these concepts rejects

Mapuche knowledge, creating a false sense of assessing the impacts of hydroelectric development. At the same time, these concepts all work to further dismantle, fragment, and destroy Mapuche life, *ixofillmogen*. The struggle for Mapuche territory is therefore always about much more than land and resources. It is about the meaning and knowledge of place, as developed by the people who have lived there for generations. The implications are clear. One immediate aspect requires grasping the importance of the ontological distance that separates Mapuche understandings of territory, water, and nature from dominant ones. This demand further requires seeing this space from the perspective of those who inhabit it, grasping Mapuche concepts, categories, and territorial knowledge through the study of things like place-names.

In this spirit, it is possible to answer the question that we posed at the beginning. Can cartography as a way of seeing and knowing the world be decolonized? We think that cartography can do this as long as it involves a constant dialogue between Mapuche knowledge and cartographic techniques. Our work puts this answer into practice, using technologies like GIS and drones to visualize and communicate Mapuche understandings of territory. At the same time, Mapuche cultural mapping demonstrates the potential for creating new cartographic languages grounded in indigenous perspectives and ontologies that fundamentally challenge the dominant cartographic rationality found in state institutions. The work presented here demonstrates the potential for new forms of cartography, identifying the challenge of developing an approach grounded in Mapuche concepts and experience.

The only way to meet that challenge is by working directly with Mapuche communities, supporting their efforts to defend *ixofillmogen* through struggles to defend their rights to land and water using their terms. Neither maps nor cartography will ever present a definitive solution to the problems of coloniality, deterritorialization, and destruction of Indigenous territories. The solutions to those problems are ontological and political. All the same, cartography can and should be used as a tool to accompany those struggles.

NOTES

1. As quoted in Díaz Gajardo 2014.

2. The authors thank the CONICYT-PIA SOC 180040 Project, which has sponsored this research.

3. Translator's note: As explained elsewhere in the text, present-day Mapuche communities are often named for the person whose name appears on corresponding land grants issued by Chilean officials.

4. Calificación del Estudio de Impacto Ambiental "Central Hidroeléctrica Doña Alicia," Comuna de Curacautín, Resolución Externa, No. 79/2015, Temuco, April 6, 2015.

5. Law No. 19.300, "General Law of the Environment," 1994. leychile.cl/Navegar?idNorma=30667.

6. Article 7, Law 1053563, "Regulations for Conducting Environmental Impact Assessments," 2012. leychile.cl/Navegar?idNorma=1053563.

7. Calificación del Estudio de Impacto Ambiental "Central Hidroeléctrica Doña Alicia," Comuna de Curacautín, Resolución Externa, No. 79/2015, Temuco, April 6, 2015, Sección VIII, para. 3. seia.sea.gob.cl/archivos/2015/04/08/58a_CH_Dona_Alicia.pdf (translated by Joe Bryan).

REFERENCES

Bengoa, José. 2000. *Historia del pueblo mapuche: Siglo XIX y XX*. Santiago de Chile: LOM Editores.

Blaser, Mario. 2009. "Political Ontology: Cultural Studies without Cultures?" *Cultural Studies* 23(5–6): 873–896. doi.org/10.1080/09502380903208023.

Calbucura, Jorge. 2015. "Resistencia: Una respuesta indígena al neoliberalismo: El caso mapuche." *Especiaria: Cadernos de Ciências Humanas* 14(25): 33–51.

Castro-Gómez, Santiago. 2000. "Ciencias sociales, violencia epistémica y el problema de la invención del otro." In *La colonialidad del saber: Eurocentrismo y ciencias sociales. Perspectivas latinoamericanas*, ed. Edgardo Lander, 145–163. Buenos Aires: CLACSO.

CEPAL/ATM. 2012. *Desigualdades territoriales y exclusión social del pueblo mapuche en Chile: Situación en la comuna de Ercilla desde un enfoque de derechos*. Santiago de Chile: CEPAL.

Citarella, Luca, ed. 2000. *Medicinas y culturas en la Araucanía*. Santiago de Chile: Editorial Sudamericana.

Comisión Verdad Histórica y Nuevo Trato. 2008. *Informe de la Comisión Verdad Histórica y Nuevo Trato con los Pueblos Indígenas*. Santiago de Chile: Comisionado Presidencial para Asuntos Indígenas.

De la Cadena, Marisol. 2010. "Indigenous Cosmopolitics in the Andes: Conceptual Reflections beyond 'Politics.'" *Cultural Anthropology* 25(2): 334–370.

Díaz Gajardo, Víctor. 2014. "Disciplinamiento, miedo y control social: Los 'otros' dispositivos de poder en la ocupación de la Araucanía." *Estudios Interdisciplinarios de América Latina y el Caribe* 15(2). www7.tau.ac.il/ojs/index.php/eial/article/view/791/942.

Escobar, Arturo. 2014. *Sentipensar con la tierra: Nuevas lecturas sobre desarrollo, territorio y diferencia*. Medellín, Colombia: Ediciones UNAULA (Colección Pensamiento Vivo).

Hirt, Irene. 2013. "Mapeando sueños/soñando mapas: Entrelazando conocimientos geográficos indígenas y occidentales." *Revista Geográfica del Sur* 3: 63–90. revgeosur.udec.cl/?p=163.

Huiliñir-Curío, Viviana. 2015. "Los senderos pehuenches en Alto Biobío (Chile): Articulación espacial, movilidad y territorialidad." *Revista de Geografía Norte Grande* 62: 47–66.

Mansilla Quiñones, Pablo. 2019. "Geografías del no ser: La zona roja del conflicto mapuche como negación de la existencia territorial." In *(Las) Otras geografías en Chile*, ed. Andrés Núñez, Enrique Aliste, and Raúl Molina, 277–294. Santiago de Chile: LOM Editores.

Mansilla Quiñones, Pablo, and Miguel Melin Pehuen. 2019. "A Struggle for Territory, a Struggle Against Borders: The Mapuche conflict in Argentina and Chile contests notions of borders promulgated by the nation-state. Their territorial dispute encompasses not only material control over land, but also a fight to define its nature and use." *NACLA Report on the Americas* 51(1): 41–48.

Mansilla Quiñones, Pablo, José Quintero Weir, and Andrés Moreira Muñoz. 2019. "Geografía de las ausencias, colonialidad del estar y el territorio como sustantivo critico en las epistemologías del Sur." *Utopía y Praxis Latinoamericana* 24(86): 148–161.

Melin Pehuen, Miguel, Patricio Coliqueo, Elsy Curihuinca, and Manuela Royo. 2016. *AZMAPU: Una aproximación al sistema normativo mapuche desde el Rakizuam y el derecho propio*. Santiago de Chile: Instituto Nacional de Derechos Humanos (INDH).

Melin Pehuen, Miguel, Pablo Mansilla, and Manuela Royo. 2017. *Mapu Chillkantukun Zugu: Descolonizando el mapa del wallmapu: Construyendo cartografía cultural en territorio Mapuche*. Nueva Imperial, Chile: Pulof Ediciones.

———. 2019. *Cartografía cultural del wallmapu: Elementos para descolonizar el mapa en territorio mapuche*. Santiago de Chile: LOM Editores.

Panez Pinto, Alexander. 2018. "Water Territory in Latin America: Contributions from the Analysis of Water Conflicts Studies in Chile." *Revista Rupturas* 8(1): 193–217.

Panez Pinto, Alexander, Pablo Mansilla Quiñones, and Andrés Moreira Muñoz. 2018. "Agua, tierra y fractura sociometabólica del agronegocio: Actividad frutícola en Petorca, Chile." *Bitácora Urbano Territorial* 28(3): 153–160.

Serje, Margarita. 2011. *El revés de la nación: Territorios salvajes, fronteras y tierras de nadie*. Bogotá: Universidad de los Andes, Facultad de Ciencias Sociales, Departamento de Antropología, CESO, Ediciones Uniandes.

6

The Ethnocartography of *Sumak Allpa*

The Kichwa Indigenous Community of Pastaza, Ecuador

ALFREDO VITERY AND ALEXANDRA LAMIÑA

Introduction

In 1978, the Indigenous communities of the Kichwa Nation of Pastaza joined together to demand territorial rights to their ancestral lands, and fourteen years later, the Kichwa made a historic march from their communities in lowland Ecuador to Quito, the capital of Ecuador, to give visibility to their claim. Thanks in part to the attention they gained with this march, the Kichwa succeeded in their struggle, and the Ecuadorian state recognized their territorial rights. Today, the territory of the Kichwa Nation of Pastaza covers 3 million acres, divided into some 160 communities with a total population of approximately 20,000 inhabitants.

To reach our current level of institutional maturity, we have spent the past thirty-five years developing political and technical capacities. In particular, due to the lack of access to cartographic data produced by the Ecuadorean state, the Kichwa communities in Pastaza have relied on ethnocartography as a tool to affirm their ancestral territorial claims. In 2000, the Kichwa initiated an ethnocartographic survey of their territory for the purpose of controlling, managing, and practicing the sustainable and just use of their natural resources based on a community-based critical analysis of their territory. These studies have served as the basis for the *Sumak Allpa* Plan (Territorial Management Plan), as well as the *Sumak Kawsay* Plan (Life Plan). In the last few years, based on these strategic plans, we have started constructing an Autonomous Territorial Government (COOTAD 2010) to exercise our individual and collective rights within our ancestral territories.

The Kichwa people place high value on the idea of self-affirmation grounded in rights established by their ancestors. Values such as dignity, autonomy, and freedom must be based on the Kichwa principle of *sumak kawsay* (community life in harmony among the *aylluguna*, or families and the habitat), and of *sumak allpa* (land of abundance and of all lives). Therefore, for the Kichwa communities, ethnocartography is not only an exercise in mapping but also a political-territorial strategy based on Indigenous concepts of harmony with the land. Kichwa ethnocartography differs from conventional cartography by leveraging traditional and ancestral knowledge to spatially represent social, territorial, cultural, spiritual, environmental, political, geopolitical, and economic elements of the land. However, ethnocartography can only be effective through a process that involves active participation by community members, leaders, and external actors, where the cartographic visions, goals, and processes are all determined by the community.

In this chapter, we describe the participatory methods deployed in our ethnocartography and analyze the social and political processes—particularly those related to making claims vis-à-vis the state—which ethnocartography has facilitated. We specifically seek to describe the principles, concepts, and values of Kichwa Amazonian society that informed our approach to community-based mapping. We begin by briefly discussing how our ethnocartographic methods emerged from the principles of *sumak kawsay*, particularly its emphasis on the management of natural resources in communitarian territories. We next explain the ethnocartography process in detail, analyzing how it emerged as a response to governmental failures to provide access to cartographic information and discussing how ethnocartography was used in tandem with other participatory methodologies. Throughout this chapter, we show how ethnocartography facilitated the documentation of community life through the Kichwa vision of natural resource management. Finally, we close with an analysis of the role of ethnocartography in the development of an intercultural political agenda to build the first plurinational province in the Ecuadorian Amazon.

Principles of *Sumak Kawsay*

Sumak kawsay, also referred to as "good living" (*buen vivir*), is the life philosophy of Kichwa Amazonian society. This essential principle guides Kichwa life in harmony with the *ayllu* (family), between *aylluguna* (families) of the community, and between communities, peoples, and other cultures. Through the practice of *sumak kawsay*, the rights of nature are respected through human coexistence with other beings, and individual and collective rights are also exercised. At the same time, Kichwa society develops and innovates its own ways of life, worldviews, spirituality, and ancestral knowledge.

Sumak kawsay relies on four core principles that guide the norms and practices of good living. *Sumak ayllu llacta kawsay* refers to the governance of *sumak kawsay* society and the construction of integrated communities. This principle guides governmental management at the level of the communities, *aylluguna*, and individuals. It also includes the values of justice, participation, social control, and accountability. *Sumak allpa* guides the management of territory, habitats, and community natural resources. From this perspective, Kichwa community territory is thought of as the living space where *aylluguna* coexist with nature in its diversity of terrestrial and aquatic ecosystems. Spiritual beings also cohabit this space.

Sumak runa yachay, meanwhile, refers to the knowledge, experiences, and practices that are the foundation of the ancestral ethnosciences that serve to develop *sumak kawsay* and achieve a life of harmony in interaction with nature. Finally, the principle of *sumak mirachina* guides the management of the economy of *sumak kawsay* based on Indigenous planning strategies and equitable, just management of community lands and natural resources, including water resources, landscapes, and ecosystems. *Sumak mirachina* is based on the following elements: sustainability, self-sustainability, equality between *aylluguna*, reciprocity, respect for the principles of *sumak allpa*, bioknowledge, interculturality, biocommerce, sovereignty and food security, sustainable management of biodiversity, and agro-biodiversity of community ecosystems.

History of Kichwa Ethnocartography

Since 1978, the Military Geographical Institute has been the official entity responsible for the design, management, and administration of the national cartography of Ecuador (IGM 1978). Under this institute, cartographic policy has been centralized for state agencies and restricted for Indigenous communities, particularly with regard to information that references border areas, which are classified as "national security zones." Moreover, during the 1970s, oil companies began operating in the Ecuadorian Amazon. These companies used detailed cartographic information to conduct prospecting activities on Kichwa territories, and the information they possessed was handled with strict confidentiality. As a result, mapping activities in Indigenous territories and Kichwa community settlements have historically been limited to special interests.

The oil boom provoked an aggressive process of land occupation and invasion by settlers from other regions of the country. This migration into the Ecuadorian Amazon was promoted by the state under the Law of Agrarian Reform and Colonization (INDA 1964). Under this law, the lands of the Ecuadorian Amazon were declared "unoccupied" in direct contradiction to the territorial claims of the Indigenous communities. As a result, serious land conflicts arose between the Indigenous communities and settlers, missionaries, soldiers, and land speculators.

Beginning in 1982, Kichwa communities and their leaders (*curacaguna*), led by the Organization of Indigenous Peoples of Pastaza (OPIP), organized to stop the growing problem of invasions into their lands. Communities organized *mingas* (collective labor activities) with the participation of both men and women to demarcate ancestral boundaries and clearly define the territorial limits between Indigenous lands and lands occupied by settlers. Since the communities did not have access to cartographic information about the territory, the demarcations were made under the direction of the elderly authorities of the Kichwa territory. Through this strategy of territorial demarcation, the Kichwa people of Pastaza managed to slow the advance of colonization until 1992, when they received official territorial recognition from the Ecuadorian state.

Community elders played a central role in our territorial demarcation because they knew the location of our ancestral boundaries and the sites of *tambus* or *purinas* (temporal sites for familial activities), family settlements built in strategic places that offered protection from outsiders. During the Kichwa mapping process, ecosystems of cultural and ecological importance were identified and evaluated so they could be conserved as sacred habitats and spaces for the reproduction of forest, rivers, and lagoons. Initially, the elders traced maps on the ground and in beach sand along the riverbanks. Using these spaces as a canvas, elders identified the rivers, mountains, forests, and ancestral *tambus*, which would later serve as spatial references for the ethnocartography of Kichwa community territory. The children and youths in the communities transcribed this information onto poster boards, thus producing the initial sketches that would inform the subsequent formal maps. All the information we collected and mapped was disseminated and analyzed during community assemblies, where community members deliberated protection and conservation strategies for the Kichwa territory. Thanks to this process of collective knowledge acquisition and production, OPIP managed to map and demarcate all the territory of the Kichwa people of Pastaza, affirming their rights over their ancestral jurisdiction.

This was a time of vibrant resistance in defense of community lands and territories. In 1992, the collective march, or *caminata*, took place under the slogan "Allpamanta, Kawsaymanta, Jatarishun" (For the earth, for life, we rise up). This historic march marked a watershed moment in the history of the Kichwa Nation of Pastaza. For the first time, various indigenous nations (Kichwa, Shuar, Achuar) were able to present the maps they had drafted while demanding recognition of their ancestral territory as a space for life and self-determination. The march was led mainly by women and elders, who assumed their historical role as inheritors of the land from their ancestors and defenders of land for their children. More than two thousand people—men, women, youths, and children—organized themselves in their communities and marched to the city of Quito (Whitten, Scott Whitten, and Chango 1997). The protesters stayed in Quito for a month and ultimately managed to secure recognition by the Ecuadorian state of 3 million acres of ancestral Indigenous territory.

Kichwa Land Management Process

Though we had received recognition of our land rights, this did not necessarily guarantee our ability to exercise and protect our collective rights. Once we gained legal recognition from the state, the debate among community leaders turned to the importance of planning and managing the territory based on a Kichwa vision of territory. For this reason, in the year 2000, we decided to develop a land management process to sustainably conserve and manage our communal natural resources and, ultimately, develop a *plan de vida* (life plan) for the Kichwa Nation of Pastaza.

We organized a series of workshops in which community leaders, local technicians, and all community members worked together to devise local territorial management plans. Topics such as access to forest resources, hunting and fishing activities, and the sustainable use of community resources were the main concerns raised in these discussions. Likewise, the topics of watershed management and conservation of water resources were discussed in depth, and the communities settled along the banks of the main rivers of the Kichwa territory were able to reach agreements on these issues.

Families also devised strategies and regulations that could be used to apply the principles of the land management plan to everyday life. In one workshop, the issue of proposed sanctions for breaching regulations was widely debated, with a focus on how ancestral concepts of justice would apply in these cases. Additionally, the issue of state natural resource management—particularly with regard to exploration of oil, minerals, and other commodities—was a heated topic of discussion, as the policies that allow for the exploitation of these resources have serious impacts on Kichwa community life. At the close of the workshop sessions, the final territorial management plan that the communities had designed was brought to the General Assembly of the Kichwa People of Pastaza for approval.

As we conducted these workshops, we prioritized the recovery of knowledge about the vision of *sumak allpa* and community-based practices of land management and ecosystem protection. The reflections in the workshops were guided by the following key questions:

> What constitutes territory from our perspective? What are its basic elements?

> How is the Kichwa territory configured?

> With what vision of life do we inhabit this territory?

> What are our ecosystems like? What are the forests, rivers, and lagoons in our territory?

> What diversity of life coexists in our ecosystems, and what is the cultural and ecological value of this diversity?

> What are the *supay* (protective beings) that inhabit the forests, and how do they interact with the *runaguna* (peoples) and other beings to balance life in nature?

> What is the relationship between the *runa* (people) and the community with nature and other beings?

> What are the ancestral practices regarding access to ecosystems, and how do we take advantage of our existing resources?

> How do we achieve and exercise self-governance in our territory?

These collective reflections allowed us to define the visions and principles of *sumak allpa*, which directly informed the ethnocartography process we would pursue in the communities.

The Ethnocartography Process

Following this series of reflective workshops, we realized it would be necessary to generate thematic maps to define the territory of the Kichwa Nation, demarcate community lands, characterize the territory's natural resources, describe the human settlements, and delineate our water basins. To achieve this, we secured support from partner agencies to train local technicians, obtain technical assistance, and develop an administrative center for the Kichwa Nation of Pastaza. The Council of the Kichwa Nation of Pastaza, through its Department of Territorial Management, was responsible for organizing and planning the mapping workshops (Lamiña and Vitery 2010). This department was equipped with the technological capability to manage geographic information, and it could also count on the expertise of an interdisciplinary team of specialists in social cartography, territorial planning, sustainable development, and territorial and environmental rights. The development of this interdisciplinary team was possible thanks to NGO support and to an agreement with the Institute for the Regional Ecodevelopment of the Ecuadorian Amazon (ECORAE), the state agency responsible for development policies in the Amazon region.

We developed the project methodology in workshops with community members and leaders, local volunteers, and technicians from the territorial management department. The *curacaguna*, community leaders who had been involved in the community-based planning process, took a leading role in educating community members about the project and engaging families in the mapping process. The technicians, who were trained in Kichwa practices and ancestral knowledge of land management and natural resources, worked closely with the members of the community to set the goals for the mapping process. This strategy helped us design a methodology that facilitated participatory work in the territory in tandem with the visions of *sumak kawsay* and *sumak allpa*, while ensuring that the communities were empowered to implement and monitor territorial management plans once the mapping process was completed.

The ethnocartographic process that eventually emerged took place in four phases: (1) initial meetings, (2) ethnocartographic design workshops,

(3) data processing and analysis workshops, and (4) presentation of findings and results. This process was based on a careful, collective analysis of the fundamental relations between the Kichwa *ayllu* (family) and the territory. The main interactions with the land occur when families carry out productive activities, such as hunting, fishing, agricultural management, and gathering of forest resources. These social and cultural relations of the Kichwa with their collective territory are carried out through ritual practices known as *paju* (skill), *sasi* (restriction), *taki* (ritual song), *muskuy* (dream), and *misha* (epiphany), among other elements of the *sumak runa yachay*.

The mapping activities took place in houses, schools, community centers, and other locations within the community. The communities provided necessary logistical resources such as food and lodging, but also looked to external NGOs and government agencies for support with materials and supplies. Community leaders organized the mapping workshops and the *curacaguna* facilitated the work, while technicians explained techniques for georeferencing satellite images and other important concepts.

All the youths, children, adults, elders, and leaders of the communities attended the various workshop activities, making the mapping process intergenerational and fostering participatory decision-making and planning. Community members designed the maps by drawing on their practices, experiences, and oral traditions, providing detailed cartographic information about the ecosystems and resources within their ancestral territory. At the same time, the geographers used standard cartographic information to complement historical knowledge with present-day data about the territory, allowing community members to accurately spatialize external or unjust interventions in their territory (Figure 06.01).

Because ethnocartography is a collective process, it allowed elders to share their knowledge and visions of life with youths and children, who in turn were encouraged to apply their technical skills to design the thematic maps. Contributions from the older generations, with their ancestral knowledge of watershed management, ecosystems, and flora and fauna biodiversity, were key elements in the preparation of land management maps. Ethnocartography thus became an empowering practice for Kichwa communities. These activities helped increase the leadership capacities of community members and created a space for co-learning, sharing of ancestral knowledge, and exchanging stories and experiences that tie people to the land. The collective character of Kichwa planning and Indigenous land management was on display throughout the entire cartographic process.

FIGURE 06.01. Participatory process of territorial management in Victoria Community, Pastaza, Ecuador, 2010. Source: Alfredo Vitery.

Applying Ethnocartography to Planning and Land Management

It is important to reclaim and restore value to the knowledge that Amazonian Indigenous peoples possess regarding the management of their territories. Through their everyday land management, the Kichwa *runa* (the Kichwa people) come to *know and learn about* their territory, allowing them to classify ecosystems and manage forest resources in accordance with their ethnogeographic knowledge. This ethnogeographic knowledge of land management is guided by the principles of *sumak kawsay* and *sumak allpa*, and it is applied in the community management of the *yaku* (aquatic ecosystem) and the *sacha* (forest ecosystem).

The term *yaku* refers to all of the aquatic ecosystems in the Pastaza, including the Bobonaza, Pinduc, Curaray, and Arajuno Rivers. Kichwa ancestral knowledge identifies four types of aquatic ecosystems: the *jatun yaku*, or principal river; the *jatunlla yaku*, or secondary river; the *ichilla yaku*, or estuaries; and the *jita*, or lagoons. The *jatun yaku* (principal river) and its secondary affluent, *jatunlla yaku*, are of particular importance for Kichwa life. These waters provide resources that guarantee food security and also act as the principal means of intercommunity communication. For their part, the *ichilla yakuguna* (estuaries) are located near human settlements and are the main supply of potable water.

Finally, the *jita* includes the lentic ecosystems, which have been formed as a result of the natural damming of water between the valleys and hills. Most of the lentic systems are far away from settlements and have therefore experienced little human intervention over time. Because of this, the lentic ecosystems are of profound ancestral importance for the communities—their surroundings are considered to be dwellings of the *supayguna* (beings that protect nature). It is in this context that the Kichwa people learn the *sacha runa yachay*, using the surrounding ecosystem as a sort of stage for enacting this process.

Sacha, meanwhile, includes the terrestrial forested ecosystems that constitute the center of the diversity of life in the rainforest. These systems are characterized by the dominance of different species of flora and fauna, different types of soil, unique topography, and a level of humidity that is common in the Amazonian forests of Ecuador. According to historical Kichwa classification, the *sacha* also includes other smaller ecosystems known as *yaku pata pamba* (flooding site), *pamba* (plain area), *turu* (swamp), and *urku* (hill).

The ethnocartographic process thus allowed communities to identify and define the ecosystems that shape their territory and also document the diversity of lives that inhabit these ecosystems. The following three images show maps of some of these different ecosystems within the Kichwa territory. All of these maps function as tools that help the Kichwa communities sustainably manage their land.

First (Figure 06.02), *yaku pata pambaguna* are alluvial plains surrounding riverbanks and lagoons. In these areas, floods deposit silt enriched with organic material, making the land especially well suited for agriculture. For this reason, *yaku pata pambaguna* are the spaces where the main *llactaguna* (human settlements) and *tambuguna* (seasonal family settlements) were historically established. The main rivers are the Villano, Curaray, Bobonaza, Arajuno, and Copataza. These areas are important for the economy of the Kichwa communities, as they allow families to harvest timber and palms to construct homes and canoes. Also, due to a concentration of fruit trees in these areas, several species of mammals and birds are concentrated in the *yaku pata pambaguna*, presenting a valuable hunting resource.

The map identifies forest resources in the *yaku pata pambaguna*, including

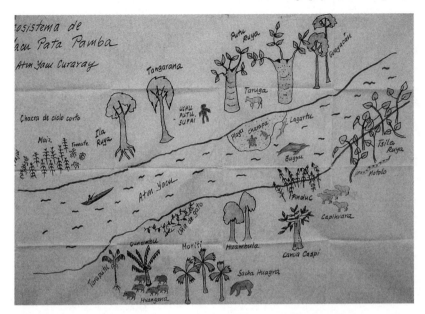

FIGURE 06.02. Participatory map of the *Yaku pata pamba* ecosystem, Pastaza, Ecuador, 2009. Source: Alfredo Vitery.

predominant flora species (such as palm and ceiba forests, medicinal plants, and species useful for construction), as well as animal species that seasonally migrate to this area (such as tapirs, peccaries, deer, capybaras, and reptiles). The map depicts a family farm where crops such as corn, potatoes, chili peppers, and tomatoes are cultivated. It also shows the riverbanks and beaches where various turtle species, a valuable food source, live. The map also includes the central figure of Uchuputu Supay, the protective being who inhabits this ecosystem. The colors and shapes used in the mapping symbolize the diversity of species within this natural environment, with Uchuputu Supay highlighted as the being that sustains this diversity.

The second map (Figure 06.03) illustrates *pamba*, a nonfloodplain forest, that is located between the hills (*urcuguna*) and the alluvial forest (*yaku pata pamba*). *Pambaguna* are crucial for the reproduction of avifauna. In these ecosystems, the *yana allpaguna* (black organic soils), which boast a high concentration of nutrients, are predominant. According to Kichwa ancestral classification, these soils are the most suitable for crops of small family farms.

The *pamba* ecosystem map reflects the high diversity of plant and especially tree species that characterizes this habitat. The map shows the presence of the Amazanga being, the generator of *sumak allpa*, the land of abundance

FIGURE 06.03. Participatory map of the *pamba* ecosystem, Pastaza, Ecuador, 2009. Source: Alfredo Vitery.

and of all lives. In this ecosystem live several species of birds, mammals, and reptiles that are crucial for Kichwa livelihood. The colors and shapes applied to this map highlight the characteristics of several species native to this environment. Among the ancestral symbols used in the map are also the figures of Amazanga and Uchutican, who are considered protective beings of this ecosystem.

Finally, *urcuguna* are forested hills that form chains that delimit the basins and sub-basins of the Kichwa territory. It is in these highlands that the headwaters of the two main rivers, Curaray and Bobonaza, originate. *Urcu*'s vegetation is diverse, and the area includes species that the Kichwa use for building, medicinal purposes, and consumption. The different *urcuguna* possess ancestral names, and some are considered sacred sites or centers of ancestral wisdom.

This ethnomap (Figure 06.04) shows the characteristics of the *urcu* ecosystem where the natural springs in the Kichwa territory originate. It also illustrates the predominant species of flora and fauna in this habitat. The varieties of palms and their fruits are used for food, and the wood from these trees is used to build houses. The map also identifies the variety of medicinal plants and fruits that are commonly collected in this area. The *urcu* ecosystem is considered to be the home of Amazanga, the protector of life in the rainforest, which is also depicted on the map.

In ethnocartographic work, the rich knowledge of community members allows for the development of effective and informative maps. Hunters contribute their knowledge of the *sacha* (forest) ecosystems, while other community members with greater knowledge of the *yaku* (aquatic system) share their knowledge to map the aquatic systems. Women contribute their knowledge

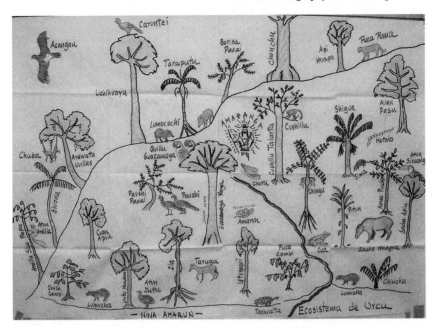

FIGURE 06.04. Participatory map of the *urcu* ecosystem, Pastaza, Ecuador, 2009. Source: Alfredo Vitery.

of community agricultural processes and the flora and fauna of the *sacha* and *yaku* ecosystems. Men and women together determine which ecosystems are particularly fragile or culturally significant, and all community members help map areas that act as the cultural stage for learning the *sacha runa yachay*.

Through this deeply collaborative and collective process, ethnocartography made it possible for the Kichwa to spatially assess how the community's lands were before, how they are now, and how they will be in the future, in line with their cultural conceptions of space. Building on this ethnocartographic process, community members were able to develop the Plan of Territorial and Natural Resources Management of the Kichwa Nation of Pastaza. This land management plan is part of the overarching Kichwa Life Plan, a plan founded upon respect for the collective and constitutional rights of the Kichwa people that articulates the social, economic, and environmental priorities of the communities.

Figures 06.05a, 06.05b, and 06.05c show a map of the territorial "zoning" of the Kichwa Commune of San Jacinto del Pindo that was the end product of a participatory mapping process (Lamiña 2014). This map uses the technical "logic" of cartography to deconstruct the normative conception of Kichwa

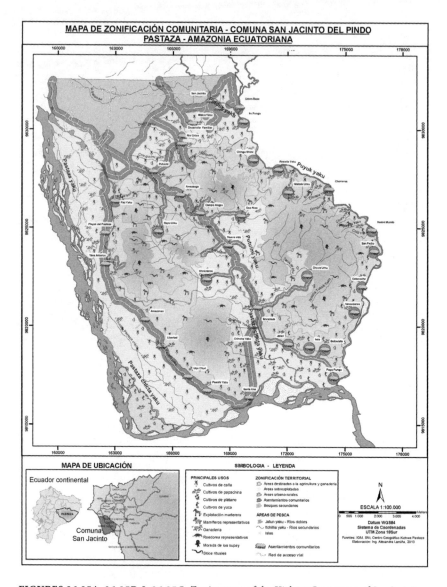

FIGURES 06.05A, 06.05B & 06.05C. Zoning map of the Kichwa Commune of San Jacinto del Pindo, 2013. Source: Alexandra Lamiña.

FIGURE 06.05B

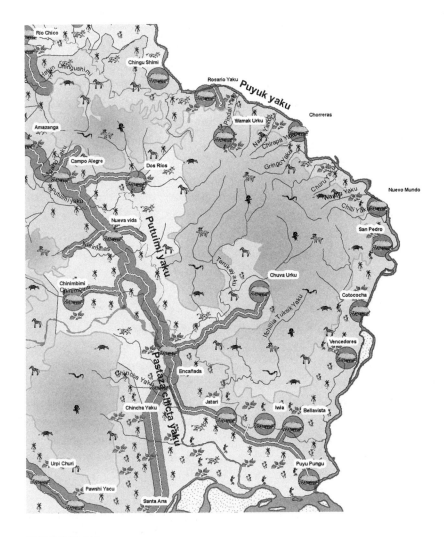

FIGURE 06.05C

territories perpetuated by the state while maintaining Kichwa iconography. For example, the map uses traditional scales, spatial georeferencing, boundary lines, and an existing road network to foster a common understanding of the space, but it also includes cultural symbols and geographic features labeled with Kichwa names.

According to Ecuadorean law, such Indigenous territorial management plans are supported by constitutional provisions that recognize the right of Indigenous peoples to self-determination within their ancestral territories. Ethnocartography thus served to provide the information necessary to construct this plan, contributing to the strengthening of our territorial, social, and economic governance. Because of the key role of ethnocartography, we recommend that this process be formally codified in state policy as the most appropriate method for developing Indigenous territorial management plans.

Conclusion: Ethnocartography and Kichwa Territorial and Natural Resource Management

Our ethnocartography has been predicated on the concept of *sacha runa yachay* (Kichwa knowledge). Ethnocartography has provided a tool for articulating the visions and guiding elements of the *sumak kawsay* (life in harmony and balance), the *sumak allpa* (forests and territories), and the *sumak mirachina* (communal economy). Together, all of this knowledge and ancestral knowledge has allowed the Kichwa *runaguna* from Pastaza to document and map the history of their territories and the transformations that have occurred in their ecosystems over time.

Within the broader process of the struggle for a plurinational province in Pastaza, ethnocartography has been a crucial, but not the only, means for us to effectively exercise our rights—not only rights pertaining to the defense, legalization, Indigenous planning, and management of land but also rights related to pursuing the Kichwa Life Plan. In this sense, ethnocartography constitutes a tool that can be continually deployed to document grassroots knowledge about the new realities that the Kichwa communities are experiencing.

However, ethnocartography is more than just technical work. For us, it has been a collaborative endeavor that brought together elders, adults, youths, children, and leaders who together own the *sacha runa yachay*. Every step of the process is participatory, from initial assessments and concept development to mapmaking, visioning, and implementation of territorial management plans. Due to the participatory nature of these methodologies, they give rise to a learning process that in turn serves to strengthen local capacities and collective knowledge. Ultimately, ethnocartography can serve as a means to fundamentally transform social, political, and economic processes for the benefit of Indigenous peoples and the respect of their cultural heritage.

REFERENCES

COOTAD (Código Orgánico Organización Territorial Autonomía Descentralización; Organic Organization Code of Territorial Autonomy and Decentralization). 2010. Retrieved from oas.org/juridico/PDFs/mesicic4_ecu_org.pdf. Quito, Ecuador: Asamblea Nacional.

IGM (Instituto Geográfico Militar). 1978. Ley de Cartografía Nacional. Retrieved from www.igm.gob.ec/work/files/LOTAIP_2014/pdf/leycartografianacional.pdf.

INDA (Instituto Nacional de Desarrollo Agrario). 1964. *Ley de reforma agraria y colonización.* Quito, Ecuador: Talleres Gráficos Minerva.

Lamiña, Alexandra. 2014. *Construcción participativa de la etnocartografía para la gestión integral del territorio y recursos naturales de la Comuna Kichwa San Jacinto del Pindo, Pastaza-Amazonía Ecuatoriana.* Bachelor's thesis, Universidad Técnica Particular de Loja, Ecuador.

Lamiña, Alexandra, and Alfredo Vitery. 2010. *Proyecto de construcción de la circunscripción territorial de la Nacionalidad Kichwa de Pastaza.* Puyo, Ecuador: Kichwa Organization of Pastaza.

Vitery, Alfredo. 2002. *Diseño participativo de la comunidad kichwa Yana Yaku (Plan de Manejo Comunitario Yana Yaku).* Puyo, Ecuador: Kichwa Organization of Pastaza.

Whitten, Norman E. Jr., Dorothea Scott Whitten, and Alfonso Chango. 1997. "Return of the Yumbo: The Indigenous Caminata from Amazonia to Andean Quito." *American Ethnologist* 24(2): 355–391. doi.org/10.1525/ae.1997.24.2.355.

7

Social Cartography and Territorial Planning in Robles, Colombia

CARLOS ALBERTO GONZÁLEZ

Introduction

The Maroon communities in the municipality of Jamundí, Colombia, were founded by *cimarrones*, slaves who escaped from the large haciendas located in the north of the *departamento* (state) of Cauca. They established their communities along the edges of rivers and developed agricultural, hunting, and other subsistence practices while remaining cognizant of the need to conserve the resources around them. The traditional farm, or finca, became fundamental for the construction of the collective identity of these *cimarrón* communities. These farms were at the center of all of the communities' relationships to the land: fruit trees were used for food and timber, plants were grown for both medicinal and spiritual purposes, and animals were both hunted and domesticated. The farm became a cultural expression of both doing and being. The *cimarrones* were eventually able to negotiate their freedom and purchase their lands from the slave owners, forming the agricultural communities we see today.

From 1996 to 1998, the *cimarrón* communities of Robles, Chagres, Quinamayó, and Villapaz, located in the southern flatlands of the Cauca River in Jamundí, were the focus of an organizational capacity-building project led by the Corporación Autónoma Regional del Valle del Cauca (CVC; Regional Autonomous Corporation of the Valley of the Cauca). CVC contracted with Fundación La Minga (known as Fundaminga), an interdisciplinary group of cartographers and scholars, to facilitate this capacity-building and mapping process. At the time, Fundaminga was actively working alongside communities in the region in their struggles for territorial rights and resource management, using social cartography as its principal methodological tool.[1]

Social cartography is informed by principles of participatory action research (PAR), which breaks with positivist assumptions about the neutrality of scientific knowledge and instead foregrounds a collective approach to

FIGURE 07.01. Participatory mapping workshop in Robles, Colombia, 2006. Source: Carlos González.

knowledge production and coproduction. From this perspective, mapmaking is understood as a collective project of knowledge production. The intergenerational dialogue fostered by social cartography leads to the emergence of "social" maps, which serve to safeguard collective memory and support local management of natural and cultural biodiversity.

Through this participatory process, social cartography was introduced to the Black communities in the Cauca Valley. Although our team had no access to mapping software or other advanced technologies, social cartography nonetheless proved to be a methodology that allowed community members to think critically about the future management of their territory and about how to most effectively preserve their culture and maintain their well-being (Figure 07.01).

In this chapter, I share our experiences with this process, discuss the outcomes of the process that still shape our communities today, and reflect on the strengths and limitations of this methodology. As I argue here, social cartography is not a "magic wand" that can immediately solve the many challenges threatening the livelihoods of Indigenous and Afro-descendant peoples in Colombia today. Rather, it is a process that, when correctly carried out, facilitates the construction of a collective vision for the future.

Traditional Biodiversity Management in the Cauca Valley

The Cauca region has a population of some 20,000 inhabitants, 98 percent of whom are Black or Afro-Colombian. Today's communities descended from several African cultures, including the Lucumí of Nigeria, the Congo and Angola of the Bantu region, the Chamba of the Ivory Coast, the Carabali of the Coast of Calabar, the Bambará of Mali, the Guagui of Niger, the Mondorgo of the Congo, the Mandinga of French Sudan, and the Ararat and the Mina from the Kingdom of Dahomey. Some surnames from other parts of Africa are also prevalent in the region, including Viafara, Aponzá, and Guazá, names that trace their origins to the Bantu and Yoruba cultures of western Africa.

The villagers participating in the mapping project are members of communities with long and rich cultural traditions, tracing back to the Maroon slaves that formed *palenques* in the region beginning at the time of independence from Spain. The *palenques* were economically self-sufficient communities that nurtured new cultural expressions through their agriculture, architecture, handicrafts, oral traditions, art, and folklore. All of these expressions of culture, when represented on maps, come together to reveal complex networks of social relationships.

Until the mid-1990s, these Afro-Colombian communities were mostly self-sufficient, still maintaining their ancestral traditions associated with sustainable agriculture and fishing in the unique marshes that are native to the area (known as *madreviejas*), which provided up to 80 percent of their food supply. The *cimarrón* approach to sustainable farming yielded a veritable pantry of agricultural products, including orange, tangerine, lemon, cocoa, soursop, and banana crops. The "economic-ecological map" (Figure 07.02) of the territory located in Jamundí, the southern, low-lying area of the valley of the Cauca River, illustrates this intense yet sustainable land-use system: the predominant color on the map is blue, representing the main channels, streams, *madreviejas*, and other wetlands of the Cauca River that have nourished traditional farms for centuries.

Two fundamental characteristics define life in the southern reaches of the Jamundí municipality. First and foremost, this area forms the ancestral territory of Afro-Colombian communities whose cultural framework is centered on spirituality, kinship ties, and social reciprocity. These notions stem from

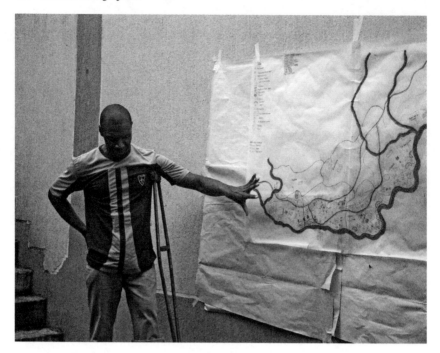

FIGURE 07.02. Social cartography map, showing ecological and economic features in Jamundí, Colombia, 2006. Source: Carlos González.

the times of slavery and were central to our ancestors' pursuit of freedom. And second, this unique *cimarrón* culture was developed in an area that hosts two of the most scarce and vulnerable ecosystems in the country and in the world: tropical dry forests and wetlands. The small patches of tropical dry forest that still remain in the area are fortunately under careful community management. The area's wetlands are thus, arguably, its most characteristic feature. The most typical landscapes seen in Jamundí are the traditional agroecosystems of Afro-descendant peoples, the old wetlands and *madrevieja* marshlands, and the Cauca River itself, which we see as "Mother Water," who gives us life and sustains the development of our communities.

The CVC also recognizes the environmental significance of this area and, in collaboration with the local Afro-descendant communities, proposed the declaration of a protected area in the region in accordance with Law 165 (established in 1994), which aims to conserve prime sources of biodiversity and environmental goods and services for current and future generations. However, today the area faces pressures and threats stemming from the arrival of "modern progress," which has four main manifestations in Jamundí. First, "progress" is seen in the sugarcane operations and cattle ranches that have consumed over 50 percent of the farmland in the area, obstructed access to wetland ecosystems, and polluted the environment through practices such as aerial spraying and the discharge of untreated wastewater. Second, "progress" comes from a fishing agro-industry that extensively cultivated "red tilapia" between 1990 and 1997, drawing labor from the Black community members, who in turn abandoned their agricultural lands. Third, "progress" comes in the form of regulations governing the waters of the Cauca River that directly affected the wetlands and caused tributaries to lose their connection with the main river, which in turn reduced traditional food production in Afro-descendent communities. Finally, "progress" takes the form of the "urban" values that were introduced into the area and created a great cultural rift between elders and young people, who began to lose their sense of identity with their communities and instead sought to emigrate to the city.[2]

Because of these external pressures on our communities, our culture, and our traditional land-use practices, from 2002 to 2003 several community-based organizations in the villages of Timba, Chagres, Robles, Quinamayó, Villapaz, and Guachinte developed a project to regain control of our territory and ensure sustainable biodiversity management practices in the Jamundí región. These organizations included Funecorobles (from Robles), Palenque Cinco (from Quinamayó), CorpoVillapaz (from Villapaz), Horacio Gómez Gallo Presbyterian Educational Institution (from Robles), the Luis Carlos Valencia Educational Institution (from Villapaz), and the José María Córdoba Educational Institution (from Timba-Valle).

As this project developed, we found that the level of food security in these Black communities was at less than 20 percent, when about a decade earlier it had been closer to 80 percent. This was due in part to the loss of an estimated 40 percent of the communities' traditional knowledge of medicinal plants. We also found that effectively all (some 99 percent) of the traditional farms were managed by the elderly, making it difficult to transmit our cultural heritage to younger members of the community. Perhaps unsurprisingly, given these realities, we also learned from the official Colombian agricultural census data for the Jamundí municipality that agricultural subsistence production had declined. In 2014, only 66.2 percent of agricultural production units, which the census defines as essentially all lands devoted to agriculture and farming, in the municipality of Jamundí were declared to have at least one production lot dedicated to self-consumption, compared to 86.2 percent in the rest of the Valle del Cauca and 70.5 percent across the country.[3] This data showed us that while farming remained prevalent in the region, fewer and fewer farms were following traditional methods of production that would ensure the food security of Afro-Colombian communities.

Social Cartography in the Community of Robles

Because of the strong history of organizing around land rights claims in Robles, in 1998 the CVC and Fundaminga chose the community as the site of the first social cartography project in Jamundí. Attendance was sparse in the first workshops, so the attendees decided to spend a few days informing more community members about the project so they could later regroup with more participants. Using this approach, we were eventually able to secure the participation of teachers, students, grassroots organizations, and other community members who may not have otherwise gotten involved in the process. Additionally, we were able to encourage more elders to attend, who contributed to the process by sharing their memories and rich traditional knowledge. In these early workshops, we focused on developing maps simply by drawing the existing reality of Robles. Little by little, however, the group began developing a more complete map, one that reflected the different versions of reality that emerged through the dialogues that the mapping exercises incited.

The first phase of the mapping process assumed a rigorous pace for approximately three months. Every seven days, Fundaminga facilitated a one-day workshop in the municipality. The work was not easy, but we were able to accomplish it by forming small working groups within each community, especially of older adults, teachers, and students, to help ensure that the community remained committed to the process. Each week, community members looked forward to discussing the discoveries made through this participatory data collection. The mapping workshops, which were truly collective knowledge-construction exercises, took place at different locations and different times of day depending on the availability of the community members. Many times, unprompted by Fundaminga representatives, community members would keep working on projects late into the night without losing their enthusiasm.

The workshops were intended to be flexible, allowing the participants to propose changes that could quickly be incorporated into the process. The excitement that was generated as participants rediscovered the nature of their environment created an atmosphere of curiosity and expectation, which in turn motivated them to take more ownership over the data collection process. For example, participants decided to bring the maps to the streets of Robles to both verify and supplement the information that had emerged in workshops. By taking the maps door-to-door in this way, workshop participants encouraged the majority of the community to directly participate in the social cartography process. Meetings were even held with local teachers to explain the process to students, so children were also involved in the mapping workshops.

Four types of maps, which will each be discussed more fully in the following sections, were developed during these workshops, with each community creating one map of each type:

1. Ecological-economic maps: These maps delimit family parcel boundaries and show places that have been used to plant crops; hunting and fishing areas; forests and mountains; and areas where medicinal plants, wood, and seeds can be found.

2. Administrative-infrastructural maps: These maps delimit our entire territory and show its internal political-administrative divisions. They also include the location of dwellings; representations of the family relations among the people who live in these homes; the location of public services such as schools, health posts, and commercial enterprises; communal buildings and areas for sports and recreation; and hazardous areas.

3. Relational network maps: These maps illustrate the networks that weave the people of a territory together with what exists both within and outside each network. For example, relational network maps show sites where agricultural products are sold, locations where cultural practices are carried out, sacred sites, recreational spaces, places where traditional festivities take place, and landscapes with significant natural beauty.

4. Conflict maps: These maps describe the relationships community members have with nature; with the state; and with mining, timber, oil, and sugarcane industries. These maps provide stark illustrations of the socio-environmental disasters facing our communities.

In addition to the above, we also developed rough sketches and (nongeoreferenced) maps to illustrate both our historical memory and our desired future.

ECOLOGICAL-ECONOMIC MAPS

Ecological-economic maps show the areas of environmental importance for the community, highlighting traditional farms, wetlands, the Cauca River, natural springs, sites of deforestation on riverbanks, beaches along the Cauca, sites of agrochemical contamination, the Salvajina reservoir, the smaller river basins, and sites for community recreation, such as waterfalls and ponds (including the Charco la Torre, the Charco Redondo, and Las Dos Agüitas), which are especially important for the youth and children. We also show local small businesses on the map, since these constitute important resources in terms of domestic production and consumption.

The ecological-economic maps demonstrate the great ecological and economic value of the Robles tributary to the Cauca. It not only serves as an attractive recreational area for young people, but the maps showed how it is also the main source of water for domestic consumption, irrigation, recreation, livestock nourishment, fishing, hunting, and provision of firewood from fallen branches and trees that grow in the riverbed. During the workshop, participants were able to learn important information that was previously unknown to the young people. For example, in one meeting, elders explained that the Robles used to run through the community in the 1940s and 1950s, but as the community expanded, the course of the river was changed. In addition to representing how the physical characteristics of the community lands had changed over time, the mapping process also made us aware of new economic practices in the community, as it revealed local microenterprises that now complement the traditional farm as productive units for the families of Robles. These include the sale of lottery tickets, banana leaves, medicinal plants, and floral bouquets made by local families.

The map also included the Salvajina dam, which forms a reservoir located outside the territory in the municipality of Suárez. The dam was originally built in 1982 to regulate the flow of the Cauca River, but it was later retrofitted to be used for the generation of electricity. Still, even though it was located outside Robles, it was included on the map because of its negative impact on the wetlands, traditional farms, and other local cultural traditions of the communities. The reservoir blocks the natural flow of the Cauca River, preventing it from overflowing into the floodplain in the winters and depositing the rich silt that is needed as fertilizer for the community's traditional farms. The dam also prevents the river from recharging the wetlands, which is necessary for the water to be oxygenated and for the fish population to replenish. This intervention in the natural systems of the area produces a state of food insecurity for the community of Robles. Without this natural fertilizer and these productive wetlands, families are left to depend on what little food they can produce from their small patio gardens. The dam upstream in the Cauca River has thus become a socio-environmental disaster, causing erosion, loss of land, and displacement of the poor. The *cimarrón* communities have lost around 200 hectares of traditional farmland due to the erosion of the Cauca River.

ADMINISTRATIVE-INFRASTRUCTURAL MAPS

The administrative-infrastructural map provides an inventory of temporary and permanent housing in both rural and more developed areas of Robles, including building materials used and the number of floors of each structure (Figure 07.03). We also mapped the locations of local and external institutions as well as channels that facilitate communication, such as alleys, roads, trails, and coverage areas of public infrastructure services. To augment this information, we conducted a population census to better understand how the demographic composition of the community had changed over time. Finally, we mapped the areas where the community had already expanded as well as potential areas for future growth, being sure to note areas of environmental risk.

As we developed this map, we learned from elders that the original communal territory used to be more extensive than what the municipal administration of Jamundí had indicated. The reason for this reduction in communal lands was the establishment of the firm Colapia S.A., one of the most important producers of red tilapia during the late 1980s and early 1990s. The company had provided employment opportunities, leading to increases in household incomes and the replacement of traditional adobe structures with homes built from brick and cement. However, because of the establishment of the factory, community members abandoned their traditional farms. To compound the negative impacts of this halt to traditional agriculture, the tilapia production also prompted intense changes in the local ecology and aquatic systems. This disruption of historical practices of traditional farming has been nothing short of a social disaster for the community.

RELATIONAL NETWORK MAPS

To develop the relational network maps, we located and described sites of mythical and spiritual significance. This included the cemetery, which is considered a transitional space between life and death; the "loma de la cruz," a noteworthy hill with spiritual significance; the *madrevieja* marshes that are

FIGURE 07.03. Administrative-infrastructural map of Jamundí, Colombia, 2006. Source: Carlos González.

the site of the *bunde* ritual, during which community members set a raft with candles afloat as a gift to Mother Nature; and other sites important to Afro-Colombian memory and history, including the Candileja, El Duende, La Pata Sola, and La Viudita, among others (Figure 07.04). We also mapped sites along roads and trails that should be avoided at night due to the presence of the dead. Finally, we located places where magical plants grow as well as the homes of traditional healers.

The participants in the workshop also mapped sites in neighboring communities where cultural events are carried out, such as the Adoración al Niño Dios in the Black community of Quinamayó. This ceremony takes place each February, instead of December, as February was the only time when slaveholders allowed enslaved Blacks to celebrate Christmas. In addition, the maps showed the nearby cities of Cali, Jamundí, and Santander de Quilichao, all places where local products are sold. The community of Robles once had a large and diverse market, but this market was gradually replaced by one in the neighboring community of Timba that was connected to the local railway system. While traditional farms still supply products for the local market in

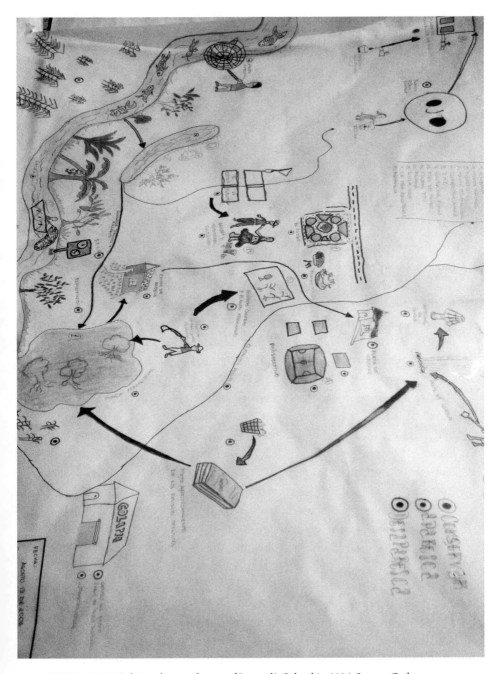

FIGURE 07.04. Relational network map of Jamundí, Colombia, 2006. Source: Carlos González.

Robles, pressure from the sugarcane industry; the loss of traditional seeds; and the replacement of permanent, traditional foods by transitory crops (such as chili, passion fruit, papaya, and soursop, as called for by government programs such as the Cadenas Hortofrutícolas initiative) are all real issues that threaten the sustainability of Afro-descendant and peasant farms. The mapping exercise thus allowed community members to better understand how the breakdown of traditional trading patterns has impacted the *cimarrón* communities.

CONFLICT MAPS

Conflict maps were the final map products that the communities produced during the workshops. During our discussions, participants identified two key historical events that led to the socioeconomic and ecological transformation of the region: (1) the construction of the state-owned Represa (Dam) Salvajina in 1982 and (2) the practices of the private agroindustrial company Piscifactoría Colapia, which operated from 1992 to 1997. As mentioned above, Colapia introduced the region to the "red tilapia," a fish species from Indochina, which it cultivated extensively along a 20-kilometer stretch of the Cauca River. This same river, as mentioned above, was manipulated and regulated by the Salvajina Dam. The fish farms provided employment for around five thousand local community members, who were attracted to this work because it was easier and provided a higher income than traditional farms. However, this shift led to a sharp decline in local food production, and when Colapia closed in 1997, those same five thousand jobs were lost.[4]

Prompted by the discussion of these two transformative events, workshop participants began to trace all of the conflicts that currently impact their community. Among others, these included the tensions over fencing between farms and the advent of new diseases in crops, especially in economically important crops such as bananas and coffee. The discussion also addressed challenges that came from the lack of institutional support, lack of credit, and lack of subsidies for small farmers. As the last step in the conflict mapping, participants mapped poorly maintained stretches of local roads.

As a result of this mapping activity, workshop participants were better able to rank the multiple challenges threatening their community. They decided that the most serious problems were a lack of organizational capacity and low participation in communal projects from residents. In line with these conversations, the participants agreed that to most effectively move forward, it was necessary to (a) pursue a development plan for the village, (b) develop projects to increase self-esteem and reduce apathy among community members, (c) raise awareness of community norms, (d) inspire professionals to share their knowledge with other community members, and (e) develop an ethno-educational plan to motivate local youths to participate in community-building activities. These social cartography workshops, therefore, fostered the development of community-based maps but also facilitated critical discussion, which in turn laid the foundation for future projects and efforts in defense of Afro-Colombian territory.

Conclusion

Ultimately, the social cartography project served to facilitate community-based planning and conservation and also led to alliances with national and international universities for collective knowledge production. As a participatory process dealing with agriculture and conservation, the project also strengthened efforts to research some noteworthy native species in the area, including a type of possum called the *chucha* (*Didelphis marsupialis*) and the medicinal plant known as *pipilongo* (*Piper tuberculatum*). In terms of empowerment, the project also opened channels for direct dialogue between the communities and the CVC, providing community members with a more central role in regional environmental planning and municipal comprehensive planning in Jamundí and fostering new, important connections with other organizations. Indeed, it was in part because of the mapping project that we were able to block the development of a proposed sanitary landfill in Jamundí (the Pan de Azúcar project). We believe that it also helped community members successfully mobilize to protect the La Guinea wetlands from development. Finally, and more broadly speaking, our social cartography project encouraged participation from children, youths, adults, and elders in the efforts to reconstruct local historical memory and strengthen the defense of Afro-Colombian territory and rights.

Social cartography is not a panacea. The technology itself cannot solve the organizational weakness of communities, nor can it by itself produce the projects and developments that communities may be envisioning. However, social cartography allows us as researchers to work collaboratively and humbly in line with future plans and visions born within the communities alongside which we partner—visions that may align with different understandings of how time and space function. In this way, it breaks down barriers that try to differentiate between those who "have knowledge" and those who "do not know," giving way instead to new forms of representation and knowledge that operate outside of these constraints.

NOTES

1. "Diagnóstico socioeconómico de Robles (1998–2000)" 2000.
2. "Diagnóstico socioeconómico del territorio" 2006.
3. "Censo Nacional Agropecuario 2014" 2016.
4. "Diagnóstico socioeconómico del territorio" 2006.

REFERENCES

"Diagnóstico socioeconómico de Robles (1998–2000)." 2000. Cali, Colombia: Fundaminga and CVC.

"Diagnóstico socioeconómico del territorio." 2006. Cali, Colombia: Alianza Funecorobles, Palenque Cinco, CorpoVillapaz. Project report.

"Censo Nacional Agropecuario 2014: Actividad agropecuaria y población en territorios de grupos étnicos del Valle del Cauca." Bogotá: Departamento Administrativo Nacional de Estadística (DANE), April 2016.

PART III

FIGURE 07.04. Relational network map of Jamundí, Colombia, 2006. Source: Carlos González.

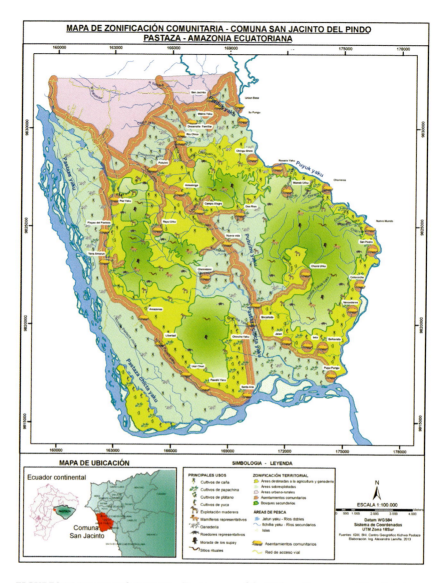

FIGURES 06.05a, 06.05b & 06.05c. Zoning map of the Kichwa Commune of San Jacinto del Pindo, 2013. Source: Alexandra Lamiña.

FIGURE 06.05b

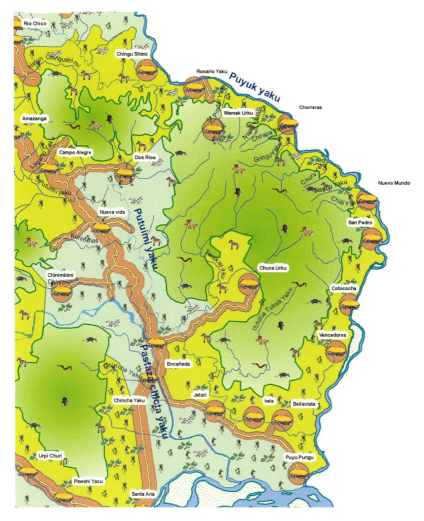

FIGURE 06.05c

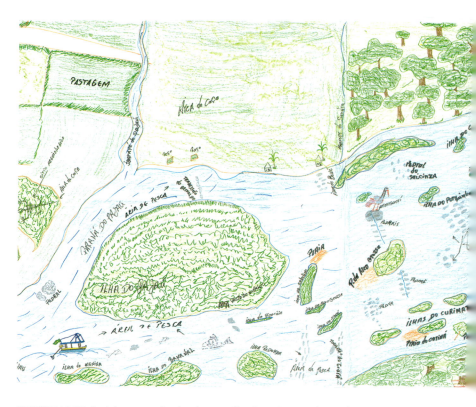

FIGURE 08.05. Social cartography sketch map of land use, Pimental, Brazil, 2015.
Source: Gabriel Locke.

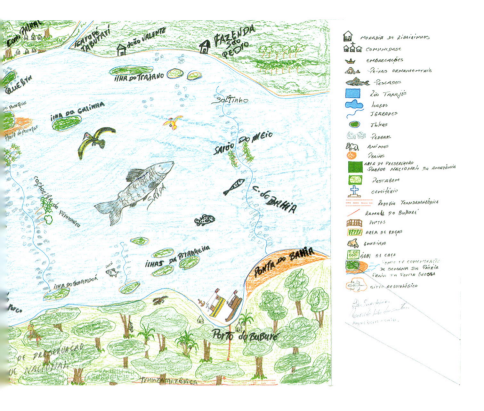

FIGURE 08.06. Social cartography sketch map of the community, Pimental, Brazil, 2015. Source: Gabriel Locke.

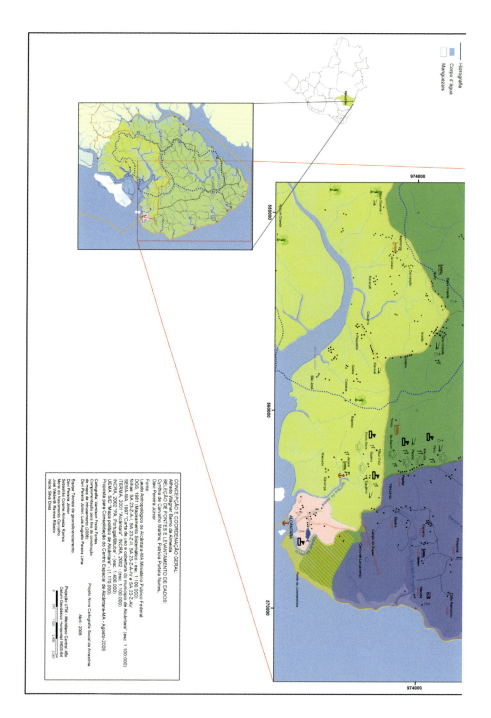

FIGURE 11.02. Map showing expansion plans for the Brazilian Space Program produced by the Brazilian anthropologist Alfredo Wagner Berno de Almeida for the Federal Public Prosecutor's Office. Source: PNCSA.

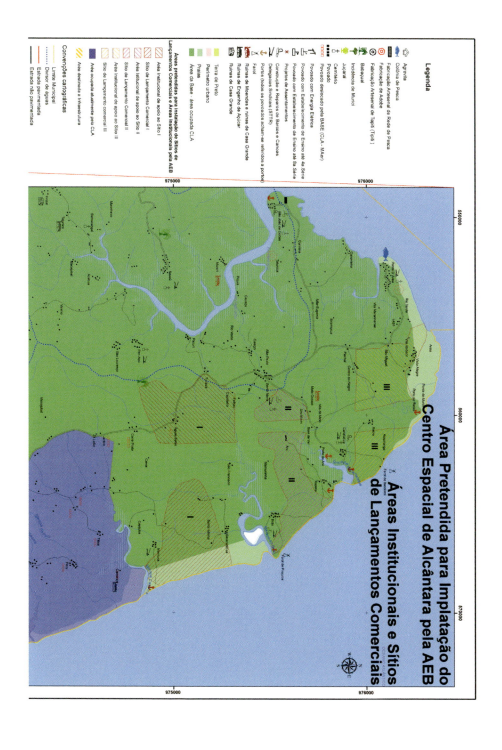

FIGURE 02.03. Calendar-map from the Yurutí del Vaupés Indigenous community in the Colombian Amazon. Source: Fundaminga.

FIGURE 05.02. Map of places of spiritual significance, Lof Hueñivales, Community Benancio Huenchupán, Chile. Source: Pablo Mansilla.

8

New Social Cartography and Ethnographic Practice

ALFREDO WAGNER BERNO DE ALMEIDA

Introduction: Social Science and New Social Cartography

Social science research often involves going "into the field" to observe the everyday activities of "research subjects," such as members of traditional and Indigenous communities. The implications of such researcher-subject relationships are both real and significant, as fieldwork occurs in diverse social spaces where social agents engage in deeply significant and complex practices. Moreover, these various social actors may have different, and at times competing, perceptions of spatial phenomena as they construct diverse meanings of material landscapes.

It is within such complex social contexts that our work in new social cartography is situated. The concept of "new social cartography," an innovative methodology for social science research and practice developed at the New Social Cartography Project of the Amazon (PNCSA), departs from the prevailing understandings of Western cartography. Instead, we find it critically important to consider the social and political positions of mapmakers, as these actors construct dominant definitions of territory and its boundaries on behalf of the state and other external authorities. In so doing, we challenge any illusions that social science research such as ours can ever produce an empirical, "knowable" reality. New social cartography goes beyond simply describing a territory or delineating boundaries on maps to instead view cartography as a critical practice for the defense and control of territories.

Our use of the word "new" thus reflects how we seek to account for different perceptions of space and encourage a plurality of meanings to ensure that our work is founded on situated knowledge that is grounded in local realities. The concept of a "new" social cartography suggests constant movement and change, premised on our understanding of mapping as an explicitly political process shaped by social realities instead of an "objective," "empirical," "normative," and "positivist" social science method.

FIGURE 08.01. Social cartography workshop in Nossa Senhora do Livramento, Brazil, 2018.
Source: Murana Arenillas Oliveira.

FIGURE 08.02. Social cartography workshop in Nossa Senhora do Livramento, Brazil, 2018.
Source: Murana Arenillas Oliveira.

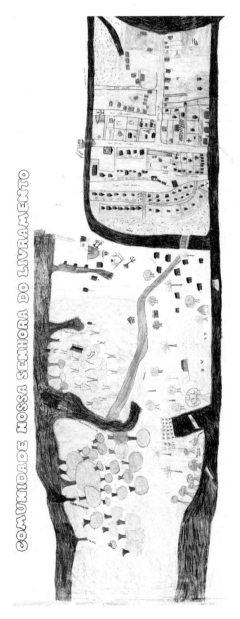

FIGURE 08.03. Social cartography sketch map from Nossa Senhora do Livramento, Brazil, 2018. Source: Murana Arenillas Oliveira.

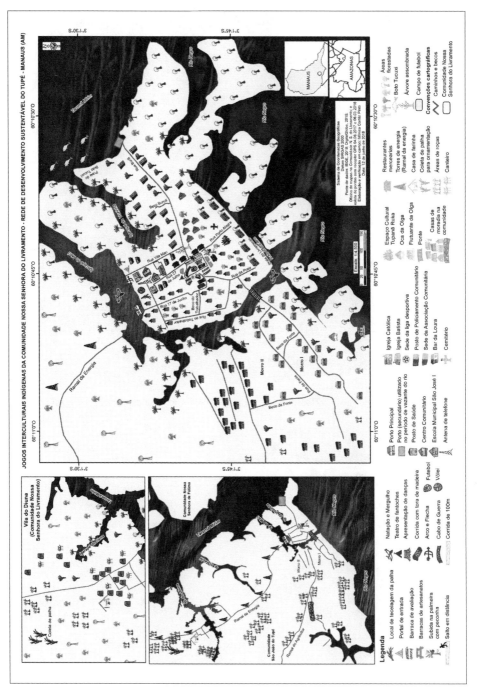

FIGURE 08.04. Final social cartography map from Nossa Senhora do Livramento, Brazil, 2018. Source: Mônica Cortez Pinto.

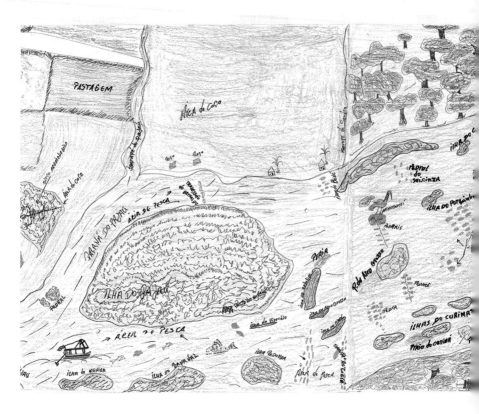

FIGURE 08.05. Social cartography sketch map of land use, Pimental, Brazil, 2015. Source: Gabriel Locke.

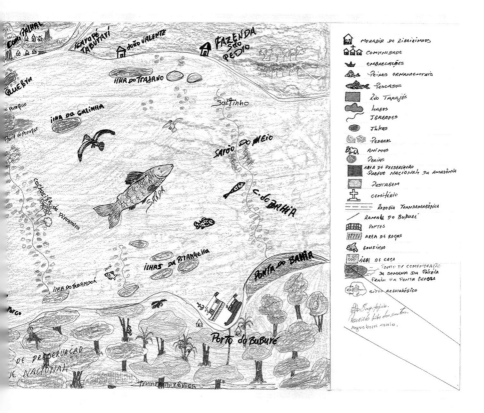
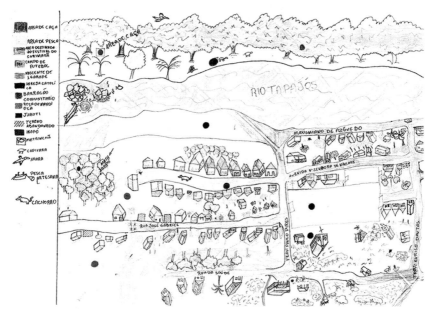

FIGURE 08.06. Social cartography sketch map of the community, Pimental, Brazil, 2015.
Source: Gabriel Locke.

Social Science Research, Collective Mobilization, and New Description

In deploying cartography to illuminate situated knowledge, we see it as a means of facilitating encounters that may result in new ways of thinking. As Pierre Bourdieu (1999) argues, "confrontations" of experiences and reflections take place in all aspects of social life and stem from the different perspectives associated with different social positions. Such an approach to understanding how people encounter and perceive the world around them signifies a "new description"—a new type of social science research that resembles ethnography in seeking (albeit in a limited way) to describe the social lives of peoples and communities classified as "traditional" through interviews and direct observation. Because even though traditional communities are politically marginalized, they nonetheless demonstrate a deep awareness—arguably, a deep consciousness—of their territorial boundaries, and they are fully capable of describing and reproducing this knowledge.

The "consciousness" of phenomena such as geographic boundaries arises from two distinct dimensions: the physical dimension where territorial knowledge is situated, and the psychological dimension where self-awareness resides. As I describe here, social agents explicitly demonstrate their territorial consciousness through the claims they make to the state. This coupling of knowledge stemming from physical reality with psychological awareness challenges the identity- and territory-based classifications that have historically been imposed by colonial powers and reproduced through mechanisms such as censuses, registries, legal codes, and maps. In other words, the growing consciousness in traditional communities, expressed through collective actions and through processes of identity formation, is now increasingly in tension with the more simplistic and racialized categories of identity, such as significations of "black," "yellow," "white," or "brown," that are used in the national census.

In Brazil, this challenge to racialized categories of traditional communities stems from an intense period of political mobilization in the 1980s, which saw the emergence of new social movements as well as the formation of new categories of identity. As a result of this mobilization, expressions of collective identities featured prominently during the 1986–1987 deliberations in the National Constituent Assembly and were later incorporated into the 1988 Federal Constitution. As traditional communities reflected on their relationship with the state during this period, they demonstrated deep knowledge of their constitutional rights.

Many scholars view these collective actions as attempts to build political units that are formalized, institutionalized, and integrated in networks that facilitate ongoing dialogue with the state and with other collective units. Yet through the "aggregate effects" (Céfaï 2007, 8) of collective actions, the significance of such movements for ethnic and territorial rights extends beyond mere demands for recognition from the state. Instead, such collective actions drive a growing self-consciousness, which in turn becomes the foundation for everything from political solidarity and new forms of political relationships to a shared agenda for making claims before the state and common understandings of the boundaries of collective territories.

In other words, by recognizing the struggle of the Other as linked to one's own struggle, each individual is able to reconstitute her history and reimagine her own "origin." This understanding of individual identity filtered through the framework of collective experience provides the basis for group cohesion, which in turn is the precursor to political action. As they rethink their histories, traditional peoples—who are acutely self-aware and standing shoulder to shoulder in transformative action—increasingly see themselves as parts of a whole that is mobilizing around a common purpose and struggle. It is this sense of political legitimacy that allows them to produce new collective histories and imagine alternative futures. What is more, this increased sense of legitimacy also facilitates representation of significant landscapes and new critical understandings of spatial and social relationships between natural places and built environments, thus giving rise to an entirely "new description" of collective territories. Even as traditional communities develop collective strategies, however, they remain aware of their differences and particular interests. Because of this, the participatory maps produced within the context of such mobilizations reflect social diversity and multiple points of view but also a shared experience of conflict and a recognition of the simultaneously distinct and collective nature of local realities.

The Politics of Territory and Identity

In Brazil, the work in social cartography is informed by the 1988 Constitution and Convention 169 of the International Labour Organization (ILO), both of which serve as the legal foundation for the rights claims pursued by traditional peoples and communities.[1] By leveraging these legal instruments, traditional communities have been able to mobilize in pursuit of their territorial rights while confronting arguments that their oppressors have historically used to justify inequalities in resource allocation. Since the 1980s, Indigenous and traditional peoples in Brazil have focused on affirming their rights to access natural resources and pursue common uses of land while simultaneously furthering their demands for land titles and pushing for more effective designations of traditionally occupied spaces.

By linking their claims to traditionally occupied lands with expressions of collective "traditional identities," these social movements are pursuing what Hobsbawm and Ranger (1983) refer to as a politics of "invention of tradition." That is to say, Indigenous peoples and Quilombolas,[2] *quebradeiras de coco babaçu*,[3] river dwellers (*ribeirinhos*), *faixalenses*,[4] and other collective identities—have gained greater visibility by linking their identity formations with their economic struggles. In so doing, their territorial claims have become part and parcel of their self-consciousness as they construct a collective identity while rejecting the imposed classifications of their culture invented by the Brazilian census. These processes therefore become codependent: political mobilization around a specific territory is fundamental to consolidating the collective identities of traditional peoples, and these identity formations, in turn, ensure the physical and social reproduction of these communities within their territories.

As Edward Said (2012) argues, social mobilizations such as those pursued by the traditional and Indigenous peoples of Brazil seek to define what actually is or is not "traditional" by setting social boundaries and delimiting spatial domains. From this perspective, new social cartography departs from historical narratives that insist on the primacy of continuity with the past. Rather, since continuity with the past is largely imagined in invented traditions, new social cartography produces ethnographic descriptions that celebrate cultural diversity by breaking with linear notions of time.

Social cartography, then, is rooted in the political mobilization of marginalized social agents (Pudal 2009, 187) and is based on what some scholars have referred to as the "art of resistance" (Scott 2008). This "art of resistance," along with the concept of a "culture of resistance" (Said 2012), allows us to better understand the political actions of marginalized groups, which often take place in domains that are rarely recognized as political. From this perspective, political life is not merely associated with official or assimilated political-organizational forms with headquarters, members, statutes, general assemblies, and the like. Instead, political life also emerges in groups, communities, peoples, and other units of mobilization that seek to build new political relationships and practices through a new description of their own realities.

By pursuing their political claims through such units of mobilization, traditional communities are leading the way to new understandings of the political. In particular, by politicizing the "traditional," Indigenous and traditional communities break with linear conceptualizations of time. These mobilizations allow for the articulation of political positions based on local rootedness coupled with environmental consciousness, thus making it possible to link economic claims with identity-based struggles. As Said (2012) suggests, a culture of resistance is premised on reclaiming, renaming, and reinhabiting land, which in turn fosters new ways of thinking and asserting rights claims.

Emergence of a "New" Social Cartography

Social cartography has the potential to shape new ways of thinking and innovate new political practices, promoting a conception of land and boundary making that is rooted in equality rather than hierarchies of power. However, state agencies have also appropriated the concept of social cartography to justify their approaches to land demarcation and demonstrate their supposed respect for traditional peoples and communities. This is deeply problematic, since mapping processes must be based on a deep consciousness of territorial boundaries and political struggles to produce "useful knowledge." If not, the mapping process may lead to an arbitrary acceptance of territorial rights as defined by official criteria rather than by the community itself. Because of this misappropriation, in 2004 we chose to characterize the PNCSA approach as a "new" social cartography. In so doing, we sought to distinguish our work from the ostensibly participatory mapping pursued by the state by highlighting our critical, and new, perspective on social cartography.

One example of the ways in which new social cartography brings forth multiple understandings through cartographic confrontations is seen in the work in the Indigenous community of Nossa Senhora do Livramento, located in the Tupé Sustainable Development Reserve in the Brazilian Amazon (Figures 08.01–08.02). The mapping project in this community intended to give visibility to the Intercultural Games that are held annually in Livramento. These games provide a space to present and preserve traditional dances, stories, and other symbolic practices that are now threatened in this area of the Amazon. By moving beyond the ordinary meaning of the term "cartography" and eschewing both traditional cartographic symbology and the Cartesian coordinate system, the mapping workshops contributed to the struggle for recognition and cultural expression by providing a new description of the community (Figures 08.03–08.04).

A second project emerged from the threats faced by *ribeirinha* communities along the Tapajós River due to the construction of the Tapajós River Hydroelectric Complex. The goal of this mapping project, which took place in a series of workshops in 2015, was to document the social history and resource uses in Pimental to support the land rights claims of the residents. The fishers and other residents of Pimental exercised agency in defining what was relevant to include on *their* map of *their* land, thus ensuring that the maps were directly derived from their own local realities and lived experiences (Figures 08.05–08.06). Life in these traditionally occupied lands is not static and unchanging, but rather profoundly dynamic in nature, and new social cartography provided the fishers with a means of critical analysis in their struggle against state and private interests driving the development of the hydroelectric complex.

These projects illustrate how traditional peoples and communities are incorporated into the process of knowledge production, fostering research relationships that have led to "new descriptions." By challenging dominant approaches to cartography and developing what we refer to as a "new" social cartography, we have fundamentally changed our ways of thinking about social science research. We have been able to forge new research relationships, drawing on the power of social cartography to describe and analyze complex and evolving realities.

NOTES

1. See Decree of the Secretariat of the Heritage of the Union (SPU) No. 89 of April 15, 2010. *Diário Oficial da União* (Brasília: Brazilian Federal Government, April 6, 2010), 91–92.

2. Descendants of Afro-diasporic communities formed by escaped slaves. See Pereira, this volume.

3. "Babaçu coconut breakers" are Indigenous women in Brazil who collect and "break" babaçu coconuts to harvest the flesh and shell for a variety of sustainable agricultural and economic uses.

4. *Faixalenses* are traditional peasants in the central-south region of Paraná who follow a collective production system, including collective use of land for animal production and environmental conservation.

REFERENCES

Bourdieu, Pierre. 1999. "Understanding." In *The Weight of the World*, 607–626. Stanford, CA: Stanford University Press.

Céfaï, Daniel. 2007. *Pourquoi se mobilise-t-on? Les théories de l'action collective*. Paris: Éditions La Découverte.

Hobsbawm, Eric, and Terence Ranger. 1983. *The Invention of Tradition*. Cambridge: Cambridge University Press.

Pacheco de Oliveira, João. 1999. "Entrando e saindo da 'mistura': Os índios nos censos nacionais." In *Ensaios em antropologia histórica*, 124–151. Rio de Janeiro: Editora UFRJ.

Pudal, Bernard. 2009. *Un monde défait: Les communistes français de 1956 à nos jours*. Paris: Éditions du Croquant.

Said, Edward W. 2012. *Culture and Imperialism*. New York: Random House.

Scott, James. 2008. *La domination et les arts de la résistance*. Paris: Éditions Amsterdam.

9

Social Cartography and the Struggle for Multiethnic, Urban Indigenous Lands

The Case of the Beija-Flor *Aldeia* in Rio Preto da Eva, Brazil

EMMANUEL DE ALMEIDA FARIAS JÚNIOR

Introduction

Starting in the 1950s, Indigenous people living in urban areas in Brazil began forming *aldeias*, Indigenous communities or Indigenous "associations." Even though these groups were quite distinct from one another, often speaking mutually unintelligible languages and maintaining different cultural practices, they united through shared struggles for territory and collective claims to Indigenous identity. This phenomenon was first reported in the classic work of Roberto Cardoso de Oliveira on the Terêna (1960, 1968); more contemporary scholarship includes research by Silva (2001), Sales (2008, 2016), and Maximiano (2008), among others.

This chapter describes the case of Beija-Flor, a 42-hectare urban Indigenous territory in the municipality of Rio Preto da Eva, located 80 kilometers from Manaus in northern Brazil. Beija-Flor was ceded to the Indigenous people of Rio Preto in 2008 by way of a municipal dispossession law, but the eight Indigenous groups living in the *aldeia* are still fighting to protect their urban territory. I focus, in particular, on their use of social cartography to successfully assert their territorial claims, while at the same time negotiating internal conflicts and confronting pressures caused by urban expansion as well as attempts at land expropriation. I discuss a project developed through a collaboration between the community and the New Social Cartography Project of the Amazon (PNCSA) (Almeida, Sales, Lima et al. 2008), which illustrates how urban Indigenous communities use social cartography as a tool in the fight for spatial justice and recognition.

I have closely followed the ethnic mobilization of the Indigenous people of Beija-Flor for fifteen years, initially as a student at the Federal University of Amazonas and later as a researcher with the PNCSA. Since my responsibility as a social scientist has not ended with the project described here, I have continued to serve the community as an adviser on community development projects such as reforestation, beekeeping, vegetable production, and construction of community spaces for meetings and rituals. In 2006, when I joined the PNCSA, the Indigenous struggle for legal territorial recognition had already been going on for more than a decade. During my work, I witnessed the dramatic events impacting the residents of Beija-Flor. The Indigenous people experienced intimidation and death threats, contamination of waterways, destruction of houses, and land invasions. Because of these imminent and existential threats to their territory, Fausto Andrade, the leader of the Sateré-Mawé Indigenous group in Beija-Flor, invited the PNCSA to develop a participatory mapping workshop with the ultimate goal of producing an Indigenous map to be disseminated on the PNCSA website.[1] Even though I served as principal researcher, the project was premised on an equitable relationship with residents based on shared responsibilities and co-authorship. That is to say, we sought to break with the traditional researcher-subject dichotomy, attempting to ensure that the residents of Beija-Flor would also feel like protagonists and authors in this process.

History of Beija-Flor

The initial Beija-Flor Indigenous Community, known as Beija-Flor I, was formed between 1997 and 2007 by eight ethnic groups: Tukano, Sateré-Mawé, Dessana, Mura, Arara, Mayuruna, Baniuwa, and Baré. The legal foundation for such a formal Indigenous community composed of distinct peoples emerged in the 1970s, when initial interethnic political agreements were established in an effort to minimize possible differences and internal conflicts. Two strategies in particular were used to consolidate the community and transform it into a supportive space for distinct ethnic groups. The first consisted of—grouping disparate cultural elements under a common umbrella, thus forming a collective identity as Indigenous peoples. This strategy was oriented toward neighboring residents and the city of Rio Preto da Eva, seeking to project a united front and common territorial claim. The second strategy consisted of forming familial units based on ethnic groups, which became reflected in the division of work within the community. After the successful consolidation of Beija-Flor I, Indigenous leaders began to mobilize other Indigenous communities in the same municipality to form other such *aldeias*. Two new communities eventually emerged on the banks of the lower Rio Preto and Rio Urubu in Rio Preto da Eva, taking the names Beija-Flor II and Beija-Flor III.

However, despite the careful planning, tensions did arise between the different groups, as recounted by Chief Fausto Andrade of the Sateré-Mawé:

> In the beginning of founding the Beija-Flor Community, since various relatives from different ethnicities were invited, we had some difficulty with communication—being from different tribes, with different languages. So we had a problem, too, with communication! But little by little, we tried to overcome it, to understand each relative, their thoughts, too. And there were some problems that tribes had with those of other ethnicities; they would say, "Mine is stronger, mine is better, yours is weaker. I am a good fisherman, I am a good hunter, you are not like me!" So we had this type of conflict, this problem in the beginning. But afterward we started to understand and respect each decision of the relatives. (Chief Fausto Andrade, thirty-three years old, Sateré-Mawé ethnicity, oral interview mapping workshop, October 19 and 20, 2007)

In Beija-Flor, internal conflicts often end up without a resolution, or with an agreement *not* to seek a solution. Otherwise, one of the parties involved in the conflict would have to remove themselves from the area, which would cause the group to weaken and lead to a shortage of workers. In the rare cases when a family did have to leave the area, the Fundação Nacional do Índio (FUNAI; National Indian Foundation, the national agency responsible for Indigenous affairs) was called upon to carry out the "transfer" of the family. However, such internal conflicts tend to dissipate when communities face external threats, causing rival groups to unite to protect the natural resources that guarantee their physical and social reproduction.

The unity among Indigenous groups in Beija-Flor emerges from the construction of a collective identity as Indigenous peoples. This "political alignment" (Cohen 1978) between distinct ethnic groups does not signify abdication of ethnic identities; on the contrary, this sort of situational organizing provides a means of establishing difference with the Other through the reconstitution of a distinct ethnicity (Barth 2002). As Barth (2005, 15) argues, ethnicity represents "the social organization of cultural differences." In the case of Beija-Flor, this alignment among distinct Indigenous peoples has produced a new conceptualization of indigeneity and a new sense of belonging. Identity as Indigenous peoples has been configured as a "unit of mobilization"

(Almeida 2006), allowing different ethnic groups to join together in a new form of political organization during a moment of struggle for territory. At the same time, residents in these communities shift between different forms of representation, sometimes reflecting their identity as Indigenous people and other times reflecting the peculiarities of their ethnic group. As I illustrate, during the mapping workshop attended by the PNCSA, the distinct Indigenous groups carefully considered how to represent unified Indigenous narratives yet also distinct ethnic identities on their maps.

Conflicts over the Recognition of the Beija-Flor Indigenous Lands

The 41.63-hectare property where Beija-Flor I is now located originally belonged to the American merchant Richard Melnyk, who, according to residents in the community, verbally granted them rights to the land in the early 1990s. As the elder Joaquim Sampaio recalled:

> He [Richard Melnyk] told me: "You go there and work, I set aside an area for you Indigenous people to work making handcrafts, planting, and so on." And we came here, we planted, because there was no one left here anymore. This area was abandoned. I started to work. My son was eleven years old at the time. We started to plant, little by little. (Joaquim Sampaio, sixty-six years old, Tukano ethnicity, oral interview mapping workshop, October 19 and 20, 2007)

However, because of the legal uncertainty associated with their land rights, the Indigenous residents of Beija-Flor I continuously faced pressure to abandon their territory. In the late 1990s, they experienced the first of various attempts at territorial expropriation by Antônio Tadeu Drumond Geraldo and his wife, Arlene Glória Alves Monteiro, who sought to expel the community and convert the land into residential lots. To confront these attempts, the Indigenous peoples appealed to the Federal Public Prosecutor's Office and other supporters to guarantee their territorial security.

In the subsequent court proceedings, Glória claimed she had purchased the land on October 2, 1997, from Richard Melnyk. As evidence, she presented a receipt of sale and purchase ostensibly between herself and Melnyk. However, the receipt was signed by Tadeu, who had claimed power of attorney and therefore the authority to dispose of Melnyk's property. The receipt showed that Tadeu had sold the 41.63 hectares to his wife for a sum of R$2,000.00 (two thousand Brazilian reais, or about US$537), an amount far below market value. Records from the legal proceedings also showed that Melnyk had previously attempted to revoke Tadeu's powers of attorney, but they had been deemed irrevocable by the courts. Melnyk had also placed a notice in the newspaper *A Crítica* on July 15, 1994, announcing that Tadeu was no longer his proxy, to no avail.

With the death of Melnyk in 2001, Tadeu returned to the scene and claimed the land in the name of his wife. Over the course of this conflict-ridden relationship, employees contracted by Tadeu intruded on part of the land with tractors, proceeding to demolish houses, destroy crops, and pollute the canal that passed through the community. According to Tadeu, his intention was to subdivide the Indigenous territory into private lots, but he could not "invest in that area because the Indians are still there. They invaded those lands."[2] He was supported by the former mayor of Rio Preto da Eva, Anderson José de Souza, who, according to Chief Fausto, offered to pursue legal dispossession of the land in return for a concession of two hundred of the private lots.

Tadeu's attempts to dispossess the Indigenous people of their territory also relied on verbal threats and racial slurs. According to Certificate of Incident #631/98, recorded in Book #007/98 dated August 28, 1998, Glória made a series of claims against Chief Fausto, the leader of the Beija-Flor Indigenous Community, for allegedly committing illegal "land invasions." In Manaus, a large part of the urban area emerged in the late 1970s and 1980s through land occupation, which is referred to as "invasions" by state and municipal governments in order to criminalize and depoliticize the landless movement. Through our "ethnography of documents" (Acevedo Marin and Castro 2004, 144) carried out prior to the mapping project, we also found frequent use of deprecating terms such as "pseudo Indians," "invaders," "mere renegade invaders," and "*caboclos*" in court documents. In an effort to question residents' Indigenous identity and undermine their claims to territory, Glória also referred to the leader of the community as a "renegade Indian."

In addition to pursuing his claims in court and through pejorative language, however, Tadeu also sought to leverage the authority of maps to assert his legitimate representation of the "region" (Bourdieu 2005). In Tadeu's mind, these ostensibly objective cartographic representations would make his case seem legitimate to both the Indigenous people and the possible buyers of the lots. Most famously, he had a map prepared that referred to the parcel as "Belo Horizonte," identifying the proposed lots with crosses while

FIGURE 09.01. Map of proposed Belo Horizonte land lots developed by Antônio Tadeu Drumond Geraldo, 1998. Source: Prefeitura Municipal de Rio Preto da Eva.

eliminating any reference to the existing Indigenous community (Figure 09.01). According to Sampaio:

> One time (Tadeu) showed (the map) to me: "Mr. Joaquim, here is the map! This blue map!"—It was a blue map, his map, ... where each one [buyer] would receive a lot, each lot marked with a cross, there were crosses all over the area! He showed it to me. "But it's your business, I don't know anymore," I said to him. He has a map ... every time that he is here in this city, he says, "I'm going to open the land lots, I'm going to expel the Indigenous people"—he would talk like that every time, but he doesn't enter anymore. That's the man, Tadeu! (Joaquim Sampaio, sixty-six years old, Tukano ethnicity, oral interview mapping workshop, October 19 and 20, 2007)

Confronted by Tadeu's cartographic representation of the land as commercial property, the Indigenous communities decided to develop their own maps based on their own understandings of the area. By defining the boundaries of their territory through the authoritative vocabulary of cartography, they would collectively develop their own representations to challenge Tadeu's map. If Tadeu were to appeal to his map in making a claim over the territory, the Indigenous communities decided they must similarly make their claims through cartography. In making this decision, the Beija-Flor Indigenous Community entered what Almeida (1994) refers to as a "war of maps." Indigenous and other collective identities have been invisibilized by the so-called civilizational processes of the Brazilian state, making it necessary to make our distinct collective identities and our claims explicit. Since technical instruments such as maps are typically invoked to grant authority to representations of space (Bourdieu 2005), the residents of Beija-Flor would now deploy these same instruments to produce "objective" representations of their territory in an explicit challenge to the dominant conceptualization of private property rights.

New Social Cartography and the Indigenous Map

In June of 2007, Chief Fausto contacted the PNCSA, requesting that we provide technical assistance to a social cartography project organized by the communities of Beija-Flor. The first mapping workshop would focus on Beija-Flor I, and two subsequent workshops would be held in Beija-Flor

FIGURE 09.02. Participants in the mapping workshop, October 19–20, 2007, *Aldeia* Beija-Flor, Rio Preto da Eva, Amazonas, Brazil. Source: PNCSA Archive.

II and III, respectively. I would serve as lead researcher representing the PNCSA, heading a team that also included Glademir Sales dos Santos and Ana Kátia Santana Cruz from Programa de Pós-Graduação em Sociedade e Cultura da Amazônia-PPGSCA/Universidade Federal do Amazonas-UFAM; Nadja Christine de Castro Souza from Programa de Pós-Graduação em Direito Ambiental-PPGDA/Universidade do Estado do Amazonas-UEA; and Willas Dias da Costa from Programa de Pós-Graduação em Educação-PPGE/UFAM. In addition, Luis de Oliveira of the Sateré-Mawé ethnicity would be taking video footage of the workshops.

The first workshop took place in Beija-Flor I on October 19–20, 2007, with seventy people in attendance, including thirty-four adults and thirty-six children from Beija-Flor I, II, and III (Figure 09.02). The workshop was covered by the journalist Thaís Brianezi and the cameraman Alexandre Baxter from the local news station Canal Futura. The participation of Canal Futura was made possible through a partnership with PNCSA that aims to produce television programs about traditional peoples and communities and their experiences with social cartography. The collaboration has resulted in the five-part series *The Amazon: A New Cartography*, with each episode focusing

Social Cartography and the Struggle for Multiethnic, Urban Indigenous Lands 153

on a different geographical area, including Rio Jauaperi, Cunuri, Iauaretê, and Belém in addition to Rio Preto da Eva.

The workshop began with oral histories told by elder participants, emphasizing the life trajectories of different families leading up to their arrival in Rio Preto da Eva. They explained that they settled Beija-Flor upon the invitation of Richard Melnyk, they provided detailed accounts about the conflict over the land, and they recounted the origins and meanings of significant religious and cultural practices, such as the "Ritual of Jabuti and Dabacuri" practiced by the Tukano indigenes of the upper Rio Negro. We also collected narratives about life in Rio Preto da Eva and cases of discrimination against the residents. Between workshop sessions, community members performed traditional songs and dances, illustrating the specific ethnicities of the performers but also demonstrating how the distinct groups had overcome their differences to form an "ethnic unit of mobilization" (Almeida 2006). As Indigenous musicians played flutes, others were telling stories of violence and lamenting the destruction of the river, plantings, and houses, leading both to tears and calls for revolt. In this way, the workshop served to consolidate the community, strengthening residents' bonds of solidarity and determination to confront those who sought to usurp their territories.

On the second day of the workshop, the participants drew sketch maps to develop their representation of the Beija-Flor I Indigenous Community (Figures 09.03 and 09.04). They first delineated areas where they collected plants used to make handcrafts, including *açai, bacaba, caracru, chumburana, inala, "lágrima de nossa senhora," morototó, patauá, pachiuba, puká, pupunha, taboca, tento, tucumã, tucumãi*, and *turi*. This resource mapping also included points located outside the community, such as locations of *arumã* fibers utilized by the Tukano people of the upper Rio Negro to make strainers, baskets, hampers, and mats. Next they sketched the locations of homes ("huts") identified by different colors, with each color corresponding to a distinct ethnic group: black indicated the huts of people of Tukano ethnicity; blue, Mayuruna ethnicity; orange, Baniwá ethnicity; brown, Dessana ethnicity; yellow, Baré ethnicity; green, Mura ethnicity; red, Sateré-Mawé ethnicity; and gray, Arara ethnicity (Figures 09.05 and 09.06).

Community members also decided to draw the entrance to the community, the bathing sites, the site where the Jabuti Ritual takes place, the Adventist Church, the trails, the bridge, the forested areas, the active fields (which include the chicken coops), "old fields" (identified as historic sites), medicinal plant gardens, the flour mill, the vegetable garden, and the old site for raising boar. In addition, they marked sites of conflict, such as the polluted

FIGURE 09.03. Elaboration of sketch maps, October 2007, *Aldeia* Beija-Flor, Rio Preto da Eva, Amazonas, Brazil. Source: PNCSA Archive.

FIGURE 09.04. Presentation of the sketches drawn by the participants in the mapping workshop, October 2007, *Aldeia* Beija-Flor, Rio Preto da Eva, Amazonas, Brazil. Source: PNCSA Archive.

FIGURE 09.05. Part of the sketch map developed by participants of the mapping workshop, October 2007, *Aldeia* Beija-Flor, Rio Preto da Eva, Amazonas, Brazil. Source: PNCSA Archive.

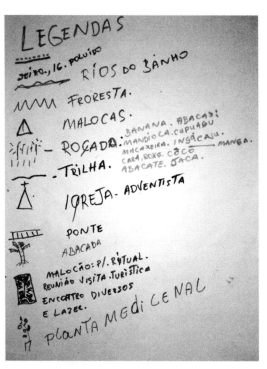

FIGURE 09.06. The color legend developed by participants of the mapping workshop, identifying the colors that correspond with the distinct ethnic groups in Beija-Flor I, October 2007, *Aldeia* Beija-Flor, Rio Preto da Eva, Amazonas, Brazil. Source: PNCSA Archive.

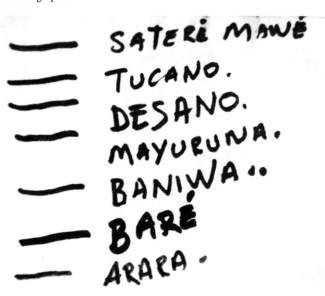

FIGURE 09.07. Legend from one of the sketches produced during the mapping workshop, October 2007, *Aldeia* Beija-Flor, Rio Preto da Eva, Amazonas, Brazil. Source: PNCSA Archive.

canal, the intrusions, the plaque with bullet holes, and the unpaved road, assigning colors and symbols to the different spatial features (Figure 09.07).

During the mapping workshop, we also gave a course on basic concepts of Global Positioning System (GPS) so community members could register the geographic coordinates of places important to them. Only men decided to take the GPS course, but women and children were also involved in the actual process of delimiting the territory and selecting the points to be recorded. Participants eventually traversed the entire physical boundary of the area belonging to Beija-Flor, with Iranir Gomes da Costa of the Marubo ethnicity taking readings using an E-Trek GPS unit and Willas Dias da Costa of the PNCSA recording the coordinates (Figure 09.08).

Based on the GPS coordinates and the sketch maps, and also using Google Earth imagery, Luis Augusto Pereira Lima of PNCSA developed a georeferenced map using the Geographic Information System (GIS) ArcGIS 9.2. After conferring with the community, we decided to use a Google Earth image as a base map to highlight the location of the Indigenous land within the urban context. In addition, we developed a booklet containing the testimonies and the original sketch maps drawn by the people of Beija-Flor I.[3] After completing revisions requested by the community, including adding more places for

FIGURE 09.08. Documenting coordinates with GPS, October 2007, *Aldeia* Beija-Flor, Rio Preto da Eva, Amazonas, Brazil. Source: PNCSA Archive.

collection of seeds and forest materials for handcrafts as well as sites of recent intrusions and conflicts, we printed one thousand copies for distribution in Beija-Flor as well as to universities, social movements, governmental agencies, and the Attorney General of the Republic.

The Indigenous map provides a stark contrast to Tadeu's map (Figure 09.09). While Tadeu's map reflects commercial interests and imagines the area subdivided by residential lots, the Indigenous map represents the same area by a polygon showing partial forest cover. The area currently encompassed by Beija-Flor I used to be larger,[4] but as the city grew, urban development began to encroach into the forest where the Indigenous groups live, causing rapid deforestation and pollution of one of the principal canals traversing the city. However, the map demonstrates how the area under extended Indigenous occupation has retained its forest cover. This is because the land use is restricted to small areas for cultivation and collection of seeds and nonwood materials to make handcrafts. In this way, the Indigenous map of the Beija-Flor community represents a way of life distinct from those of their neighbors in Rio Preto da Eva.

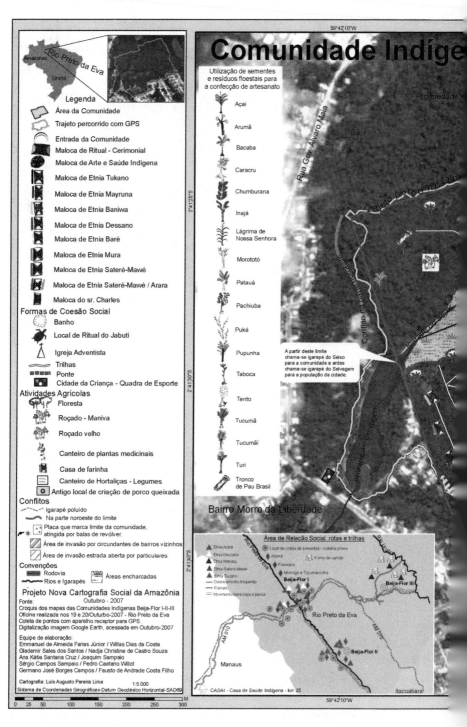

FIGURE 09.09. Map of the Beija-Flor I Indigenous community, Rio Preto da Eva, Brazil, 2007. Source: PNCSA Archive.

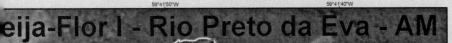

Conclusion

Beyond presenting an alternative spatiality, residents of Beija-Flor were also able to use the map and the booklet to advance their territorial claims. By referencing what Chief Fausto refers to as "our map," community members successfully pressured the municipality of Rio Preto da Eva to expropriate the land in the name of "public interest." According to Article 2 of Municipal Organic Law #302, the expropriation was "intended to grant definitive tenure to the residents, farmers, and other existing occupants" of the territory occupied by the people of Beija-Flor. As their land tenure was finally guaranteed via this municipal ordinance, their legal status was also changed from "community" to "*aldeia*." Residents now refer to "*Aldeia*" Beija-Flor in speaking about the Indigenous territory and even reissue birth certificates and other documents to reflect their new legal status.

With the formal recognition of the Indigenous territory of Beija-Flor I as an *aldeia* "under the dominion of the Indigenous community" according to national law, FUNAI can include this Indigenous land in its registry and implement public policies directed toward Indigenous peoples. In 2013, the municipality of Rio Preto da Eva granted an area of 4 hectares contiguous to the Indigenous land to the communities. This area contains an important waterway that passes through both the urban area and the Aldeia Beija-Flor, reflecting the municipality's acknowledgment of Indigenous ability to maintain riparian forests and waterways.

Ultimately, the social cartography process was crucial to the representation—both visually and legally—of a distinct urban way of life constructed through unity among different ethnic groups. The mapping workshop served as a space for the Indigenous groups of Rio Preto da Eva to critically consider the cultural, linguistic, and spiritual aspects of their identities, allowing them both to embrace and to place these elements within the complex spatiality of a large and growing city. The formal recognition of the Indigenous land strengthened the position of the Indigenous peoples in Rio Preto da Eva, ensuring their legal tenure in the face of repeated attempts at expropriation by those who think that Indigenous land is available for occupation and urban development.

NOTES

1. See novacartografiasocial.com.br.
2. According to a report in the Manaus-based newspaper *A Crítica*, cited by Prazeres (2007).

3. The booklet can be downloaded from novacartografiasocial.com.br.
4. On April 14, 1994, according to the Exchange Deed signed at the Quarto Ofício de Notas Notary in Manaus, Amazonas, Book 333, Pages 70–71, Richard Melnyk—represented by Power of Attorney by Ivan de Sá—traded 40 hectares of the aforementioned area for 370 hectares that belonged to the City Hall of Rio Preto da Eva. According to the certificate issued by the land registry office, dated April 15, 1994, "following the Exchange Deed, enacted by Mr. Richard Melnyk and the Municipal Government of Rio Preto da Eva, only 41.63 hectares remain." Quarto Ofício de Notas Notary in Manaus, Amazonas, Book 333, Pages 70–71; author translation.

REFERENCES

Acevedo Marin, Rosa E., and Edna Castro. 2004. *No caminho das pedras de Abacatal: Experiência social de grupos negros no Pará*. Belém, Brazil: NAEA/Universidade Federal do Pará (UFPA).

Almeida, Alfredo Wagner Berno de. 1994. *Carajás: A guerra dos mapas*. Belém, Brazil: Falangola Editora.

———. 2006. *Terras de quilombo, terras indígenas, "babaçuais livres", "castanhais do povo", faxinais e fundos de pasto: Terras tradicionalmente ocupadas*. Manaus, Brazil: PPGSCA-UFAM.

Almeida, Alfredo Wagner Berno de, Glademir Sales dos Santos, Luís Augusto Pereira Lima, et al. 2008. *Estigmatizacão e território: Mapeamento situacional das comunidades e associações indígenas na cidade de Manaus*. Manaus, Brazil: Casa 8.

Barth, Fredrik. 2005. "Etnicidade e o conceito de cultura." *Antropolítica* 19(2nd semester): 15–30. Niterói, Brazil: UFF.

———. 2000. "Os grupos étnicos e suas fronteiras." In *O guru, o iniciador e outras variações antropológicas*, 25–68. Rio de Janeiro, Brazil: Contra Capa.

Berreman, Gerald D. 1980. "Etnografia e controle de impressões em uma aldeia do Himalaia." In *Desvendando máscaras sociais*, ed. Alba Zaluar Guimarães, 123–174. Rio de Janeiro, Brazil: Editora Francisco Alves.

Bourdieu, Pierre. *O poder simbólico*. 2005. Rio de Janeiro, Brazil: Bertrand Brasil, 2005.

Cohen, Abner. 1978. "Organizações 'invisíveis': Alguns estudos de casos." In *O homem bidimensional: A antropologia do poder e o simbolismo em sociedades complexas*, 115–147. Rio de Janeiro, Brazil: Zahar Editores.

"Decisão vai beneficiar indígenas: Decisão da câmara municipal acabará com uma batalha que já durava 17 anos." 2008. *A Crítica*: Caderno Cidades, 2 de outubro.

Farias Júnior, Emmanuel de Almeida. 2009. *Terras Indígenas nas cidades: Lei Municipal de Desapropriação no. 302, Aldeia Beija-flor, Rio Preto da Eva, Amazonas*. Manaus, Brazil: UEA Edições.

Gusfield, Joseph R. 1975. *Community—a Critical Response*. New York: Harper and Row.

"Indígenas lutam por terras sem herdeiros." 2007. *A Crítica*. Edição No. 2066 de 04/07.

"Índios reclamam por terras." 2007. *A Crítica*: Caderno Cidades. Edição No. 2102 de 09/08.

Leach, Edmund Ronald. 1996. *Sistemas políticos da Alta Birmânia*. São Paulo, Brazil: Editora da Universidade de São Paulo.

Macedo, Guilherme Martins. 2004. "Esboço do Projeto Artesanato e formas de produção de identidade: Uma comunidade indígena urbana do Amazonas." Unpublished manuscript.

Maximiano, Claudina Azevedo. 2008. *Mulheres indígenas em Manaus: Identidade étnica e organização como forma de construir comunidade*. Master's thesis in Sociedade e Cultura na Amazônia. Programa de Pós-Graduação em Sociedade e Cultura na Amazônia, Universidade Federal do Amazonas.

Oliveira Filho, João Pacheco. 1999a. "A população ameríndia: Terra, meio ambiente e perspectivas de transformação." In *Ensaios em antropologia histórica*, 155–163. Rio de Janeiro, Brazil: Editora UFRJ.

———. 1999b. "Uma etnologia dos 'índios misturados': Situação colonial, territorialização e fluxos culturais." In *A viagem da volta: Etnicidade, política e reelaboração cultural no nordeste indígena*, ed. João P. de Oliveira, 11–39. Rio de Janeiro, Brazil: Editora Contra Capa Livraria.

Oliveira, Roberto C. de. 1960. *O processo de assimilação dos Terêna*. Rio de Janeiro, Brazil: Edição Museu Nacional, Série Livros I.

———. 1968. *Urbanização e tribalismo: A integração dos índios Terêna numa sociedade de classes*. Rio de Janeiro, Brazil: Zahar Editores.

Prazeres, Leandro. 2007. "Índios apelam ao Governo Federal." *A Crítica*, Edição No. 2114 de 21/08.

Rio Preto da Eva-Amazonas-Brasil. 2008. *Lei No. 302, de 29 de outubro de 2008*. Dispõe sobre autorização ao Poder Executivo Municipal para desapropriar, em caráter amigável ou judicial, áreas de terras que menciona, e dá outras providencias.

Santos, Glademir Sales dos. 2008. *Identidade étnica: Os Sateré-Mawé no bairro da Redenção, Manaus-AM*. Master's thesis in Sociedade e Cultura na Amazônia. Programa de Pós-Graduação em Sociedade e Cultura na Amazônia, Universidade Federal do Amazonas.

———. 2016. *Territórios pluriétnicos em construção: A proximidade, a poiesis e a praxis dos indígenas em Manaus-AM*. PhD diss., Sociedade e Cultura na Amazônia. Programa de Pós-Graduação em Sociedade e Cultura na Amazônia, Universidade Federal do Amazonas.

Silva, Raimundo Nonato P. da. 2001. *O universo social dos indígenas no espaço urbano: Identidade étnica na cidade de Manaus/AM*. 2001. Master's thesis in Antropologia Social. Programa de Pós-Graduação em Antropologia Social, Universidade Federal do Rio Grande do Sul.

10

Participatory Cultural Mapping in Nvwken, Mapuce Territory, Argentina

Exploring Other Forms of Territorial Representation

MARÍA LAURA NAHUEL

Introduction

This chapter explores participatory cultural mapping, a methodology that disrupts normative approaches to territorial representation so as to insert new forms of understanding into land management processes. Our intercultural and interdisciplinary research team has been fine-tuning this methodology since 2006, based on shared experiences in Waj Mapu[1] (Mapuce Territory) in Argentina. Our team consists of members of the Mapuche Confederation of Neuquén (CMN), the Human Rights Observatory of Indigenous Peoples (ODHPI), the Mapuce Norgvbamtuleayiñ Education Center, and the Popular and Intercultural Education Center (CEPINT).

We chose to focus on participatory cultural mapping as a research methodology that can be used to represent "Kimvn Mapuce," or Mapuce wisdom. As Raúl Díaz (2003, 9) argues:

> Participatory cultural mapping manages to produce community knowledge through the "scientific" development of "other" cartographies. On the one hand, it is a type of a performative pedagogy that consists of critically reading the official maps, unraveling the colonization of space, both materially and symbolically, in an attempt to visualize the geographical markers of economic, social and cultural domination. On the other hand, it is a performative pedagogy that seeks to transform reality in order to know it; that is to say, this sort of pedagogy tries to reoccupy the space through its visualization in maps that are developed collaboratively, to be used on the one hand as legal instruments and on the other as educational instruments for the strengthening of Mapuce identity.

Throughout the land we know as Abya Yala, which is also referred to as "America," maps have historically been used as tools for the powerful to dispossess Indigenous peoples of their rightful lands. Colonial powers have justified their resource exploitation, land occupation, wars of invasion, and destructive land planning practices all in the name of supposed scientific and technological advancements. As a result, modern states have similarly drawn their own arbitrary borders and devised their own arbitrary constructs to delineate the differences between the colonizers and the colonized subject.

The current political, economic, cultural, and judicial context of our work has led us to think carefully about how the state's historic monopoly over cartography has served to subjugate the ancestral and millenary wisdom of our people, the Mapuce. In particular, new multinational resource extraction projects, which are endorsed by the Argentine government, threaten our livelihood and subject us to a constant state of tension and uncertainty. This reality has led us to develop territorial defense strategies as well as plans for achieving *kvme felen*, or a state of good living. Mapuce participatory cultural mapping plays a key role in this process.

Mapuce kimvn (sometimes also called *kimvn mapuce*) is the Mapuce wisdom that serves as the basis of our existence as an Indigenous people with our own epistemology. All of the activities involved in our participatory cultural mapping are rooted in this wisdom. As Valdez and Pereyra (2011, 5) state, *mapuce kimvn*

> ... covers all forms of knowledge—the technologies, knowledge, skills, practices and beliefs—that allow the community to deploy its life. But it can also be understood in terms of making the assertion of ethnic identity viable, so it is a dynamic knowledge that responds to a changing environment.

The reconstruction of Mapuce epistemology on the basis of this wisdom thus serves as a means to both reassess and protect the Mapuce knowledge that has been transmitted from generation to generation. Effectively, *mapuce kimvn* acts as a sort of compass that guides contemporary Mapuce peoples like us toward other ways of representing ourselves—other ideas of territory, other types of maps, other symbols, other pedagogical forms, other forms of education, and other ideas of tourism. Collectively, these new forms of representation ensure our decolonization.

As the foundation of our participatory cultural mapping activities, *mapuce kimvn* has placed the concept of "Waj Mapu" (Mapuce Territory) at the center of this analysis. Waj Mapu is a complex and dynamic concept in the Mapuce cosmovision, involving both spatial and spiritual elements to show how territorial occupation is at once a spiritual and material practice. By using the lens of Waj Mapu, we have put forward a critique of the state's official approaches to cartography, specifically with regard to the territorial survey in the province of Neuquén that the Argentine government carried out during the application of National Law 26.160/07.

As we analyzed the state's maps, we were able to see how they compared to the maps that our community members made of their territory. Community members could clearly see how the army and the dominant classes were using the state's "official" maps to serve their land acquisition. The lands they wanted to occupy—our lands, which we have occupied for generations— were represented on these maps as vacant property, available for capitalistic development. Reviewing the state's approach to cartography was therefore a crucial pedagogical experience during our mapping workshops. It allowed us to learn about and appropriate the same tools of power, such as GPS and GIS technologies, for our own purposes.

This chapter reviews participatory cultural mapping within the context described above. The first section, which we call "Kiñe" (One), outlines the Mapuce conception of territory and provides a brief history of our people to understand the context within which the cultural mapping has emerged in the province of Neuquén. The next section, "Epu" (Two), describes the role of maps for the imposition of state power in Argentina. It also analyzes how maps made by landowners linked to the government are used to justify repression, as well as how an emerging understanding of mapping has become a strategy for Mapuce empowerment and struggle in this context. Finally, the third section, "Kvla" (Three), describes some of our experiences with participatory cultural mapping in the Mapuce communities of Lof Paichil Antriao and Lof Quintriqueo in the province of Neuquén, in the Argentine region of Patagonia.

One of the most important aspects of mapping Lof Paichil Antriao was analyzing a historical sequence of maps to show how the dispossession of land had escalated over time. Being able to visualize this process with maps helped validate the Mapuce territorial claims and provide a basis for our legal defense. Similarly, another important aspect of the mapping process was the development of "conflict maps," which were used to assess possible proposals for territorial restitution. A final aspect concerned Mapuce pedagogy and internal debates regarding self-representation. In Lof Quintriqueo, we had important critical discussions about using cartographic technologies while still maintaining our skepticism toward official cartography. In these conversations, we also discussed the importance of renaming spaces within the community's territory.

This chapter, therefore, seeks to revalue, resignify, and visibilize Mapuce epistemology and performative pedagogy in line with Mapuce concepts of "territoriality." In the hands of the Mapuce people, cultural mapping consciously seeks to make space for other forms of representation. Such new forms allow us to recover the right to represent ourselves instead of being subjected to the representations that others impose on us, while at the same time allowing us to produce a "geopolitics of Mapuce knowledge" that reflects another idea of territory, composed of other experiences, worldviews, and maps. Our "other" cartography represents the Mapuce culture as members of the communities have narrated, created, re-created, and enriched it over time.

Kiñe: Waj Mapu and Its Characteristics

Two fundamental principles have shaped Mapuce philosophy for millennia: (1) respect for the forces of nature (*punewen*) and (2) the promotion of community life. Mapuce philosophy sees Mapuce culture as part of nature, not the ruler of nature, so it holds a deep respect for the rights of nature and the natural world within a larger framework of collective rights.

The concept of Waj Mapu is an approach to conceiving territorial space[2] that combines spiritual and material elements, including the following:

- *Pu ce* (people)
- *Pu gen ko* (guardians of water)
- *Pu gen kvxaj* (guardians of fire)
- *Pu gen kvrvf* (guardians of the wind)
- *Pu gen mawiza* (guardians of the mountain)
- *Pu gen piren* (guardians of the snow)
- *Pu gen maijan pijan* (guardians of the volcano)

In Waj Mapu, these elements are interrelated and combined in different dimensions, increasing the *newen* (strength) of the *ixofillmogen* (biodiversity). In our language, the entirety of Mapuce territory is called Waj Mapu or Wajontu Mapu. "Waj" means a sum or a totality, and "Wajontu" refers to the idea of the "all-encompassing," which reflects the circular way in which Mapuce life is organized and Mapuce thought is governed. Thus, "Waj Mapu" or "Wajontu Mapu" can be interpreted as the "cosmos" or "universe."

In the Mapuce universe, there are different dimensions in which *pu newen*, or different interrelated forces with both tangible and intangible elements, complement one another. According to the knowledge of our philosophical leaders, there are those who speak of eight dimensions and others who say that there are twelve or more dimensions. These discrepancies, we believe, must correspond to the transmissibility of knowledge and the particularity of the various territorial identities that make up the Mapuce people. Four of these eight to twelve dimensions are further explained below:

> *Pvjv mapu*: *Pvjv mapu* is a dualistic dimension. On the one hand, it corresponds to one of the spatial, immaterial dimensions of the Waj Mapu, and on the other, it is the dimension where the material territory (*xufken mapu*) exists, which is where we develop our community life.

> *Wenu mapu*: *Wenu mapu* is understood as the "land from above." Here, all the life-forms of the *pvjv mapu* are spiritually reproduced.

> *Miñce mapu* or *Nag mapu*: These terms refer to underground or subterranean systems, which contain various life-forms such as oil, gas, and mineral resources.

> *Ragiñ wenu mapu*: This is the dimension that encompasses all other dimensions.

The Waj Mapu also has an order called *az mapu*, from which the particular form of Mapuce social order is configured.[3] All dimensions of the Mapuce universe have their own *az mapu*, or their order and organization. When the *az mapu* is attacked by *pu ce* (people), the rulers of the Waj Mapu, the *gene* (guardians), will punish the offenders. Generally, this punishment takes the form of *kuxan*, which means "pain" or "illness." As the Maci[4] Victor Caniullan says of the *kuxan*, "There are many diseases that are spiritual in nature and there are many diseases that are social in nature, but all of these could manifest in a physical way."[5] Since the Mapuce coexist with the different forces of nature in a space that contains multiple worlds, we must fulfill our responsibility to "be well," or to achieve a state of well-being. Our role as a people is regulated by the *az mapu*, which orders us to respect and protect all forms of life, because as the *kimce* (sages) say, "Kisu gvnen kvlelayiñ" (We do not go along alone).

Kvme felen (good living), the expression of *az mapu* in the communities of Neuquén, serves as a frame of reference for Mapuce community life and a framework for our self-governance, but the concept also offers another view of life and other categories of analysis that merit consideration and respect within Western culture. The key words in *kvme felen* express the fundamental rights of the Mapuce people: territory, autonomy, and community. Drawing on the complexity of the Waj Mapu concept, we suggest new categories of analysis, including ancestral occupation, traditional occupation, and ancestral and permanent forms of communication and circulation. We see these ideas as categories that reflect our existence, our permanence, and our rightful land possessions.

Epu: Assessing the Situation of the Mapuce People in Puelmapu

STATE REPRESSION THROUGH CARTOGRAPHY

Before the consolidation of the Argentine and Chilean states at the end of the nineteenth century, the territory of the Mapuce people extended across a large expanse of the southern end of the South American continent, stretching from the Atlantic Ocean to the Pacific Ocean. As such, the borders drawn by the Argentine and Chilean states a little more than 130 years ago fragmented this original Mapuce Waj Mapu. The axis of union of the Waj Mapu, the Andes mountain range, was demarcated and broken up with imaginary lines traced in fire and blood, resulting in the death of thousands of our *futa ke ce*, our ancestors. In the words of the renowned *logko* Antonio Salazar, of the Pewence area, the living memory of the Waj Mapu persists on both sides of the Andes:

> They had been in Ñorquinko, and from there they went to Gulumapu. . . . They had the Mapuce on the run in this way, from one place to the next. I've always known this story, because my grandfather was in that group. They were all trying to make their way back to where we are. Chile together with the Puelmapu was a single territory. For us, Gulumapu is the land others have called Chile. The state separated it, dividing it along the ways the water falls. Water falls over there for Chile, it falls in Puelmapu, and then it comes here to Argentina, or at least so says the *wigka* [invader]. That's why this territory here is one entirety, it is one Waj Mapu . . . Before if you wanted to live here, or if you came from there, nobody stopped you. The *wigka*

made the territory like this, they made the division between Chile and Argentina.⁶

This demarcation of the Chilean and Argentine states forced thousands of Mapuce to flee from one side of the mountain to the other, seeking refuge to save their lives. The first genocide⁷ that the Argentine state committed against the Mapuce was commanded and executed by General Julio Argentino Roca in 1879, with the legislative support of Law 947. What is more, this genocide was financed by British capital, the foremost beneficiary of Mapuce land appropriation. As a result of the genocides committed on both sides of the Andes, our population was dramatically reduced and dispersed throughout our ancestral territories.

During this time, the formation of the "ideal" citizen was firmly rooted in the national project of a whitening and Europeanizing Argentina. This Creole conscience, which privileges the European "contributions" to Argentine culture and dismisses and silences Indigenous voices, is constantly evident in today's speeches and is reflected in the ways that the Mapuce have been repressed and persecuted in recent years. Argentina still looks to Europe and the United States as cultural "role models" and strives to align its politics with that of these modern-day capitalist and Eurocentric powers.⁸

To speak of Waj Mapu in the present means to continually recall our history, to think of our time as a free people before the crimes against humanity committed against our ancestors; before the military campaign of the end of the nineteenth century; and before the torture we endured in concentration camps, slavery, trafficking, subjugation to Christian ideology, and the military regimes. On the heels of all this violence, the state "granted" small allocations (called *reducciones*) of inhospitable land with little agricultural value to the Mapuce, relegating our communities to dispersed settlements in isolated lands pushed up against the mountains, far from our places of origin. Other people now occupied the lands where we Mapuce once lived, stripping us of the freedom to travel around our rightful territory, such as in the case of Lof Paichil Antriao, which will be discussed later.⁹ These repressive mechanisms of control ultimately served to incorporate the stolen land into the incipient Argentine nation-state to be used for livestock production and real estate speculation.

The state's production of official cartography facilitated both the symbolic and the territorial appropriation of the lands that belong to the Mapuce people. These official maps served both to strip the Mapuce of their land and to legitimize the state's general demonization and repression of the Mapuce people. State maps were thus key mechanisms used to sow fear among the

Mapuce and justify the actions of the conservative sectors of the Neuquén society.

This point is illustrated by the fierce repression of the Currumil community in Quillén, Pewence, which took place in 2009. This repression was part of the provincial government's strategy to delegitimize our struggle and, along with it, to invisibilize the identity and territorial claims of the Mapuce in Patagonia. The mass media disseminated a map found online that showed a portion of Mapuce territory as an area of danger, accusing the Mapuce of wanting to secede to create a separate state. We did not develop this map, but nonetheless the image was exploited as an instrument of power used to generate fear, divide public opinion, and legitimize further actions of state violence against the Mapuce.

The provincial government in Quillén also formed an association called ADELEY (Association in Defense of the Law) that accused the Mapuce of being linked to armed separatist groups such as the Revolutionary Armed Forces of Colombia (FARC) and Basque Homeland and Liberty (ETA). This accusation of an alleged association had real and destructive consequences for the Mapuce, leading the province to launch twenty criminal cases in 2009 and accuse more the 350 individuals in civil cases. Around the same time, the regional government passed a resolution demanding that the Mapuce sever their connections with armed groups of Chile. On top of all this, another resolution was brought forth that called for all who "claim territorial possession" within Argentina to be eliminated from the list of recipients of government benefits.[10]

These events show how our conception of space, specifically our notion of Mapuce territory, was condemned and misrepresented by the *wigka* through various ideological campaigns. The objective of these campaigns, moreover, was distinctively similar to that of military campaigns in late nineteenth-century Argentina. Although we now have a legal framework that offers us some protection (National Law 26.160/07), we are still deeply concerned that our ancestral lands continue to witness state violence and ongoing legal struggles for native peoples.

USING MAPS AS A STRATEGY FOR EMPOWERMENT AND STRUGGLE

In 2009, the Mapuce Confederation of Neuquén (CMN; Mapuce government in Neuquén), the National Institute of Indigenous Affairs (INAI), and the

National University of Comahue (UNCo) signed an agreement to implement National Law No. 26.160, an emergency ordinance that intended to:

> Declare an emergency with regard to the possession and ownership of the lands traditionally occupied by the Indigenous communities of the country. . . . Suspend for the term of the declared emergency, the execution of sentences, procedural or administrative acts, whose object is eviction or unemployment . . . the National Institute of Indigenous Affairs must carry out the technical-legal-cadastral survey of the situation regarding ownership of the lands occupied by the Indigenous communities. (Author's translation)

However, this agreement was rejected by the Provincial Deputies Block of the Movimiento Popular Neuquino (MPN; Neuquén Popular Movement) in the legislature of Neuquén, two months after the repression in Quillén. The accusations against the Mapuce described in the previous section thus furthered the persecution and denial of Indigenous communities in Neuquén and gave the provincial government an excuse to halt legislation that would promote Indigenous territorial autonomy.

It took seven years for Law 26.160 to be applied in Neuquén, but its effects are limited, since the provincial government is responsible for its implementation, without any requirement for active participation by the Mapuce governmental body in the region. This arrangement sets up a conflict between the provincial state, which has failed to collaborate with the Mapuce in applying the law, and the Mapuce participatory cultural mapping project. Despite the legal protections offered to them on paper, the reality is that more than a dozen communities have yet to be recognized by the provincial state. Instead, the territory that rightfully belongs to these communities is categorized as "fiscal land," signaling its availability to tourism companies, large commercial farms, and others with access to power and money that have interest in these lands.

To summarize, those of us living in the fifty-nine Lofs (communities) within Neuquén currently find ourselves in a state of constant conflict and uncertainty regarding our territory. This ongoing tension manifests itself through:

- Lack of land title and obstacles to achieving legal representation
- Lack of adequate demarcation of the Mapuce "reserves" and objections to some demarcations that do not match the area historically occupied by the communities

- Intrusions and encroachments from outsiders on Mapuce lands
- Abuses related to the private exploitation of natural resources, including public works or development projects promoted by state entities
- Negative environmental impacts of natural resource exploitation
- Deficit in the quantity and quality of land assigned, which prevents sustainable development
- Repression and judicialization of Indigenous demands
- Challenges to preserving the cultural heritage of the Mapuce people.

Although the territorial survey in Neuquén began in August 2013, communities that lack legal status have been entirely left out of this process. The only areas included in the survey were places where Indigenous communities already held title to the land, and places where there was clear and undeniable physical presence of Indigenous community life. To make matters worse, Provincial Decree 1184/2002, sponsored by former governor Jorge O. Sobisch, allowed the provincial state to decide who is or is not Mapuce, and who does or does not belong to a Mapuce community. With this decree, the provincial state sought to strip Indigenous peoples of their agency by denying their right to self-identification, thus refusing to recognize both the legal status and the actual existence of several communities in the province.

KIÑEL MAPU: EXPLORING THE SPATIAL AND "GEOCULTURAL" TERRITORIAL IDENTITIES OF THE MAPUCE PEOPLE

Despite the challenges presented above, the strength of the Mapuce people has allowed us to reconstruct our own autonomous spaces and organizational forms. One of the best examples of this is the formation of "zonal councils," a process that proved crucial to granting a new significance to the multitude of Indigenous territorial identities in the province of Neuquén.

During the 15th Mapuce Parliament (called Gvbamtuwvn), which the Neutral Mapuce Confederation convened at the end of 2000, the idea of zonal councils was proposed as a way to usher in a new form of locally based spatial organization and representation of the Mapuce of Neuquén. In this meeting, *kiñel mapu* was suggested as a Mapuce organizational framework that could be used to categorize all territorial identities within Neuquén. This concept, and the names of the various geographic areas represented in zonal councils, fundamentally altered Mapuce practices of spatial configuration as well as

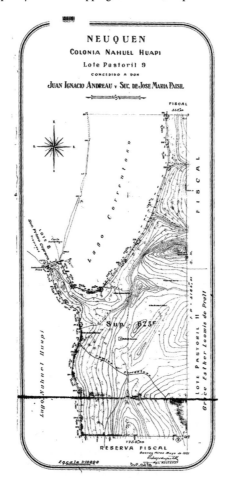

FIGURE 10.01. Map of the area of lot 9, which was "granted" to the Mapuce in 1935. Source: María Laura Nahuel, 2018.

the Mapuce way of pursuing self-affirmation and self-recognition through exercising territorial rights.

Currently there are six Mapuce territorial geographic units across the province of Neuquén with names that reflect their natural environments: (1) Xawvnko (union or confluence of the waters), (2) Pikunce (people from the north), (3) Pewence (*pewen* people), (4) Wijice (people from the south), (5) Lafkence (people from the lakes), and (6) Ragiñé ce (people of the center). These designations serve as a means to both recover and reassert the Indigenous rights that the *wigka* continues to suppress. Moreover, assigning these place-names provides a way for Mapuce people to manage our own territories and resources, maintain and safeguard our spiritual spaces, strengthen our regional economies, and ultimately conceptualize our own *kvme felen* (good living) in line with our cosmovision and cultural values. As I outlined in the introduction, participatory cultural mapping is a key methodology that allows us to achieve these goals.

Kvla: Mapping Projects

SURVEY IN LOF PAICHIL ANTRIAO

We carried out participatory cultural mapping from 2010 to 2011 in Lof Paichil Antriao, a community that had seen an entire city built by outsiders within its territory. The main objectives of the project included (1) demonstrating and making visible the historical and current existence of the Lof in this territory, (2) documenting the processes of dispossession and displacement that the Mapuce community had suffered for decades, and (3) making proposals to the state for territorial restitution and reparations.

Many years ago, members of Lof Paichil Antriao established their community life in the Lafkence area in the department of Lagos. Although the Mapuce are Indigenous to these lands, President Julio A. Roca issued a presidential decree in 1902 to measure the lands the Argentine state had "conquered" in this area and then "grant" lot number 9, which consisted of a reduced area of only 625 hectares, to the Mapuce (Figure 10.01). From 1902 to the present, this community has survived multiple processes of dispossession and reduction of its territory, which by 2000 had shrunk to a mere 125 hectares. As a team member said during one of the mapping workshops, "Not only do they confine us to [a single lot], but they also developed a city on top of our land and continually try to evict us from territory we have held for generations."

Defending its territory has taken a toll on the community, which has had to endure sixteen criminal cases filed against more than forty-eight community members, who have been ironically accused of "usurping" their ancestral territory. The ongoing conflict affecting the Mapuce in Lof Paichil Antriao prompted the ODHPI to request that our intercultural research team carry out the participatory cultural mapping with this community.

The mapping project took place in two stages. The first stage focused on maps elaborated by the Lof members based on their oral histories, as well as an analysis of maps and reports prepared in the 1920s and 1930s by Emilio R. Molla and Susana Lara of the former National Parks Directorate. The second stage consisted of map production using Geographic Information System (GIS).

In the second stage of the project, we decided to use the same technical tools that the government uses to fragment and appropriate our territory. By using the language of GIS, we hoped to provide the state with a technical analysis that would justify our proposal for historical reparations. Our claim for reparations was based on the fact that Mapuce territory was appropriated, divided into lots, and sold to outside interests, prompting the gradual expulsion of the population of the Lof from their own lands. Over time, lot 9 had transformed into the urban center of Villa La Angostura, a city widely coveted by domestic and foreign investors with real estate interests.

Given the complex history and political context, the mapping project served as an invaluable tool for collecting evidence, testimonies, and important documents and plans that supported the community's rightful claim over their lands. During the project, we managed to document the knowledge of Lof members through oral histories. These histories not only recounted their experiences of dispossession and eviction but also sparked a dialogue about future plans for good living. The project thus relied on a dualistic cultural/technical knowledge: it used ancestral Mapuce knowledge as a guiding framework for understanding the past, present, and future of the community, but also used modern-day technical knowledge of legal processes, demarcations, survey methodologies, and cartographic technologies to represent that framework. Both sets of knowledge were needed to develop plans for good living for Paichil Antriao, a Lof that is constantly forced to reaffirm its identity, its territory, and its autonomy in the face of imposition from the Argentine state.

MAPUCE EMPOWERMENT:
THE EXPERIENCE OF THE KONA OF LOF KINXIKEW

Lof Kinxikew is located in the Lafkence area (zone of the lakes) of Villa La Angostura. It is an area of native forests where the great lake Nahuel Huapi stands out in the landscape. Families across the territory participate in fairly regular migrations between its different zones, moving from low-lying areas in winter to higher-elevation areas in summer in search of pasture and water. The need to train community members to produce "other" maps is in large part a response to these migrations, as they spark a sense of urgency to cover and document all of our communal territory as people are passing through it.

We began the mapping at the end of winter, when community members were living in the lower-elevation areas, or the winter zone. We held workshops on technical tools such as GPS, GIS, and map literacy with the *koha* (a term that refers to youth who are active and eager to help), so that they themselves could record the geographic coordinates of the sites that they wished to protect and reaffirm. The first part of the workshop focused on how the Mapuce cosmovision conceives of territorial space. Pety Piciñam, a philosophical leader in the community, spoke about the history of genocide against the Mapuce people and the division of the Mapuce territory along either side of the Andes. Then we drew a map to show the ancestral territory of the Mapuce people and how it had been gradually reduced to its present state.

To close the workshop, we gathered together to collectively interpret three "official" maps. The first was a map of Argentina's national borders that the Argentine Army developed in 1873. This map was very significant for our discussion, since it helped the *koha* better understand the military invasion of their territories that Pety Piciñam had referenced earlier. The second map we considered was the Cuyiñ Manzano survey map of 1884, the first map of the area produced by trained land surveyors. As *koha* Pascual Kinxikew, a young person who participated in the workshop, described, this map showed the grid system imposed on the land, with its lots enclosing three entire *tolderías*, or traditional Mapuce settlements. This second map further corresponded to documents the research team found in the Cadastre Directorate of Neuquén (ordinance survey office). Finally, the third map we discussed was a more recent topographic map of Cuyiñ Manzano, from 1949. This map was especially interesting because of the toponyms it used and the altimetric and planimetric measurement systems it leveraged to produce something that could be considered "official cartography." We were also able to refer to the coordinates from this map to facilitate our use of GPS.

Interpreting these official maps in conjunction with the participatory mapping process helped residents understand how the army and the ruling classes had historically used maps to learn about and dominate Mapuce territory. This analysis led us to the "cultural" component of our mapping process, underscoring the importance of documenting those elements of the land that are not included in any official maps but are nonetheless of vital importance for the Mapuce.

We then reviewed the map prepared by community members in the mapping workshop in order to decide where to walk and take geographic coordinate readings. We stopped at important locations where some community members shared stories, and we took GPS points of the *ruka* (the houses), *mallines*, *lawen* (Mapuce medicine), and *newen* (various energies and apparitions). Members of the first walking group documented several locations of medicinal herb plants and sites of biodiversity, but the participants decided to hold a second walk with a *maci* to more precisely document additional locations of medicinal herbs. Through this work, the *kona* became increasingly enthusiastic and felt empowered to use these new technical tools for the benefit of the community.

In addition to empowering the next generation to take ownership and pride in our ancestral lands, renaming different places within our community is another very important part of our work. The official cartography produced at the end of the nineteenth century and earlier has been of great importance for our work, since Mapuce place-names that community members had forgotten (because of the imposition of other names later on) are preserved in these products. Original Mapuce place-names were not names of people; rather, they were names that reflected the characteristics of the landscape—its *az mapu*, the shape of the land. This is how Lof Kinxikew recovered the original name of the Paso Coihue sector, which was formerly called Weke Malal, meaning "sheep corral."

THE NEED TO INNOVATE WAYS OF REPRESENTATION

In our workshops, we discussed at length how to prepare maps based on the drawings of the members of Lof Pu Lof, since what is captured in their drawings has multiple meanings. Because several individuals participated in the drawing process, their maps are filled with movement and colors, and they use a variety of symbols that reflect their admiration for the spaces they represent. This led us to discuss how to avoid making maps that are just flat sheets using conventional symbology on a Cartesian grid, since these maps only reflect international norms that the Mapuce do not recognize as their own.

We have been involved in participatory cultural mapping projects in Neuquén for more than seven years, and over time, noticeable changes have occurred in our approach to representing the territories. In the territorial mapping work that was carried out in Lof Linares, for example, the spaces we mapped were represented as a mosaic in a CorelDRAW® graphic design program. The subsequent maps will be represented in the same way, until we arrive at the mapping work of Lof Paichill Antriao, which will incorporate the design of several thematic maps made in GIS.

Upon finishing the mapping workshops, we had produced a collection of maps that sought to show Mapuce ancestral territory, areas of conflict within the territory, present-day community land uses, a spatial representation of Mapuce cosmovision, the history of dispossession that Mapuce have suffered since the late nineteenth century, and finally our proposal for territorial reparations. These were initially designed to be published in a formal socio-anthropological report, but during our process we decided to create a DVD instead to present the territory to members of the Lof, students, and the general public in a more moving and interactive format. We agreed that the design of this interactive tool should be as circular as possible to most accurately represent Mapuce thinking, even though this is difficult to achieve with screens that have a rectangular format. Nevertheless, we are committed to developing pedagogical tools that are reflective and respectful of Mapuce values.

In our team discussions, another important consideration arose: the question of how to spatially represent time and show that it is not linear. Interactive digital tools allowed us to effectively go to the past, stop in the present, and then go to the future—an experience akin to listening to a *kimce* tell a story with circular language, returning from the past to talk about the present and then think about the future. This conversation, in turn, made us think critically about where to start the Mapuce history we were mapping. At what point in the long history of the Mapuce people should our viewer enter? Some team members considered it important to start the presentation with a review of the ancestral territory, while others argued that current legal issues were most immediate and critical and that, as such, the presentation should start by reviewing the current territorial conflicts.

These differences of opinion were ultimately resolved with an agreement to start the presentation with an image of the symbol that has represented us as the "Pueblo-Nación Mapuce" since 1992, the Wenufoye (Mapuce flag). The richness of its symbols and significance, we all agreed, was the best image to use at the beginning of the interactive DVD. By starting with an image of the Wenufoye, the program is rooted in the symbol that the *maci* Victor Caniullan developed to exemplify the principal parts of the Waj Mapu: the Kujxum with four rulers in different times-spaces, presented through images and stories told by Mapuce community members.

Conclusion: Challenges and Expectations for the Future

Throughout the participatory cultural mapping process, one of the principal challenges that our team faced was how to create new ways of representing our ancestral territory by breaking with the rules of legibility that seek to homogenize spatial representations. To accomplish this, the task before us is to continue developing new forms of mapping as we continue to recover our ancestral forms and symbols. This need to develop our own forms of symbology has emerged as a priority among the Mapuce as a result of the participatory cultural mapping workshops. These symbols—our own symbols—allow us to continue respecting our territorial identities and avoid falling into the trap of homogenization and reproduction of imposed representational forms.

Part of our vision is to expand the participatory mapping project to other Mapuce communities and continue to build upon the work described here. To do so, we urgently need to share these mapping techniques so that the *kvme felen* can move forward. Unfortunately, real economic limitations stand in the way of us reaching this goal, and to our knowledge, no NGOs in Argentina allocate resources for mapping projects. Despite these limitations, we have accomplished important and valuable work with contributions from our comrades.

Act 26.160, the law that obliges the state to stop evictions and calls for the territorial surveys of all Indigenous peoples of Argentina, is currently in force. As discussed throughout this chapter, the Mapuce continue to see a stark contrast between the techniques of participatory cultural mapping and those mapping techniques promoted by the National Institute of Indigenous Affairs and other national and provincial government entities. This disagreement about the appropriate way to map our lands has come to no resolution to date. As the territorial surveys continue and the disagreements between Mapuce communities and provincial administrations magnify, it will become more and more necessary to rethink the ways in which governments attempt to exercise authority over Indigenous communities through cartography. Our hope is that such a process will lead to the end of governmental manipulation of Indigenous peoples and will put into place a new approach that ensures that communities can embrace the role that history calls for them to assume: that of masters of their own fate.

Ultimately, we remain optimistic that in this search for *kvme felen*, we are making progress toward keeping the memory, culture, identity, and territoriality of the Mapuce people alive. As we make these advances, we see the Mapuce participatory cultural mapping process as key. It is a process that makes it possible for us to reclaim the right to represent ourselves as we reject the symbology and spatial representations that others have imposed upon us. In the hands of the Mapuce people, cultural mapping thus opens the door to imagining a *new* type of cartography, one that dismisses homogenization and erasure to embrace "other" forms of representation.

NOTES

1. All Mapuchezugun text in this article will use the alphabet devised by the Mapuce linguist Anselmo Raguileo.

2. This concept is more or less understood to mean a "totality," or as a "complement of

pairs that go together," and also as "everything related to everything." It is important to point out, as other authors say (such as Pereyra and Valdés or Benigar) that this translation is particularly challenging because talking about other worldviews inherently means that there are no "right" words for what you want to translate, a limitation that ultimately impoverishes or distorts meaning.

3. Valdes and Pereyra (2011), in a presentation on the cosmovision and the role of women in the *mapuce kimvn* transmission network.

4. Maci is the term for a Mapuce philosophical leader that is capable of communicating with other forces of nature. The *maci* also oversee Mapuce medicine practices.

5. In a radio show about diseases, Mapuradio 2010.

6. Interview with *logko* Antonio Salazar, 2006.

7. "Genocide means any of the acts mentioned below, perpetrated with the intention of destroying, in whole or in part, a national, ethnic, racial or religious group as such: a) Killing of group members, b) Serious injury to the physical or mental integrity of the members of the group." Diana Lenton, quoted in Bayer 2010, 29.

8. Quijano 2005, 236.

9. The term "Lof" (community) refers to both rural and urban communities, since 80 percent of the Mapuce population lives in urban areas.

10. Anteproyecto de ley 6596, decreto provincial 070/09.

REFERENCES

Alvarez, Gregorio. 1985. *Neuquén, historia, geografía, toponimia.* Vol. 5. Neuquén, Argentina: Editorial Gobierno de la Provincia de Neuquén.

Aranda, Darío. 2010. *Argentina originaria: Genocidios, saqueos y resistencias.* Buenos Aires: Editora Lavaca.

Bauer, Francisco. 2007. *Aportes para descolonizar el saber eurocentrista.* Córdoba, Argentina: Editorial La Cañada.

Bayer, Osvaldo, ed. 2010. *Historia de la crueldad argentina: Julio A. Roca y el genocidio de los Pueblos Originarios.* Buenos Aires: Ediciones El Tugurio.

Benigar, Juan. 1978. *La Patagonia piensa.* Neuquén, Argentina: Siringa Libros.

Clifton Goldney, Adalberto A. 1956. *El cacique Namuncurá: Último soberano de la Pampa.* Buenos Aires: Editorial Buenos Aires.

Coraggio, José Luis. 2008. *Economía social, acción pública y política: (Hay vida después del neoliberalismo).* Buenos Aires: Ediciones CICCUS.

Díaz, Raúl. 2009. "Del saber del espacio al espacio del saber: Confección de mapas comunitarios y crítica de la cartografía 'oficial' como artefacto hegemónico de representación y dominación territorial." Ponencia presentada en el V Congreso Nacional y III Internacional de Investigación Educativa. Cipolletti, Argentina. seminariociudad.sociales.uba.ar/wp-content/uploads/sites/125/2013/03/DIAZ-Del-saber-del-espacio-al-espacio-del-saber.pdf.

Di Risio, Diego, Marc Gavaldà, Diego Pérez Roig, and Hernán Scandizzo. 2012. *Zonas de sacrificio: Impactos de la industria hidrocarburífera en Salta y Norpatagonia.* Buenos Aires: América Libre.

Foucault, Michel. 2012. *El poder, una bestia magnífica: Sobre el poder, la prisión y la vida.* Buenos Aires: Editores Siglo Veintiuno.

Giglio, Silvia. 2007. *El Huerquén: Interculturalidad y Educación: Una experiencia en escuelas rurales.* Neuquén, Argentina: Editorial Universitaria Educo.

Harvey, David. 2001. *Espacios del capital: Hacia una geografía crítica.* Translated by Cristina Piña Aldal. Madrid: Ediciones Akal.

Heras, Ana Inés, and David Burin, eds. 2008. *Trabajo, desarrollo, diversidad: Políticas y metodologías de desarrollo local con acento en la generación de empleo, trabajo e ingresos.* Buenos Aires: Ediciones CICCUS.

Lander, Edgardo, comp. 2005. *La colonialidad del saber: Eurocentrismo y ciencias sociales: Perspectivas latinoamericanas.* Buenos Aires: Ediciones CICCUS.

Mandrini, Raúl, and Sara Ortelli. 1993. *Volver al país de los araucanos.* Juvenile fiction series. Buenos Aires: Editorial Sudamericana.

Mignolo, Walter. 2008. "La opción de-colonial: Desprendimiento y apertura: Un manifiesto y un caso." *Tabula Rasa* (Bogotá, Colombia) 8: 243–281.

Moreno, Francisco P. 2004. *Apuntes preliminares sobre una excursión al Neuquén, Río Negro, Chubut y Santa Cruz.* Buenos Aires: Ediciones El Elefante Blanco. Originally published 1897.

Moyano, Adrián. 2015. *Crónicas de la resistencia mapuche.* Buenos Aires, Argentina: Editorial Chiribote.

Nahuel, Jorge. 2010. *Un sistema de gobernanza de Áreas Protegidas desde nuestras cosmovisiones.* Neuquén, Argentina: Confederación Mapuche de Neuquén. Available at idl-bnc-idrc.dspacedirect.org/handle/10625/49496.

———, ed. 2013. *Huellas y senderos: Informe final de los resultados del Relevamiento Territorial, histórico, social y cultural de la comunidad mapuche Lof Paichil Antriao.* Puelmapu, Argentina: Observatorio de Derechos Humanos de Pueblos Indígenas (ODHPI).

Offen, Karl. 2009. "O mapeas o te mapean: Mapeo indígena y negro en América Latina." *Tabula Rasa* (Bogotá, Colombia) 10: 163–189.

Quijano, Aníbal. 2005. "Colonialidad del poder, eurocentrismo y America Latina." In *La colonialidad del saber: Eurocentrismo y ciencias sociales: Perspectivas latinoamericanas,* ed. Edgardo Lander, 201–246. Buenos Aires: Consejo Latinoamericano de Ciencias Sociales (CLACSO).

Rodríguez de Anca, Alejandra, Jorgelina Villarreal, and Cristina Valdez. 2013. "Otros mapas, otras territorialidades: Reflexiones a partir de experiencias de mapeo cultural participativo en Territorio Mapuce." Ponencia presentada en I Jornadas Norpatagónicas de Experiencias Educativas en Ciencias Sociales para la Escuela Secundaria. aacademica.org/i.jornadas.norpatagonicas/41.

Roux, Curruhuinca. 1986. *Sayhueque: El último cacique.* Buenos Aires: Editorial Plus Ultra.

———. 1993. *Las matanzas del Neuquén: Crónicas mapuches.* Buenos Aires: Editorial Plus Ultra.

Salamanca, Carlos, and Rosario Espina, eds. 2012. *Mapas y derechos: Experiencias y aprendizajes en América Latina.* Rosario, Argentina: Editorial de la Universidad de Rosario.

Salgado, Juan Manuel, María Micaela Gomiz, and Verónica Huilipan. 2008. *Informe de situación de los Derechos Humanos del Pueblo Mapuce en la Provincia del Neuquén.* Neuquén, Argentina: ODHPI.

———. 2009–2010. *Informe de situación de los Derechos Humanos del Pueblo Mapuce en la Provincia del Neuquén.* Neuquén, Argentina: ODHPI.

———. 2013. *Informe de situación de los Derechos Humanos de los Pueblos Indígenas en la Patagonia.* Neuquén, Argentina: ODHPI.

Sletto, Bjørn. 2014. "Mapas y memoria en la Sierra de Perijá, Venezuela: La cartografía participativa y el rescate del territorio Yukpa." *Antropológica* 58 (121–122): 89–121.

Sletto, Bjørn, Joe Bryan, Marla Torrado, Charles Hale, and Deborah Barry. 2013. "Territorialidad, mapeo participativo y política sobre los recursos naturales: La experiencia de América Latina." *Cuadernos de Geografía* 22(2): 193–209.

Valdez, Cristina, and Petrona Pereyra. 2011. "Cosmovisión y rol de la mujer en la red de transmisión del Mapuce kimvn." Ponencia presentada en VIII Congreso Internacional de la Asociación Argentina de Estudios Canadienses "Pueblos Indígenas: Conflictos y poder en la educación y la cultura." November 7–11, Córdoba, Argentina.

Wallerstein, Immanuel, ed. 2006. *Abrir las ciencias sociales.* Mexico City: Editorial Siglo Veintiuno.

Walther, Juan Carlos. 1948. *La conquista del desierto: Síntesis histórica de los principales sucesos ocurridos y operaciones militares realizadas en la Pampa y Patagonia, contra los indios (años 1527–1885).* Buenos Aires: Editorial Círculo Militar.

Zeballos, Estanislao S. 1961. *Callvucurá y la dinastía de los piedra; Paine y la dinastía de los zorros; Relmu, reina de los pinares.* Buenos Aires: Editorial Hachette.

———. 2004. *Episodios en los territorios del sur (1879).* Estudio preliminar, edición y notas Juan Guillermo Duran. Buenos Aires: Editorial El Elefante Blanco.

11

Political Appropriation of Social Cartography in Defense of Quilombola Territories in Alcântara, Maranhão, Brazil

DAVI PEREIRA JÚNIOR

Introduction: The Quilombolas and the Slave System

The municipality of Alcântara is located on the coast of the state of Maranhão in northeastern Brazil, 22 kilometers from the state capital, São Luís. According to Brazilian census data, the municipality has 114,000 hectares of land, of which 62,000 hectares (54.3% of the total land in the municipality) were expropriated from Quilombola communities and allocated to the Brazilian Space Program in 1980 and 1991. Alcântara has approximately 21,852 inhabitants, of which 6,400 (29.2% of the total population) live in the city of Alcântara. The other 15,452 people (70.8% of the total population) are dispersed throughout more than two hundred Quilombola communities within the municipality.

According to the certification criteria of the Palmares Cultural Foundation, a public institution responsible for formal recognition of Quilombola communities in Brazil, the municipality is subdivided into three large Quilombola territories, including the Ethnic Territory of Alcântara, which was affected by the Alcântara Space Base;[1] Cajual Island;[2] and Santa Teresa, or Itamatatiua,[3] in addition to three National Institute of Colonization and Land Reform (INCRA)[4] settlements: Ibituba and Portugal, located at the southern end of the municipality, and São Pedro.

The first Black people to arrive in Alcântara came as slaves in the eighteenth century to replace Indigenous slave labor on large sugarcane, cotton, and rice plantations. During the colonial period, the city of Alcântara was the main stronghold that gave birth to Maranhão's aristocracy. According to Jerônimo Viveiros (1977), the city was home to four senators of the empire, four barons, and a multitude of "intellectuals," politicians, doctors, military officers, and others—trained at the best educational institutions in Europe. However, what no one mentions is that this elite colonial population of Alcântara built its fortune, social status, and political power by exploiting slave labor. Many of the families who benefited from slavery to amass their fortunes, social prestige, and political power remain powerful to this day, more than a century after the abolition of slavery. Proudly and without restraint, like other Brazilian elites who have benefited from slavery, they continue to enjoy wealth produced at the expense of the lives of Blacks who were brought to Alcântara as slaves.

The economic crisis and subsequent overthrow of the colonial production system—resulting in the flight of landowners from Alcântara to Europe, Rio de Janeiro (the capital of the empire), and even São Luís (the capital of the province)—led to the proliferation of *quilombos*, an Afro-diasporic social organization that was originally formed by escaped slaves. Before they left Alcântara, the slave masters took everything of value from the old *casas-grandes* (big houses) and abandoned their slaves and the lands they occupied. Freed from the oppressive power of their masters, the former slaves were able to take control of the land and establish their own land-use norms and natural resource management systems (Pereira Júnior 2012, 47).

In particular, the Afro-diasporic communities in Alcântara replaced the mercantilist mode of production based on the great plantations with a system of common use, thus gaining control of both the means of production and the labor force within their territory. Common use is based on tacit agreements that provide everyone living in a given territory with equal opportunity to cultivate the land and access natural resources. Under a system of common use, people grow their crops in a collective fashion by involving several families in the same productive enterprise, with each family having the right to a portion of the crops produced.

By the mid-nineteenth century, Quilombolas and Indigenous people had formed a large, autonomous ethnic territory, and the old plantations had been transformed into a mosaic of small family units where production was oriented toward subsistence and internal markets. In addition to the plantation lands, former slaves had also adopted the old surnames of the aristocracy. Their use of former landowners' family names served to legitimize themselves as landowners, justifying their control over their lands as heirs to the colonial aristocracy.

However, the process of *aquilombamento* in Alcântara resulted in a diversity of forms of spatial organization that emerged from the disintegration of the great plantations (Almeida 2006a). Ex-slaves and freedmen also remained on the lands either through donation, acquisition, or abandonment by the *sesmeiros*, settlers who had been ceded land by the Portuguese king that was ostensibly "abandoned or uncultivated." This led to different forms of appropriation of land by Black people, including *terras de preto, terras de santo, terras de índio, terras de parente, terras de ausente, terras de santa, terras de santíssima*, and *terras de pobreza* (Black lands, holy lands, Indigenous lands, familiar lands, absentee lands, terras de Santa, sanctified lands, and impoverished lands). Although they are characterized by common use of land and natural resources, these territorialities reflect the complex and varied forms of autonomy experienced by Black people during colonial times. Furthermore, these diverse territorialities help explain why the collective social memory of these groups start with the moment they achieved autonomy, thus erasing the memory of captivity.

Thus, Quilombolas redefined how to use land, replacing the slavery model with an autonomous production system of family labor and the common use of both land and natural resources as its central axis. It is this understanding of territory and community that has informed the struggle surrounding the Brazilian Space Project and led us to use social cartography to defend our territories. The official maps of Alcântara used by the Brazilian Space Agency (AEB) are produced according to the interests of the state, rendering Quilombola communities "invisible" with the aim of denying their rights. However, for us Quilombolas, our identity is firmly rooted in our relationship with territory. Since our physical, social, cultural, and religious survival is not possible without our territory, we turned to social cartography to challenge these dominant representations of Quilombola territory.

The Quilombolas, State Racism, and the Rocket Launch Base

The conflict involving the Brazilian Space Project and the Quilombola communities of Alcântara has persisted for nearly forty years. Driven by deep-seated structural racism, the Brazilian government has failed to comply with the Constitutional Charter of 1988, which recognized Quilombolas' right to territory, and has shown blatant disregard for international agreements to which the country is a signatory. In an effort to expropriate Quilombola territory in Alcântara, Decree 7.320 of 1980 allowed the government of the state of Maranhão to declare an area of 52,000 hectares of land belonging to generations of Quilombolas as an area of public interest. The land, deemed by the state as an "empty demographic," was transferred to the military for the purpose of implementing the Alcântara Launch Center (CLA). The military later used its political influence to expand the area by an additional 10,000 hectares, formalized in a federal decree drawn up in the 1990s by the administration of former president Fernando Collor de Melo.

This expropriation of Quilombola territory for military use led to the compulsory displacement of 312 families from twenty-one communities to seven *agrovilas* (small urbanizations) in 1986–1987, preventing the Quilombolas from reaching their sacred sites to worship and care for their ancestors. Moreover, the government used another decree (number 72.571) to reduce the *módulo rural* (minimum agricultural plot size, according to the Brazilian Land Statute) from 35 to 15 hectares in Alcântara. The reduction of the minimum agricultural plot size represents one of the many contradictions of the Brazilian Space Project. If Alcântara were indeed a demographic void, why would there be reason for such a reduction?

These actions show how the Brazilian Space Project was planned and built on a foundation of structural racism. The CLA never took the Quilombola communities into consideration. Instead, agents of the state have always represented Quilombolas through a rhetoric permeated by eugenics theories from the nineteenth century, reproducing the idea that *quilombos* are backward communities that hinder the nation's modern development.

In 2006, the Brazilian Space Agency (AEB) presented a proposal to Quilombola leaders, communities, and social movements from Alcântara to convert the CLA into the Alcântara Space Center (CEA). Unlike the CLA, the CEA would serve a purely commercial purpose, providing rentable platforms for launching spacecraft. By transforming the area into a commodity, this proposal was contrary to the intent of the original expropriation of Quilombola lands for public utility purposes rather than commercial ends. Instead of staying true to the original purpose of the space program, in 2006 the Ministry of Defense and the Ministry of Science, Technology, Innovation and Communication (MCTIC) created a binational company, Alcântara Cyclone Space (ACS) in partnership with Ukraine, to offer rocket launch sites for rent. In doing so, the program would enter the multimillion-dollar restricted market for spacecraft launches, making it clear that the government's primary concern is economic gain rather than national security.

According to ACS, there would be no need for new compulsory displacements, since the rental launch sites and institutional support areas would be located outside of the Quilombola settlements. However, from the perspective of the communities, the prospective development of these sites is nonetheless a threat to their territorial integrity. Even if these sites do not impact inhabited areas, they affect places intended for agricultural fields and intrude upon communities' access to the sea, leaving inhabitants unable to practice fishing. This situation would completely inhibit economic activities in the area where the enterprise would be located.

A map was included in the AEB proposal and clearly illustrates the intrusive plans of the AEB and the MCTIC. The polygons located on the right side of the map—extending from the north to the south and marked in pink, blue, and yellow—are areas intended for commercial launching platforms, impacting 2,690 hectares of land. The polygons on the left side of the map (in green) represent areas intended for "institutional support" for each site, which, if developed, would restrict access to 2,690 hectares of Quilombola land. The polygon located to the south (with the acronym CLA) shows the Quilombola area impacted by the launch center.

Starting the Social Cartography Process: The "War of Maps" between Quilombolas and the Military

While the Brazilian government's attempt to illegally build the CEA in 2007 was halted by the Federal Public Prosecutor's Office, which recognized the Quilombola claim to the area, with the formation of the ACS, the rules of the game in Alcântara changed. The creation of ACS was intended to integrate the Brazilian Space Program into the space commodity market, transforming the Quilombola territory into areas of commercial interest in the process. In response, the Quilombolas, social movements in Alcântara, and labor unions mobilized, placing increased pressure on the state to fulfill the provisions of Article 68 of the Brazilian Constitution and comply with the International Labour Organization (ILO) Convention 169 concerning Indigenous and tribal peoples.

Prior to initiating the lawsuit, the Quilombolas sought to create an associative formal legal instrument to secure definitive title to their lands in accordance with Decree 4.887, which in Brazil regulates the criteria and procedures for titling Quilombola territories. To develop the legal statement, the Quilombolas held a series of community "consultation" workshops. The 150 Quilombola communities were divided into ten local hubs, taking into account geographic proximity and family networks. A total of 596 community representatives participated in the workshops and signed the attendance lists: at the final plenary session, held on October 15, 2007, 340 community representatives were present.

During the consultation workshops, time was set aside to develop so-called

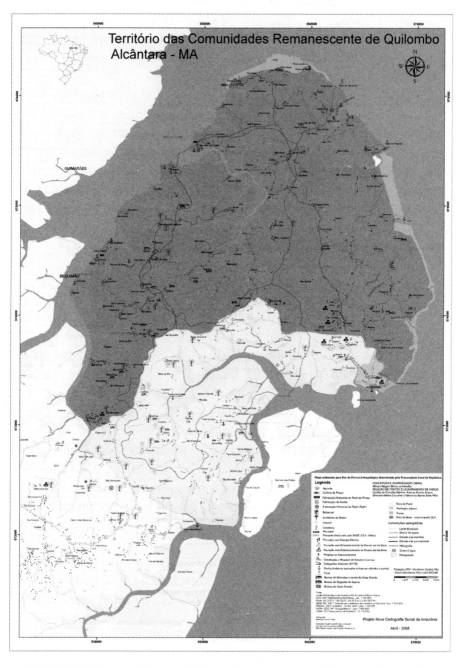

FIGURES 11.01A, 11.01B & 11.01C. Map of the ethnic territory of Alcântara, Brazil, published in the anthropological report. Source: Almeida 2006a.

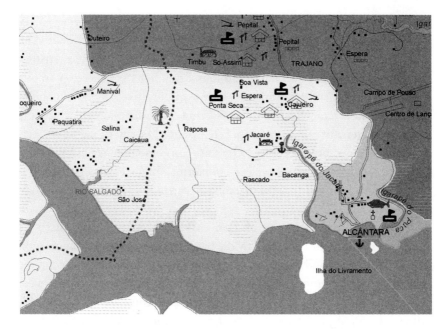

11.01B

11.01C

map narratives, during which community members would describe the region where their communities were located. The map narratives focused on recounting the social relations between the Quilombolas and their territory and natural resources, facilitating profound moments of reflection among the community members. Through these map narratives, the Quilombolas demonstrated their collective dissatisfaction with the ways in which the Quilombola territory of Alcântara was represented in official maps. To challenge the official representation of Alcântara as a demographic void, the communities decided to pursue a type of "countermapping" (Peluso 1995) of their territory. This required that the mapping be carried out by the Quilombolas themselves.

Following the series of consultation workshops, community leaders, via the Movement of Those Affected by the Base (MABE),[5] requested courses on GPS, photography, and the basics of GIS from the Group for Socioeconomic Studies of the Amazon (GESEA) and the New Social Cartography Project of the Amazon (PNCSA). These courses provided community leaders with advanced training in cartography and georeferencing as well as technologies such as Global Positioning System (GPS) and Geographic Information Systems (GIS), giving them the skills necessary to develop their own maps and to monitor their territory. The coordinators of the PNCSA requested that I, as a Quilombola and as someone from Alcântara, serve as the lead community researcher on the project. In addition, we also brought other young Quilombola leaders into the project because they could easily travel throughout the territory and monitor the activities of the CEA.

Since the social cartography project was conducted during the most intense phase of the conflict surrounding the Alcântara Space Center (CEA), we opted to carry out all of the work ourselves. This would serve to counter accusations by the Brazilian government that our resistance was influenced by NGOs and outsiders, and it would allow us to move freely throughout the territory without arousing suspicion. We decided to divide the work into two phases: in the first phase, we would produce an "overlay map," which would allow us to compare the official maps used in the AEB proposal with maps published in an anthropological report produced by the Brazilian anthropologist Alfredo Wagner Berno de Almeida in 2003 for the Federal Public Prosecutor's Office (Almeida 2006a; Figure 11.01a, 11.01b & 11.01c).

We produced the overlay map by digitizing the polygons of the AEB proposal into shapefiles, which we then transformed into the same coordinate system as the anthropological report. By overlaying the two sets of shapefiles, we were able to visualize the scale of the impact of the CEA on the Quilombola territories of Alcântara (Figure 11.02). This "war of maps" (Almeida 1994) completely contradicted the state's argument that Alcântara was a demographic void. While the AEB map showed only 10 communities, by overlaying the anthropological map, we identified more than 150 communities in just the area affected by the Brazilian Space Program

The overlay study, coupled with the map narratives developed previously, led to intense reflections on our vulnerability in the face of those who exercise a powerful monopoly over map production. After all, depending on the interests of those in power, discourses on communities' existence (or lack thereof) can be either undermined or strengthened. Likewise, the size of large rural properties, the presence of natural resources and minerals in different territories, or any number of other important data points can be profoundly manipulated in the mapmaking process. This process of reinterpreting state maps contributed significantly to legal proceedings against companies that had illegally invaded Quilombola territory.

Social Cartography for Territorial Protection

According to the map contained in the AEB proposal (Figure 11.04), the first of the "institutional support areas" would be located in areas of cultivation belonging to the communities of Folhau, Tacaua, Águas Belas, Rio Verde, Galego, Corre Prata, Peri-Açu, Mamuna, and Baracatatiua. This institutional area would support the "commercial launch site" located on the coastal strip between Baracatatiua and Mamuna. This site would prevent access to the sea for nearby communities such as Baracatatiua and Mamuna. In addition, it would significantly reduce areas for planting near the coast. Access to the sea and farming areas would be completely compromised for 160 families.

The second institutional area was intended to support the second launch site (represented in blue in Figure 11.04) and would occupy an area used for cropland, making it impossible for residents from the following communities to practice agriculture: Santa Maria, Mato Grosso, Vila do Meio, Porto do Aru, Aru, Tapera, Bom Viver, Brito Mamuninha, and Canelatiua. The second launch site would be located between Brito and Tapera, making it difficult for communities to access the sea while also occupying a significant piece of land near the coast used for agricultural purposes. This site would prevent more than 260 families from having free access to the sea and family farming areas.

The third and last of the institutional areas was designed to support launch site number three, shown in pink on the map (Figure 11.04). This site would

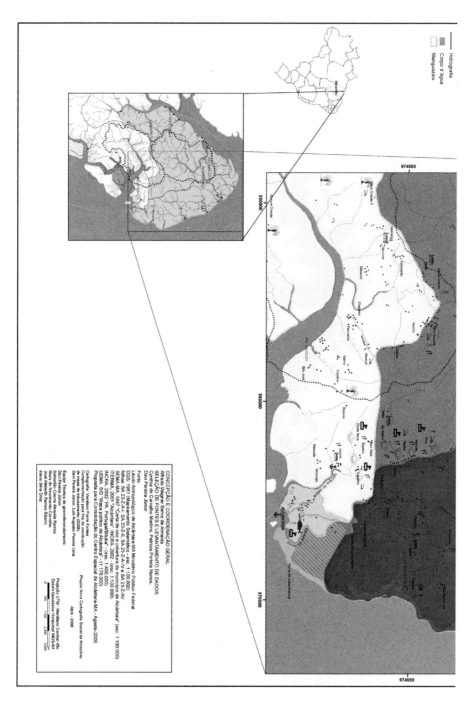

FIGURE 11.02. Map showing expansion plans for the Brazilian Space Program produced by the Brazilian anthropologist Alfredo Wagner Berno de Almeida for the Federal Public Prosecutor's Office. Source: PNCSA.

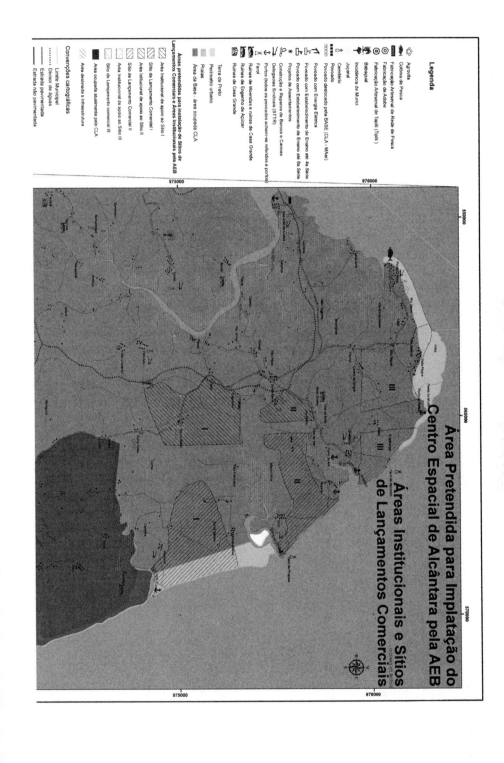

occupy planting areas of the following communities: Vila Valdecir, Vista Alegre, Areia, Retiro, Canelatiua, Rio Green, São Miguel, Vila Maranhense, Centro de Alegre, Ponta de Areia, and Mãe Eugênia. The site would take over the entire coastal area between Canelatiua and Areia, preventing access to the sandbar and the sea for inhabitants of nearby communities and occupying a large section of land traditionally used for agriculture. In practice, it would be impossible for more than 180 families to access the sea, farming areas, and natural resources.

With the map overlay process concluded, the team of social cartographers and MABE leaders now began to discuss how to move forward. We decided to first return to the communities to verify that the overlay map was consistent with their view of Quilombola territory in Alcântara; following this, we would map conflict areas in more detail. The conflict mapping consisted of georeferencing areas where conflict was occurring between the Quilombolas in Mamuna and Baracatatiua and the companies contracted by Alcântara Cyclone Space, which had devastated areas intended for agriculture in these two communities. We decided to stay in Mamuna, one of the best-organized communities where MABE had provided political training to raise awareness of the struggle.

To develop the maps, we gathered spatial information through GPS, photography, and direct observation along the perimeter of the ACS work with the assistance of residents who, with their intimate knowledge of local paths, guided us through the area. Still, the destruction of the land was so severe that even older residents lost their points of reference. We only avoided getting lost because the community is located along the shoreline and the sound of the waves led us back to the beach. Sometimes, in order to avoid drawing the contractors' attention to what we were doing, we hid the GPS devices and cameras. Since we were all from the community, we were hardly even noticed by the workers.

With the field data collected in Mamuna, we were ready to develop our first conflict maps. We plotted all of the spatial data on the maps, including permanently closed public access paths, new roadways, cleared crops, deforested riparian forests, and areas where babassu palms had been felled. In addition, we georeferenced the position of all the companies' equipment within the territory to represent the spatialization of the conflict (Figures 11.03a, 11.03b, and 11.03c).

Then we developed a photomap (Figures 11.04a and 11.04b) that uses photographs, GPS data, and ethnographic descriptions to visualize the various conflict areas in the territory. We georeferenced the locations of the photos and then linked each photo to a short description of the destruction perpetrated by the ACS contractors in the area between Mamuna and Baracatatiua. This made it possible to visualize the damage that had occurred as well as its precise location. In this way, we entered into not only a "War of Maps" with the military but also a battle for the right to produce knowledge about ourselves. This became a critical moment of self-awareness for us.

From this moment on, we began to use social cartography as a political instrument to aid in the communities' struggle. Our maps express how we conceive of our relationship with territory, using our own modes of representation. These are organic maps in which conflicts and triumphs are expressed through spatialization, allowing us Quilombolas to map our own conflicts. Our maps have gained attention, since they also serve as a way of politically positioning the group in relation to its territory, and as a way of making conflicts visible in the sense articulated by Farias Júnior (2010, 96; author translation): "Social cartography makes it possible to politicize maps once dominated by technocratic stratagems controlled by government agencies and multinational corporations. The map has been incorporated into social struggles, evincing religious factors, gender factors, and the dispute over natural resources."

When a community decides to map their own territory, they are challenging the state's power to map and contesting its monopoly over the definition of territory and its classification. In other words, they are engaging in a struggle for the power to map and the right to define territory. In our case, we were able to make political use of the maps: MABE incorporated the maps into a report sent to the Maranhão Federal Public Prosecutor's Office, denouncing the development of the space base and the destruction of Quilombola land. This report with the conflict maps served as the basis for a ruling issued in the federal courts of Maranhão in 2007 and 2008 banning the ACS from building the proposed launch sites in Quilombola territory and thus preventing the compulsory displacement of hundreds of families.

The mapping project represented the last phase in a forty-year struggle to protect Quilombola territory. Today the Quilombolas assist other groups of traditional peoples and communities that face invasions of their territories, drawing on our experience that mobilization is needed to enforce laws protecting traditional peoples. As the Quilombola leader Leonardo dos Anjos said in an interview, referring to the mobilization and mapping process carried out by the Quilombola communities of Alcântara: "We have the right to remain in the lands where we live and work, and that we occupy as a traditional community."

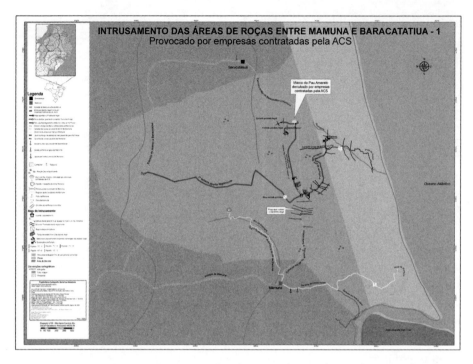

FIGURE 11.03A, 11.03B & 11.03C. Social cartography map showing locations of conflicts with the Alcântara rocket base, Alcântara, Brazil, 2007. Source: PNCSA.

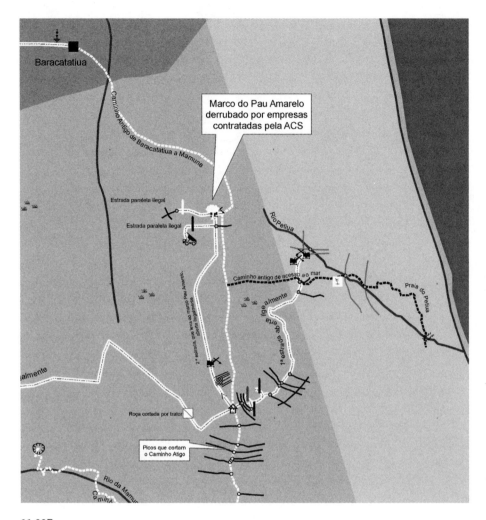

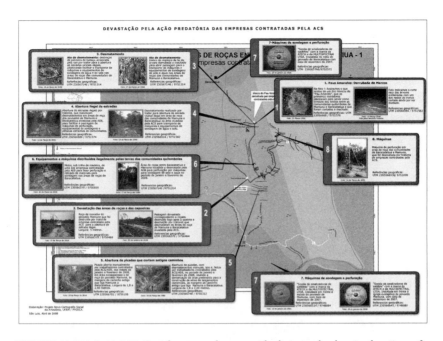

FIGURE 11.04A & 11.04B. Social cartography map with photographs showing locations of conflicts with the Alcântara rocket base, Alcântara, Brazil, 2007. Source: PNCSA.

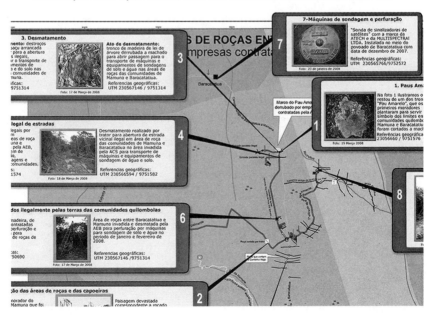

11.04B

Final Reflections

As the lead Quilombola researcher, I frequently traveled to the Quilombola communities affected by the space base. To my surprise, whenever we would arrive in a Quilombola settlement, community members would ask our driver, Vilson Serejo, why the researcher had not come. I was "invisible" to them because they did not expect to see a Black researcher. As soon as they realized who I was, I was quickly incorporated into the community. My apparent invisibility also facilitated my travel to areas affected by the conflict with ACS. By traveling with other Quilombolas, I was able to enter devastated areas and use GPS and camera georeferencing tools to document the damage caused by the company without drawing the attention of ACS employees.

For an external researcher, it is necessary to overcome mistrust to develop a relationship with the group he or she intends to study. My identity, and the fact that I am from Alcântara, without a doubt greatly facilitated my relations with the Quilombolas affected by the space base. As the work progressed, community members and leaders began to treat me as a Quilombola; at the same time I was able to present myself as a researcher when speaking with outsiders. This put me in a unique position as a researcher. The object of analysis was my own social world, forcing me to consider my own affective relations and ways of thinking and acting when I interacted with other community members.

Conducting a scientific investigation with one's own social world as the object of study requires reflexivity. My biggest challenge was taking a critical approach to scientific knowledge production, managing the potential impacts of the research, and establishing relations without exercising symbolic violence. I wanted to avoid confusing my own personal perspective with the position of the group or getting stuck in a spontaneous sociological investigation. Even while belonging to the group, it is essential for the researcher to build a good research relationship with the group. Otherwise, the researcher risks not being able to adequately interpret issues impacting the group, much less developing representations that accurately express the position of the group. My experiences in Alcântara showed me that research requires a relationship based on trust, independent of the position that the researcher occupies in relation to the group.

Ultimately, our social cartography project challenged the Brazilian state's monopoly over map production, asserting our right to make our own maps in defense of our own territory. Without land, our lives and our identity are at risk. The Brazilian state has long used maps to justify its various assaults on our territories, but through social cartography, we are better able to visualize and analyze the threats to our lands.

NOTES

1. In the case of the territory of those affected by the space base, the necessary procedures for titling (in accordance with Article 4.877/2003) have already been carried out. The territory has had an anthropological report since 2003; the Technical Identification and Delimitation Report (RTID) was officially published on November 4, 2008, via the National Institute of Colonization and Agrarian Reform (INCRA) on pages 110 and 111 of Section 3 of the *Diário Oficial da União* (Official Gazette of the Union), no. 214. The territory is composed of approximately 159 communities and occupies an area of 85,000 hectares. The only thing lacking for the completion of its title is the political will on the part of executive powers to duly sign the decree.

2. The towns located on Cajual Island are included in a certificate of recognition issued by the Palmares Cultural Foundation, dated January 25, 2006.

3. The certification of this territory was issued by the Palmares Cultural Foundation on May 5, 2006, and is duly documented in General Registry no. 0006, record no. 553, page 62. This is case no. 01420.000040/1998/88 regarding approximately forty settlements located in the municipalities of Alcântara and Bequimão.

4. All acronyms are created from the original Portuguese name of an organization.

5. The MABE was founded in 1999 by the Quilombola communities of Alcântara affected by the space base. It is an institution of a political character that represents all of the Quilombola communities of Alcântara, affected or not by the Brazilian space program.

REFERENCES

Almeida, Alfredo Wagner Berno de. 1994. *Carajás, a guerra dos mapas: Repertório de fontes documentais e comentários para apoiar a leitura do mapa temático do Seminário-Consulta "Carajás: Desenvolvimento ou Destruição?"* Belem, Brazil: Falangola Editora.

———. 2006a. *Os quilombolas e a base de lançamento de foguetes de Alcântara.* Vol 1. Brasília: Ministério do Meio Ambiente (MMA).

———. 2006b. *Os quilombolas e a base de lançamento de foguetes de Alcântara.* Vol. 2. Brasília: MMA.

Berreman, Gerald. 1975. "Etnografia e controle das impressões em uma aldeia do Himalaia." In Alba Zaluar Guimarães, *Desvendando máscaras sociais*, 123–175. Rio de Janeiro: Francisco Alves, 1980.

Farias Júnior, Emmanuel de Almeida. 2010. "Cartografia social e conhecimentos tradicionais associados à reivindicação de territorialidades específicas no baixo rio Negro: Os quilombolas do Tambor." *Caderno de Debates Nova Cartografia Social: Conhecimentos Tradicionais e Territórios na Pan-Amazônia* 1(1): 90-97.

Geertz, Clifford. 1990. *A interpretação das culturas.* Rio de Janeiro: Zahar Editores.

———. 1999. *O saber local: Novos ensaios em antropologia interpretativa.* Petrópolis, Brazil: Editora Vozes.

Lopes, Danilo da Conceição Serejo. 2014. *A Base Espacial e as comunidades quilombolas de*

Alcântara. Annals of the 64th Meeting of the Sociedade Brasileira para o Progresso da Ciência. Available at sbpcnet.org.br/livro/64ra.

Peluso, Nancy. 1995. "Whose Woods Are These? Counter-Mapping Forest Territories in Kalimantan, Indonesia." *Antipode* 27(4): 383–406.

Pereira Júnior, Davi. 2008. *Luta dos quilombolas pelo título definitivo: Oficinas de consultas*. Nova Cartografia Social da Amazônia fascículo 25. Manaus, Brazil: Editora da Universidade Federal do Amazonas. Available at novacartografiasocial.com.br/fasciculos/movimentos-sociais-identidade-coletiva-e-conflitos/?cp_movimentos-sociais-identidade-coletiva-e-conflitos=3.

———. 2009. *Quilombos de Alcântara: Território e conflito: O intrusamento do território das comunidades quilombolas de Alcântara pela empresa binacional Alcântara Cyclone Space*. Manaus, Brazil: Editora da Universidade Federal do Amazonas.

———. 2010. "Quilombolas de Alcântara na Rota do 4887: Uma fábula da história do racismo institucional à negação de direitos pelo estado brasileiro!" *Caderno de Debates Nova Cartografia Social: Territórios Quilombolas e Conflitos* 1(2): 101–110.

———. 2011. "Tradição e identidade: A feitura de louça no processo de construção da identidade da comunidade de Itamatatiua—Alcântara maranhão." In Cynthia Carvalho Martins et al., *Insurreição de saberes: Práticas de pesquisa em comunidades tradicionais*. Manaus, Brazil: Universidade do Estado do Amazonas–UEA.

———. 2012. *Territorialidades e identidades coletivas: Uma etnografia de Terra de Santa na Baixada Maranhense*. Master's thesis, Programa de Pós-Graduação em Antropologia da Universidade Federal da Bahia, Salvador, Brazil.

Viveiros, Jerônimo de. 1977. *Alcântara no seu passado econômico, social e político*. Maranhão, Brazil: Fundação Cultural do Maranhão.

Commentary: What Sort of Territory? What Sort of Map?

JOE BRYAN

What is a territory? The question pops up repeatedly across the chapters in this volume. After all, what are mapping projects if not attempts to define territory? The problem, as several of the authors suggest, is that mapping affords a partial understanding of territory at best. At worst, mapping runs completely counter to Black and Indigenous concepts of territory with potentially devastating results. That outcome makes the question of what a territory is all the more pressing, to say nothing of what work mapping does.

We are used to thinking of territory as a closed object, a thing that can be mapped, recognized, and demarcated. The dominance of this concept is reinforced by mapping, beginning with the use of GPS units and other cartographic technologies to locate material instances of use and occupancy by Black and Indigenous peoples. Legal developments reinforce this approach, pushing titling and demarcation as a remedy to the lack of protection for Black and Indigenous rights. Mapping did not precede legal mechanisms like the International Labor Organization's Convention 169 or the Inter-American Court's rulings on property rights for Indigenous and Black communities. Rather, mapping coevolved with these reforms (Wainwright and Bryan 2009). In much the same way, the vast majority of mapping projects in Black and Indigenous communities begin in response to grabs for land and resources. Mapping, like a land claim, is an important *defensive* response, a tactical reaction to a series of imposed conditions under which Indigenous and Black communities must struggle. The territories that emerge from those conditions ought to be read accordingly, as responses that are specific to the context and means through which they come to be rather than expressions of a precolonial concept or ethnic difference. That is to say that territory is not at all a closed object, defined by an internal, self-organizing logic of ethnic identity or customary use. Instead, it denotes a broader terrain shaped by power and relations of force. Maps that show territories as closed, bounded objects are but a symptom of those relationships (Wynter 2006).

What sort of territory do maps produce? How one responds to that question has a great deal to do with whence that response is formulated. The chapters in this volume think from a diversity of contexts, provisionally aligned by their shared use of mapping as a means to defend highly localized territories while confronting a common threat of dispossession. The responses in this volume should be read in terms of their open-ended diversity. Still, the consistency of the forces they face—dispossession, land grabs, death—offers some room for generalizing. In that spirit, this chapter expands on the idea of territory by drawing on some of the themes raised in other chapters, reading their uses of mapping as charting zones of encounter and contact across differences and characterized by awkward, unequal, unstable connections that create new kinds of relations (Rivera Cusicanqui 2012, 2018; see also Tsing 2005). But first, a detour.

Mapping the Destruction of Territory

Most everything that I have learned about maps has come from making maps with communities in a wide variety of settings that range from Newe Sogobia to Wallmapu, and many points in between.[1] Each of the chapters in this volume starts from a similar position, moved by a sense of the importance of what is variously termed land or territory to their unique, collective ways of life. In nearly every one of those experiences, the immediacy of mapping was framed in response to historical and ongoing threats of dispossession. While focused on land and resources, communities invariably saw dispossession as something larger—the destruction of an entire world grasped through relationships between people and land, forests, animals, and so much more. Nonetheless, the initial focus of mapping was often guided by a strong sense that an immediate remedy to that threat routed through legal recognition of territory as a right. Mapping plays a vital role in making territory visible as a physical area of land that can be titled, demarcated, and legally protected. Without that visibility, dispossession was often treated as the inevitable outcome. How could state officials, national societies, and corporations respect something that they could not see? In contrast, mapping facilitated recognition of Black and Indigenous territories, giving them a place in a social and spatial order founded on their dispossession. The assumed solution to that problem was therefore possession, an outcome reinforced by the emphasis on titling and demarcation. Coming from outside of the grounded normative frameworks that shape the importance of territory in Black and Indigenous communities, I had to learn the inadequacy of titling and demarcation the hard way, through mapping.

In 2002, I began research in the Indigenous Mayangna community of Awas Tingni, Nicaragua, studying the role that participatory mapping had played in their historic land claim that was eventually reviewed by the Inter-American Court of Human Rights. After a prolonged legal battle, the Inter-American Court issued a landmark ruling in Awas Tingni's case in 2001. The ruling affirmed that Indigenous peoples had the right to own lands they had historically used and occupied as an expression of their basic human right to property. In its ruling, the Inter-American Court directed Awas Tingni's adversary, the government of Nicaragua, to title and demarcate the community's land, formally registering their rights to property in national law. When I arrived in Awas Tingni one year later, invited in first by the community's lawyers and later by the community itself, the community had long since mapped their territory. The pressing question at the time was why the map did not become the territory, directing state efforts to title and demarcate Awas Tingni's claim. My initial research involved sitting in on meetings where state officials and lawyers explained to Awas Tingni that the map was not, in fact, the territory they would receive title to, at least not automatically. The Inter-American Court, the highest human rights body in the Americas, could not order the titling of Awas Tingni's claim. Titling and demarcation were instead a process to be negotiated between the community and the state.

The ensuing negotiations proved fraught. State officials' first position was to order the "verification" of Awas Tingni's map by an independent team of researchers. State officials eventually selected a team in 2003. The team was led by an established expert in the field of Indigenous mapping, the US anthropologist Anthony Stocks. Stocks had previously led efforts to map five other Indigenous Miskito and Mayangna territories west of Awas Tingni's claim. Though none of the territories had been titled, many in Nicaragua and beyond regarded the maps as a model of academic rigor coupled with community participation. In Awas Tingni, Stocks's team applied a similar method, using cultural ecology methods to map land use and occupancy with community participation. Hired on by Awas Tingni's lawyers to observe the verification study, I saw how thrilled residents of the community were to return to mapping their land. The project accelerated their ability to move through the territory, by making time and supplies available for long forays into the forest. Their delight was reflected in the resulting maps that documented their use and occupancy over a much larger area than shown in the initial claim.

Outside Awas Tingni, the reception was very different. State officials challenged the verification study, not on the basis of the accuracy of what it showed but rather on the calculus that it was simply too much land to give to too few people (Stocks 2005). Neighboring Indigenous Miskito communities echoed that rationale, arguing that larger numbers of people in their communities dictated that Awas Tingni should cede their claims to areas where their use and occupancy overlapped. Despite their differences, both claims countered the idea that territory was somehow about space for a collective way of life, however defined, and more about the proper calculus for allocating resources to people. Their arguments turned the focus of mapping away from use and occupancy and toward the question of boundaries. Who was entitled to control what lands and resources? And on what basis?

Part of this shift was already established in the Inter-American Court's ruling. Convinced by arguments made by Awas Tingni's lawyers, the Court interpreted territory as property. If there was no solid footing for recognizing territory as a fundamental human right, there certainly was for property. The Court's ruling interpreted that right as having a meaning autonomous from state definitions, thereby allowing for the concept of property as a collective right of the community. Liberal notions of property, long used to deny Indigenous peoples' rights to territory and exclude them from society, were now repurposed as means of bringing them into Nicaraguan society. It was a determination that, in practice, came down to demarcation. And in order for demarcation to proceed, there needed to be clear boundaries for it to follow.

In the Awas Tingni case, these boundaries were first drawn along ethnic lines, distinguishing Mayangna residents' use and occupancy from that of their Miskito neighbors. The resolution of overlapping claims built on that distinction, though they ended up moving the boundaries considerably. Under Nicaraguan laws passed following Awas Tingni's 2001 court case, communities were required to resolve all boundary conflicts prior to petitioning for title. In Awas Tingni's case, that effort failed repeatedly. While Awas Tingni residents saw Miskito communities projecting claims far onto Mayangna lands, Miskito communities saw Awas Tingni's growing territorial claims as a direct threat to their existence. Eventually the dispute was adjudicated by the regional autonomous government in 2007, with officials arbitrarily drawing a line on a map bisecting the overlapping area. There was no fieldwork behind the line as Awas Tingni residents had grown accustomed to. Instead, it was drawn by a fiat. As much as the result angered Awas Tingni residents, it cleared the way for titling and demarcation of the community's claim a year later in 2008. Seven years after the Inter-American Court ruling, Awas Tingni had its title.

In hindsight, it was already too late to save Awas Tingni's territory. Beginning in the 1990s, Indigenous and non-Indigenous settlers had been steadily moving onto the community's land, drawn into the forest in search of mahogany, rosewood, and other valuable tropical hardwoods. Awas Tingni residents were also logging in many of these same areas, engaged in a historical use that many outside the community saw as opposed to customary or traditional use. Since much of the wood was sold on gray markets, mixing legally and illegally cut timber, all involved were well aware of the risk of being accused of illegal activity. As titling and demarcation efforts advanced, people on all sides intensified their logging in the face of uncertainty over who would get what land. The balance shifted in 2007 when Hurricane Felix, a Category 5 storm, passed directly over Awas Tingni's territory, devastating the forest. The storm ground demarcation surveys to a halt as crews faced an impenetrable blockade of fallen trees. Miskito logging cooperatives, many of them composed of Contra War veterans well connected to regional political officials, lobbied hard to salvage the downed wood rather than let it rot on the forest floor. State officials agreed, allowing the cooperatives to log in the devastated area. By the time Awas Tingni received its title a year later, outside interests were operating across wide swaths of the community's territory. By 2008, there were three collectives of Miskito veterans logging in the community's claim. They were joined by another 37 families who similarly saw themselves engaged in the settlement of frontier lands, converting land and forest to marketable commodities (Awastingni-AMASAU 2012). Logs topped the list, followed by cattle and beans. By 2010, the number of outsiders had grown to 214 families. No line in the forest or title could stop them.

Under Nicaraguan law, state officials have the duty to evict outsiders living illegally on lands titled to Indigenous and Black communities. Nonetheless, in 2010, state officials declared that they would not carry out any evictions out of respect for the property rights of all Nicaraguans. Made by officials in Sandinista president Daniel Ortega's administration, the declaration spoke to its revolutionary commitment to land redistribution among the country's large landless and land-poor rural population. At the same time, it undercut one of the key aspects of Ortega's efforts to make good on that commitment through titling Indigenous and Black territories. The trends have developed in tandem. Awas Tingni's title was the first of eighteen issued by the Ortega administration, bringing the total number of titled Black and Indigenous territories to twenty-three. Every one of those territories faces encroachment from outsiders who have operated with growing impunity since 2010. The rate of forest loss has spiked during the same period, generating some of the highest rates in Central America (Sesnie et al. 2017). In a number of cases, frustrated community residents have themselves attempted to evict outsiders, leading to violent clashes. Settlers killed twenty-eight residents of Miskito communities in 2015. As many as three thousand more Indigenous Miskito and Mayangna people have been displaced by the violence.

None of this appears on maps circulated by Nicaraguan officials. Instead they show the twenty-three territories that occupy roughly a quarter of the country and coincide extensively with autonomous regions established to guarantee Indigenous and Black political participation. Non-Indigenous mestizos, many of them settlers, already demographically outnumber Black and Indigenous residents in both autonomous regions. In more than a few communities, including Awas Tingni, people openly wonder how much longer they will exist as such. And if they don't, what kind of new community might they make or join? Those fears capture an expansive understanding of dispossession as the destruction of an entire world, replaced with a life as minority ethnic smallholders of property.

Events in eastern Nicaragua demonstrate that the solution to dispossession is not possession. That point is often obscured by mapping's emphasis on producing bounded territories, amenable to recognition via titling and demarcation. Possession has secured a place for Black and Indigenous communities at the lowest rungs of a Nicaraguan society that remains structured by inequalities of race and class, and whose will to dispossession remains unaltered. As the Nishnaabeg theorist Leanne Betasamosake Simpson (2017, 43) notes from another time and place, distant from Nicaragua yet close to Awas Tingni and other communities like it, "Dispossession is our relationship with the state."

Territory, Reconsidered

The speed and scope of devastation of Black and Indigenous territories in eastern Nicaragua ought to give pause for reflection. In a little more than fifteen years, vast areas of forest and entire communities have been pushed to the point where many wonder just how they will continue to exist. As a number of chapters in this volume suggest, this level of dispossession accompanying mapping projects in Nicaragua is not an isolated incident. Vitery and Lamiña's chapter describes how titling Kichwa territory has come with a renewed pressure from Ecuadorian officials to negotiate access to oil, a state-owned resource, beneath their lands. Where in the past, communities demanded recognition of their land rights as a means to oppose oil development, this time around state officials insist that they can no longer say no. With formal state recognition comes the duty to act as any other property owner with regard to the claims of another. Communities in Paraguay that have won rulings from the Inter-American Court, building on the precedent set by Awas Tingni, have similarly encountered renewed threats of displacement and dispossession while they await state registration of their rights (Correia 2018). The list goes on.

Despite the differences of context and setting, the persistent threat of dispossession after titling and demarcation ought to temper the enthusiasm for mapping. Part of what is at stake is the much-clichéd relationship between the map and the territory. That relationship is typically used to flag the tense relationship between reality (territory) and representation (map). The phrase is problematic for all sorts of reasons, beginning with the idea that maps are representations of some externally defined reality. Maps are instead very much a part of reality insofar as their production and use involves practices of interpreting the world and making it conform to the image of it found on maps. To paraphrase Denis Wood's remarks, we see the world through maps with powerful, far-reaching effects on how we exist in it (Wood, 2010). The territory cannot be separated from the practices that bring it into being.

The emphasis on titling and demarcation suggests that one of the more important aspects of mapping is the drawing of boundaries. While customary use and occupancy, place-names, cultural sites, and so on may provide the basis for maps of Black and Indigenous territories, boundaries are what are recognized in strictly legal and political terms (Bryan 2011). They are what make Indigenous and Black territories commensurate with dominant notions of property. Collective ownership adds an important twist to the equation, though the emphasis on customary use and occupancy does not, especially when shorn of any connotation of tradition. What else is the settlement of frontier lands than a form of customary use and occupancy, converting "nature" into resources and land?

Boundaries do not define territories by delimiting them. They do so by drawing their elements together, organizing them spatially. Property rights can be demarcated and registered, but the overall purpose they serve is one of organizing society along familiar lines of power and economy. In much the same way, Indigenous and Black territories are invariably enframed by a national territory, located within it. Collectively, they define territory as a space structured by power relations, and not an area bounded on a map. The logic shapes Black and Indigenous mapping projects that by and large tend to be bounded by lines of ethnic and racial difference. The emphasis makes sense. Their exclusion from the political and economic life of the societies that surround them is typically justified in terms of racial and ethnic difference, using both as means of devaluing populations and the areas they occupy. Community mapping projects respond to this dynamic by asserting differences, making themselves visible. The value they create for their territories through recognition does not alter the logic of their devaluation. It doubles down on it, an effect that often plays out through the emphasis on property rights and its correlating questions of natural resource management and economic activity. The Nicaragua case demonstrates this point. Fortunately, it is not the only reading.

Boundary Work

On a 2015 visit to Awas Tingni, I sat talking with a longtime colleague who lives in the community. He had participated in every one of the projects to map the community's claim. He had also lived through the aftermath of titling, and now we sat mixing memories of past trips we had made through the surrounding forest with discussion of how many of those places no longer existed, replaced by bean fields and cattle pastures established by settlers. The conversation paused for a moment. "We will fight for this place even if it is nothing more than rocks and dirt," he said. "It's our place, just like the Court said. It's all we have." Months later, I would learn that he had abandoned his home in Awas Tingni and moved to another community to try and start life anew. It took a long time to hear his words as anything other than a desperate plea made worse by his absence.

With time, I have come to understand how his words pick up the question of what a territory is. In particular, they underscore the importance of relationships that make a collective way of life possible through their attachment to a particular place, even if all that is left is "rocks and dirt." Those relationships push against the normative importance placed on legal recognition. In the Awas Tingni case, as well as in legal approaches to Indigenous rights more generally, the emphasis on recognition structures possession of land and resources as a solution to dispossession. Instead, his words highlight the importance of connection to people and land, one that informs a sense of what the Dené theorist Glen Coulthard (2014) terms "grounded normativity," defined as an ethical framework fashioned through the practice of living in a place.

This kind of grounded normativity abounds in the practices of mapping, perhaps nowhere more so than in the production of boundaries. Boundaries are more often than not an imposition that mapping projects must engage, a requirement for titling and demarcation. This is not to say that Black and Indigenous communities do not have boundaries. They often do, though they are seldom the kinds of boundaries that make straight lines on maps or on the ground. Making the latter kinds of boundaries is often one of the more difficult aspects of mapping, frequently running counter to the ways that communities relate to one another and negotiate access to land and resources (Bryan 2011; Sletto 2009). This is why the question of what a territory is comes up so often in the course of mapping projects. In Vitery and Lamiña's case, the question was triggered by community objections to the idea of simply transforming their territory into a commodity whose resources can be auctioned off and sold. In the case from Oaxaca discussed by Cruz, the question of what is a territory leads to a reflection on how spatial knowledge is conceived as part of community life. Crucially, neither case pitches territory as a closed object, to be recognized and defended. Rather, both point to the spatial and temporal openness of territory as understood in their respective locations as an essential aspect of community life. It is a space, as Cruz points out, that cannot be mapped. That does not mean that maps should never be made. Instead, it establishes the basis for rethinking mapping altogether.

Not one of the cases discussed in this volume involves a community taking up mapping of its own accord, independent of any threat to the integrity of their "living space" (Cruz 2010). Several of the cases describe a sense of being compelled to map. In others, mapping was all but forced on communities. If they wanted to defend themselves against resource concessions, land grabbing, and so on, they had to find ways to address the cartographic logic of those proposals head-on. In nearly every case, communities have faced the risk that mapping does not interrupt the cartographic logic of parceling out land and resource rights. It only temporarily redirects it. The kinds of territory that maps help make simply won't do. But what sort of territory would work? And what sort of map?

There's no straightforward answer to those questions, due in no small part to the differences between the settings where mapping occurs. Countering oil concessions in the Peruvian Amazon is not entirely the same as countering oil concessions in the Ecuadorian Amazon, any more than defending Wallmapu—Mapuche territory—in Argentina is a match for efforts in Chile. Despite their proximity, differences persist. At the same time, they have certain features in common. All of the cases discussed counter a renewed push for land and resources associated with economic globalization. Human rights tend to follow a similar course, progressively expanding a set of universal claims through application to particular cases. Put differently, human rights and economic globalization are two aspects of the same territory, and the expansion of both is accomplished through their incorporation of differences.

The paradox of using maps to resist domination at the risk of expanding it is real. In several of the chapters in this volume, the urgency of this paradox animates the question of what a territory is. As Cruz describes in his chapter on narrative cartographies in Oaxaca, Zapotec communities' first clue that the México Indígena project was mapping a very different territory than the one they had in mind came when the US-led mapping team started surveying individual parcels (see also Bryan and Wood 2015; Cruz 2010). Cruz underscores the point that for communities in the Sierra Norte, collective ownership of land is one of the defining elements of the territory. The US Army–funded México Indígena project was mapping that space by first dismantling it, reducing it to categories and concepts that could be mapped. Cruz's discussion of the jaguars' traversal of the same space highlights the stark differences between community understandings of territory and those of the México Indígena project. In the narrative map he presents, territory begins with a survey of all that is, describing a whole by way of organizing its habitation. Rather than a closed space, the territory described is an open set of relationships. Vitery and Lamiña raise a similar point in their discussion of *sumak kawsay* as one aspect of a complex set of relations through which people are linked to their surroundings (see also Bryan 2017). The idea of Wallmapu discussed in the chapters by Nahuel and Mansilla and Melin offers another iteration of this theme.

It is tempting to see this emphasis on the unmappable or untranslatable as doubling down on the importance of difference in delineating Indigenous and Black territories. Much of what concepts like *sumak kawsay* or Wallmapu suggest exceeds culture, asserting certain ontological differences that make contrasting meanings of territory mutually exclusive. There is certainly something to that difference. Cruz's discussion of the jaguars' travels brings into being an idea of territory that is radically at odds with what appears on maps and in law. He is also careful to point out that the gap is not insurmountable. Cruz's narrative or oral cartographies are characterized by their ability to incorporate new elements, to expand and stretch as necessary to support a collective way of life. Jaguars and *supay* (Vitery and Lamiña) demonstrate this possibility, asserting an altogether different set of relationships—a different "nature-culture" as the theorist Sylvia Wynter terms it—that can serve as the basis for a different society and the kind of humanity that goes with it. Cruz's discussion of the more recent shining jaguar, captured and fitted with a telemetry collar, elaborates on this idea of a different nature-culture. Instead of simply allowing science to track the animal's movement, Cruz suggests in his chapter that the jaguar's movements provide the basis for a new form of territory that emerges at the intersection of what he terms "textual mapping" and "narrative cartographies." His proposal displaces the emphasis on valorizing Indigenous and Black territories in terms of inherent differences that establish their continuity with a precolonial past. Instead, he suggests the open-ended creation of something altogether new.

The Zone of Encounter

Cruz's account of the GPS-equipped jaguar blurs the distinction between a time of the ancestors and the present, between oral cartographies and textual mapping. He does not indiscriminately blend them together as if they were one and the same, so much as he asks us to see both the living jaguar that is also an ancestor *and* the GPS. That perspective resonates with Silvia Rivera Cusicanqui's discussion of *ch'ixi*, an Aymara word that literally describes the color created by seeing black and white spots together at the same time (Rivera Cusicanqui 2012). The concept is grounded in weaving, pulling black and white threads together that can be stretched in conversation with Cruz's discussion of meshworks made of *ixtle*, maguey fiber. Rivera uses the concept to counter the idea of Indigenous peoples as a "fenced-off ethnic identity, enclosed on ethnic maps" (Rivera Cusicanqui 2018, 126). In its place, she advances a notion of identity as a "weave of exchanges, a fabric of feminine origins and a process of becoming." The materiality of weaving is essential to her argument, as she highlights the spaces created by the interweave of different elements. Rather than emerging fully formed from a precolonial past, indigeneity, Rivera argues, is of the present, an alternative form of modernity grasped through the interplay of differences. She contrasts this with dominant interpretations of indigeneity that circulate in the Bolivian setting that she writes from that continually map Indigenous peoples as poor and rural, establishing a politics of belonging (Rivera Cusicanqui 2012). *Ch'ixi* presents a feminist counter that weaves together people's practices "as producers, merchants, weavers, ritualists, and creators of languages and symbols capable of seducing the 'other' and establishing pacts of reciprocity and coexistence among different groups" (Rivera Cusicanqui 2012, 107).

Her critique of maps notwithstanding, the practice of mapping described by Cruz and many others in this volume approximates Rivera Cusicanqui's discussion of *ch'ixi*. As community participants produce and read maps, they interweave different practices of space and cartography. Mapping does not solve problems of dispossession or facilitate recognition so much as it lends itself to bringing new territories into existence, opening up categories and concepts typically thought of as closed. In place of a universalizing trend to fold all people and places onto a single cartographic grid, mapping charts the seams where that unifying project encounters differences. The promise of Indigenous and Black mapping lies in its ability to proliferate these differences, treating them as generative without negating them, preserving their variegated nature much like woven threads that make *ch'ixi* something other than a uniform gray.

None of this is any guarantee against the dispossession, land grabbing, and death that Black and Indigenous mapping projects confront. Those forces are often too much to overcome with a map, even when backed by legal recognition of territorial rights. And yet, Indigenous and Black communities across the Americas have continually demonstrated an ability to create new spaces, new collective forms of life for themselves out of the ruins of the old. Their actions necessarily break with the kinds of linear approaches that root them in territories according to traditions, allowing them more movement than is often acknowledged. None of that diminishes the importance of territory. Given events described in this volume, territory is more threatened than ever as liberalism's propensity for dispossession pushes it further. Others, much like frontiers, are an essential category for organizing that process. As practiced in Indigenous and Black communities, mapping recenters that process, making the practice of Indigenous and Black existence, of interweaving differences, the basis for an altogether different concept of territory. It is a territory that will not be found on any map. Rather, its construction will require an altogether new way of mapping. The clues of what that practice might look like are spread across this volume. Let us see what we can make of them.

NOTE

1. Newe Sogobia is home to the Western Shoshone (Newe) people and is actively claimed by the United States. Wallmapu, actively claimed by Argentina and Chile, is the home of the Mapuche people. To say that either of these territories is located *in* the respective states is to concede a fundamental point of struggle for people in both places.

REFERENCES

Awastingni-AMASAU. 2012. "Caracterización jurídica de terceros en el territorio ancestral de la comunidad Mayangna de Awastingni—Awastingni Mayangnina Sauni Ûmani (AMASAU), Marzo–Mayo 2012: Fortalecimiento de las experiencias de ordenamiento territorial de dos pueblos indígenas en Colombia y Nicaragua." Bilwi, Nicaragua: Grupo de Trabajo Intercultural "Almáciga," Asociación de Cabildos del Norte de Cauca (ACIN), y el Ministro de Asuntos Exteriores y de Cooperación (AECID) del Gobierno de España.

Bryan, Joe. 2011. "Walking the Line: Participatory Mapping, Indigenous Rights, and Neoliberalism." *Geoforum* 42(1): 40–50.

———. 2017. "Oil, Indigeneity, and Dispossession." In *Other Geographies: The Influences of Michael Watts*, ed. Sharad Chari, Susanne Freidberg, Vinay Gidwani, Jesse Ribot, and Wendy Wolford, 157–168. Oxford: Wiley Blackwell.

Bryan, Joe, and Denis Wood. 2015. *Weaponizing Maps: Indigenous Peoples and Counterinsurgency in the Americas*. New York: Guilford Press.

Correia, Joel E. 2018. "Indigenous Rights at a Crossroads: Territorial Struggles, the Inter-American Court of Human Rights, and Legal Geographies of Liminality." *Geoforum* 97: 73–83.

Coulthard, Glen Sean. 2014. *Red Skin, White Masks: Rejecting the Colonial Politics of Recognition*. Minneapolis: University of Minnesota Press.

Cruz, Melquiades. 2010. "A Living Space: The Relationship between Land and Property in the Community." *Political Geography* 29(8): 420–421.

Rivera Cusicanqui, Silvia. 2010. *Ch'ixinakax utxiwa: Una reflexión sobre prácticas y discursos descolonizadores*. Buenos Aires: Tinta Limón.

———. 2012. "Ch'ixinakax utxiwa: A Reflection on the Practices and Discourses of Decolonization." *South Atlantic Quarterly* 111(1): 95–109.

———. 2018. *Un mundo ch'ixi es posible: Ensayos desde un presente en crisis*. Buenos Aires: Tinta Limón.

Sesnie, Steven E., Beth Tellman, David Wrathall, Kendra McSweeney, Erik Nielsen, Karina Benessaiah, Ophelia Wang, and Luis Rey. 2017. "A Spatio-Temporal Analysis of Forest Loss Related to Cocaine Trafficking in Central America." *Environmental Research Letters* 12(5): 054015.

Simpson, Leanne Betasamosake. 2017. *As We Have Always Done: Indigenous Freedom through Radical Resistance*. Minneapolis: University of Minnesota Press.

Sletto, Bjørn. 2009. "'Indigenous People Don't Have Boundaries': Reborderings, Fire Management, and Productions of Authenticities in Indigenous Landscapes." *Cultural Geographies* 16(2): 253–277.

Stocks, Anthony. 2005. "Too Much for Too Few: Problems of Indigenous Land Rights in Latin America." *Annual Review of Anthropology* 34:85–104.

Tsing, Anna L. 2005. *Friction: An Ethnography of Global Connection*. Princeton, NJ: Princeton University Press.

Wainwright, Joel, and Joe Bryan. 2009. "Cartography, Territory, Property: Postcolonial Reflections on Indigenous Counter-Mapping in Nicaragua and Belize." *Cultural Geographies* 16(2): 153–178.

Wood, Denis. 2010. *Rethinking the Power of Maps*. New York: Guilford Press.

Wynter, Silvia. 2006. "On How We Mistook the Map for the Territory, and Re-Imprisoned Ourselves in Our Unbearable Wrongness of Being, of *Désêtre*: Black Studies toward the Human Project." In *Not Only the Master's Tools: African-American Studies in Theory and Practice*, ed. Lewis R. Gordon and Jane Anna Gordon, 107–169. Boulder, CO: Paradigm.

Afterword

CHARLES R. HALE

This volume contains a series of extremely valuable individual chapter contributions that speak for themselves, and which Bjørn Sletto ably summarizes in the introduction. I will focus this brief afterword on three overarching dimensions of this project, which I consider to be especially important and valuable. These are: the ethos and practice of "collaborative" research; the benefits and potential of "social cartography" or "participatory mapping" as one prominent form of collaborative research practice; and the contributions of "radical social cartography" with Indigenous and Afro-descendant communities in the current conjuncture of Latin American political-economic landscapes.

Although the academic and institutional backing for this project was substantial from the start, this does not begin to tell the full organizational "backstory" of the book's production. LLILAS Benson Latin American Studies and Collections at the University of Texas at Austin enthusiastically supported the project as a prime expression of its institutional commitment to horizontal, collaborative research with social impact for the common good; we benefited as well from ample participation of the University of the Andes in Bogotá (Colombia), from Rights and Resources International (Washington DC), from the Projeto de Cartografia Social in Manaus (Brazil), and from various other academic institutions with which the contributors are affiliated. Yet the foundational conditions of possibility for these chapters—the authors themselves and the research processes—are long-standing relations of collaboration with community and civil society–based organizations and their associated intellectuals. In direct contrast to the mainstream mode—in which academy-based scholars collect and interpret "raw data" provided by their "subjects"—the research summarized in these chapters began with objectives defined primarily by political exigencies and unfolded using methods characterized by collaborative data collection, dialogic interpretation, and writing.

The participants in these activities were diversely positioned activist intellectuals who had to find common ground as they recorded their analysis. This kind of collaborative research often is invoked and described in a celebratory fashion, which emphasizes its benefits but downplays or eludes its complexities. These chapters, in contrast, provide a more balanced perspective, which ultimately makes a stronger argument for the endeavor. They make a persuasive case for collaborative research, not because it is easy or straightforward, but precisely because the tensions and contradictions that inevitably arise are so illuminating and generative.

Mapping is an especially apt research activity for this kind of collaborative research because the very process—collaboration among diversely positioned actors—not only brings different "perspectives" to the table but often convokes fundamentally different epistemologies that need to be expressed, understood, and negotiated. As Sletto cogently notes in his introduction, these differences require a double maneuver, which takes place in many contexts of social struggle but has especially prominent characteristics in the terrain of social cartography. On the one hand, the maps produced through social cartography are so useful and powerful precisely because they are made in the Cartesian language of the modern Western nation-state, and therefore render legible the demands of people who would often otherwise be dismissed or discounted. This is the classic counterhegemonic power of maps, deploying the same rigorously produced cartographic features to mobilize support, advance legal arguments, demand rights—that is, to wage a struggle from within. On the other hand, these same maps (or, at times, alternative versions made through the same collaborative research processes) have a very different purpose: to document and legitimate the particular "ways of knowing" that the people in question associate with their landscapes. Especially when the people in question are Indigenous and Afro-descendant, these ways of knowing will have "partial connections" to Cartesian legibility, but almost surely will overflow these epistemological boundaries, at times stretching the limits of standard mapping technologies to their breaking point. How do we map people's territories when they find boundary lines to be a dangerous simplification? When landscapes have subterranean or celestial dimensions? When distant mountains are active and animate? If the goal is to represent and amplify facets of these knowledge systems that have not been destroyed or disfigured beyond recognition by settler colonialism and racial capitalism, then Cartesian legibility in the absence of the second maneuver can become a harmful imposition. These chapters do not resolve the dilemma embodied in the need for this double maneuver; rather, they embrace it as the focus of reflection and mediation, with aspirations to strike a momentary balance between the two opposing logics, which requires constant renegotiation as conditions evolve.

The "radical" turn in social cartography practice, which the chapters in this book exemplify, is directly linked to the emergent conjuncture of social struggle. Over the past three decades, throughout the Americas, the rise of participatory mapping has coincided with what Karl Offen (2003), Roque Roldán (2005), and others have termed the "territorial turn." In response to effective mobilization from below, often aided by international actors and institutions, governments throughout the region set aside nineteenth-century models of individual and monocultural citizenship rights, opting instead for regimes of multicultural governance, characterized by the recognition of collective rights grounded in cultural difference (Hale 2019). The most expansive expressions of these multicultural rights—achieved throughout the region, especially in the latter years—were collective rights to territory and resources. Social cartography, in turn, became crucially important as a source of substantiating evidence for these claims, including the boundary demarcations, which later would become collective property lines. While these territorial rights were rarely fully achieved or implemented, they now appear in retrospect as astoundingly expansive material achievements and glimmers of hope. In recent years, by contrast, storm clouds of change at a global level have been gathering: as we reach the end of the second decade of the new century, it seems increasingly clear that the era of multicultural governance is coming to an end, replaced by regimes that actively repudiate the very idea of multicultural rights and refute the underlying premise that these rights are needed to remediate historical-structural inequities (Calla, Hale, and Mullings 2017). Although we do not yet understand the full logic or scope of the successor regime, it bears the clear marks of a toxic "racial retrenchment": not just an end to the expansion of multicultural rights, but an active refutation of these claims and a repudiation of those who make them as illegitimate and, increasingly, as "criminal." In this cultural-political state of affairs—full of danger and threat—radical social cartography takes on a momentous new valence. The "radical" aspect is a reference, in my reading, to a greater emphasis on long-standing and emergent forms of self-determination, which social cartography can help produce, refine, and justify. This does not mean that the double maneuver referred to above will no longer be necessary: one element of the great power of maps will continue to be their legibility for making demands on the state and, more generally, for speaking truth to power. Increasingly, however, the emphasis will be on fending off threats;

fortifying internal organizations; and advancing the autonomous bases for political, economic, and cultural empowerment. This book's "radical" focus is well positioned to make substantive contributions to these crucial and timely goals—helping to strengthen an Americas-wide alternative to the existential threat of this emergent phase of global capitalism.

REFERENCES

Calla, Pamela, Charles R. Hale, and Leith Mullings. 2017. "Race Matters in Dangerous Times." NACLA 49(1): 81–89.

Hale, Charles R. 2019. "Neoliberal Multiculturalism." In *The Routledge Handbook of Latin American Development*, ed. Julie Cupples, Marcela Palomino-Schalscha, and Manuel Prieto, 75–87. New York: Routledge.

Offen, Karl H. 2003. "The Territorial Turn: Making Black Territories in Pacific Colombia." *Journal of Latin American Geoography* 2(1): 43–73.

Roldán, Roque. 2005. "Importancia de los territorios colectivos de indígenas y afroamericanos en el desarrollo rural." In *Desarrollo territorial rural en América Latina y el Caribe: Manejo sostenible de recursos naturales, acceso a tierras y finanzas rurales*, ed. Rubén G. Echeverría, 135–161. Washington DC: Inter-American Development Bank.

Contributors

JOE BRYAN
Joe Bryan is associate professor in geography at the University of Colorado, Boulder. His work focuses on Indigenous politics in the Americas, human rights, and critical cartography. His most recent work addresses the role of community-based mapping in a 2001 ruling by the Inter-American Court of Human Rights. The case concerned a land claim brought by the Indigenous Mayangna community of Awas Tingni against the Republic of Nicaragua, and set an important legal precedent for recognizing Indigenous land rights. His chapter draws on his decades-long experience in Central America, critically examining the innovations of participatory mapping emerging from Indigenous communities; how these innovations shape the roles and interests of external actors; and how these radical mapping techniques influence the preservation of traditional land uses, governance, cultural relationships to land, and territorial rights in Central America. He is the author, with Denis Wood, of *Weaponizing Maps: Indigenous Peoples and Counterinsurgency in the Americas* (Guilford, 2015).

MELQUIADES (KIADO) CRUZ
Melquiades (Kiado) Cruz is a community organizer, communication technology innovator, and Indigenous scholar from the Zapotec community of Yagavila in the Rincón de la Sierra Norte of Oaxaca. His roots are in the Sierra, as are those of his ancestors, and his family continues to live there, next to the fields they cultivate. Kiado has used everything he has learned in his community as well as outside of it to reflect, motivate, and search for a different way of regenerating culture through communication. In the last few years, Kiado has worked in various sectors—civil organizations, alternative and independent media, and public institutions. Through these experiences, he has learned that the process of democratizing expression and creating

new and expanded kinds of relationships accompanies the hope that society can create new and autonomous ways of life. He has published an important critical reflection on current mapping projects in *Political Geography* (29, no. 8 [2010]: 420–421), in which he examines reasons for mapping and what sorts of maps Indigenous communities seek.

EMMANUEL DE ALMEIDA FARIAS JÚNIOR

Emmanuel de Almeida Farias Júnior holds a PhD in social anthropology and a master's degree in society and culture in the Amazon from the Federal University of Amazonas, Brazil. He is now associate professor in the Department of Social Sciences, Center for Applied Social Sciences-CCSA, and the Postgraduate Program in Social and Political Cartography in the Amazon at the State University of Maranhão, Brazil. He has also been a researcher at the New Social Cartography Project of the Amazon in Manaus, Brazil, since 2006. For the past decade and a half, he has been working as a partner with Indigenous people and Quilombolas on social cartography projects in support of their struggle to preserve collective identities, ethnic territories, and traditional natural resource management.

CARLOS ALBERTO GONZÁLEZ

Carlos González, a native of the Afro-Colombian region of the Cauca Valley in Colombia, is an ethnobotanist with a degree from the Universidad del Valle, Cali, Colombia. Currently working as an ethnobiologist at the Funecorobles Foundation in Colombia, González has twelve years of experience coordinating community projects oriented toward protection and conservation of natural resources and the culture of ethnic groups, especially in Black communities. He has also conducted social research and environmental education through cartography and ethnography with ethnic and peasant communities. He has published extensively on topics such as social cartography, biodiversity, and conservation. He sees social cartography as a means to facilitate the participation of community members in intergenerational dialogues, thus validating traditional knowledge and strengthening communities' political discourse.

CHARLES HALE

Charles Hale is the former director of the Lozano Long Institute of Latin American Studies at UT-Austin and co-organizer of the participatory mapping conference in Bogotá and the Lozano Long Workshop on Participatory Mapping at UT-Austin. He is currently dean of the School of Social Sciences at the University of California–Santa Barbara. He is internationally respected in his field of activist anthropology for his research on participatory mapping, race and ethnicity, identity politics, and consciousness and resistance. He is past president of the Latin American Studies Association (LASA) and the author of *Más que un Indio: Racial Ambivalence and Neoliberal Multiculturalism in Guatemala* (School of American Research, 2006) and *Resistance and Contradiction: Miskitu Indians and the Nicaraguan State, 1894–1987* (Stanford University Press, 1994).

ALEXANDRA LAMIÑA
Alexandra Lamiña from Quito, Ecuador, is a PhD student in Latin American Studies at the University of Texas at Austin, where she also earned master's degrees in Latin American Studies and in community and regional planning. In Ecuador, she studied geographical engineering (at the Universidad de la Fuerzas Armadas) and environmental engineering (at the Universidad Particular de Loja). Lamiña works with Indigenous organizations in the Ecuadorian Amazon to support processes of territoriality and political representation. Her research areas include social mobilization, planning, migration, and participatory mapping. She is currently researching conflicts between modernist planning and Indigenous ontologies, focusing in particular on opportunities to forge new forms of planning that incorporate Indigenous epistemologies.

PABLO MANSILLA QUIÑONES
Pablo Mansilla Quiñones is associate professor at the Institute of Geography, Pontificia Universidad Católica de Valparaíso, Chile. He was the winner of the 2013–2014 Antipode Scholar-Activist Project Award and received his PhD in geography from the Universidad Federal Fluminense, Brazil, and his master's degree in geography from the Universidad de Chile, Santiago. He is currently an associate researcher with the CONICYT project "Geohumanities and Creative (Bio)Geographies: Approaching Sustainability and Co-conservation through Rhizomatic Immersion." He is the co-author, along with Miguel Melin and Manuela Royo, of the books *Cartografía cultural del wallmapu: Elementos para descolonizar el mapa en territorio mapuche* and *Mapu Chillkantukun Zugu: Descolonizando el mapa del Wallmapu, construyendo cartografía cultural en territorio mapuche*.

MIGUEL MELIN PEHUEN
Miguel Melin Pehuen is a professor with the Universidad Católica de Temuco, Chile, specializing in intercultural bilingual education. He studied Indigenous rights, environments, and communicative processes at the

Universidad de Chile in Santiago. One of the founders and spokespersons of the Mapuche Territorial Alliance, Melin Pehuen is a native speaker of the Mapuche language of his people and currently plays a cultural role in the territorial struggles of his home community of Lofmapu Ralipitra in the commune of Nueva Imperial. He is co-author of numerous books, reports, and articles, including *Desigualdades territoriales y exclusión social del pueblo mapuche en Chile*, *Azmapu: Una aproximación al Sistema Normativo Mapuche desde el Rakizuam y el Derecho Propio* and *Mapu Chillkantukun Zugu: Descolonizando el mapa del Wallmapu, construyendo cartografía cultural en territorio mapuche*.

MARÍA LAURA NAHUEL

María Laura Nahuel is a resident of the Mapuce Lof (Community) Newen Mapu, Neuquén, Argentina, and received her undergraduate degree in geography from the Department of Humanities at the National University of Comahue, Argentina. Since 2004, she has participated in different research projects focusing on intercultural themes organized by the Mapuce Education Center "Norgvbamtuleayiñ" and the CEPINT (Popular and Intercultural Education Center) of the National University of Comahue. She is the *werken* (messenger, spokesperson) of the Confederación Mapuce Neuquina and has been involved with participatory cultural mapping workshops in several Mapuce communities. She views participatory cultural mapping as a fundamentally important tool for the construction of life plans by strengthening and reaffirming Indigenous culture and territoriality.

DAVI PEREIRA JÚNIOR

Davi Pereira Júnior was born in the Quilombola community of Itamatatiua in the south of the municipality of Alcântara. He holds an undergraduate degree in history from the State University of Maranhão (UEMA) and a master's degree in social anthropology from the Federal University of Bahia (UFBA). Pereira Júnior has been a researcher for New Social Cartography in Brazil since 2005 and has extensive experience in developing participatory cartographies with Indigenous peoples and traditional communities in Brazil. He is currently a doctoral student in Latin American Studies at the University of Texas at Austin.

WENDY PINEDA

Wendy Pineda is a specialist in geoinformatics and Geographic Information Systems. For the past thirteen years, she has worked with a number of Indigenous organizations in the Peruvian Amazon, including Pueblos

Indígenas Amazónicos Unidos en Defensa de sus Territorios (PUINAMUDT) and the Asociación Interétnica de Desarrollo de la Selva Peruana, coordinating ethnocartography initiatives, community-based environmental monitoring and Indigenous land management projects. She was territorial consultant for the former Federación de Comunidades Nativas del Río Corrientes (FECONACO) in Perú, an organization that represented three Indigenous groups, the Achuar, Kichwa, and Uranina from the watershed of the river Corrientes, an area under significant threat from oil exploration.

NALÚA ROSA SILVA MONTERREY

Nalúa Silva has a doctoral degree in social anthropology from the School of Advanced Social Science Studies in Paris. She is currently director of the Centro de Investigaciones Antropológicas de Guayana (Center of Anthropological Research) at the Universidad Nacional Experimental de Guayana, Venezuela. She has worked extensively for the last three decades with Indigenous people of eastern Venezuela, including on territorial demarcation projects with Indigenous Ye'kwana collaborators. Her work has served as a model for Indigenous territorial demarcations in Venezuela and in other countries in the region.

ÁLVARO CÉSAR VELASCO ÁLVAREZ

Álvaro Velasco is a lawyer and professor of environmental studies at the University of Nariño, Colombia, and founder and director of the Fundación Fundaminga. In the 1990s, he served as adviser to the Asamblea Nacional Constituyente de Colombia (Colombia's National Constituent Assembly) and was spokesperson for the Movement of Indigenous Authorities of the Southwest of Colombia when they successfully achieved constitutional recognition. He has developed the concept of "social polygraphy," a form of participatory research premised on knowledge production through autonomous processes of conversation and representational strategies, including "speaking maps." As the founder of Fundaminga, he is an early proponent of participatory mapping in Colombia.

ALFREDO VITERY

Alfredo Vitery is an Amazonian Kichwa Indigenous leader and current director of the Instituto de Gestión del Bioconocimiento y el Hábitat Amazónico, Pastaza, Ecuador (Institute for Biodiversity Management and the Amazonian Habitat, Pastaza, Ecuador). His professional experiences include coordination and leadership of many local and regional Indigenous organizations. He is an Indigenous scholar, serving as director of regional research projects and as an international consultant. He currently assists Indigenous Amazonian organizations in their struggle for recognition of their collective rights, including strengthening Indigenous representation in local and national political governance.

ALFREDO WAGNER BERNO DE ALMEIDA
Alfredo Wagner is Brazil's preeminent authority on social cartography; the author of numerous books and articles on the topic; and founder of the New Social Cartography Project of the Amazon, a Manaus-based research center that now includes fifteen researchers with doctoral degrees. He holds master's and doctoral degrees in social anthropology from the Federal University of Rio de Janeiro. He is currently a National Council for Scientific and Technological Development (CNPq) grant recipient; a senior researcher at the State University of Maranhão; and a professor of graduate studies at the State University of Maranhão, the State University of Amazonas, and the Federal University of Amazonas. The objective of the New Social Cartography Project is to carry out a "new cartography" for the traditional peoples and communities in the Amazon with the aim of representing both the diversity of cultural expressions and the collective identities of social movements. He has decades of experience with social mapping in Brazil and will be an important contributor to innovative practices and critical perspectives on cartography in terms of counterhegemonic resistance.

Index

Note: Page numbers in *italics* indicate images and captions.

Abuelo Jaguar (Grandfather Jaguar), 32n3
Abya Yala, 164
Achuar Assembly, 66, 73
Achuar people, 66–67, 69–74, 75, 101
A Crítica newspaper, 149
ADELEY (Association in Defense of the Law), 170
administrative-infrastructural maps, 121, 123
Adoración al Niño Dios, 124
Afro-descendent peoples. *See specific groups and places*
agriculture: and Beija-Flor mapping project, 148, 153; and biodiversity management in Cauca Valley, 117, 119; and calendar-maps, 41; and *cimarrones* of Jamundí, Colombia, 115; and defense of multiethnic urban lands, 160; and Kichwa ethnocartography, 107; and Mapuche communal life, 92; and Mayangna lands, 207, 210; and Quilombola countermapping conflict, 191, 194; and repression of Mapuce people, 171; and social polygraphy, 37–38; and territorial planning in Robles, Colombia, 121–123, 124–126; and traditional knowledge, 38, 41; and Ye'kwana-Sanema mapping project, 47–48
agrovilas (small urbanizations), 186
Alcântara, Brazil, *188–189*, 190, 194–195, *196*
Alcântara Cyclone Space (ACS), 186, 194–195, 200

Alcântara Launch Center (CLA), 185–186, *199*
Alcântara Space Center (CEA), 186–187, 190–191, *199*
aldeias, 145, 147, *152, 154, 155, 156, 157*, 160
Alianza Territorial Mapuche (ATM), 82
Almeida, Alfredo Wagner Berno de, 151
Álvarez, Rodolfo, 39
Amazanga, 107–108
The Amazon: A New Cartography (television series), 152–153
American Geographical Society (AGS), 19
ancestral lands and knowledge: ancestor veneration, 20–21; ancestral relational maps, 38–39, 41–43; and biodiversity management in Cauca Valley, 117–118; and drilling concessions in Peruvian Amazon, 68; and expropriation of Quilombola territory, 186; and FECONACO mapping project, 79; and Kichwa collective life, 99; and Kichwa ethnocartography, 100–101, 103–104, 105–108, 112; and Kichwa land management, 97–98, 102–103; and Mapuche mapping project, 174–175, 175–177, 177–178; and Mapuche resistance to dam projects, 93–94; and reconceptualizing territory, 213; and repression of Mapuce people, 168–170; and shining jaguar tale, 31, 32n3; and social polygraphy, 39–43; and Ye'kwana-Sanema mapping project, 52, 54
Andean Cordillera, 85
Andrade, Fausto, 146–147, 149, 151–152, 160
Anjos, Leonardo dos, 195

annexations, 83, 87, 93
anthropology: and coproduction of knowledge, 10; mapmaking–ethnography relationship, 11; and mapping destruction of territory, 205; and Mapuche mapping project, 178; and Mapuche resistance to dam projects, 83, 86, 93; and oral cartography Rincón Zapoteco, 24; and Quilombola countermapping conflict, 190–191, *192*, 201, 201n1; and Quilombolas countermapping conflict, *188–189*; and Ye'kwana-Sanema mapping project, 46, 50–51
aquaculture, 84. *See also* pisciculture projects
Arajuno River, 105–106
Arara people, 146, 153
Araucanía, 87
"art of resistance," 140
assimilation, 7, 30, 90, 93, 140
astronomy, 50
Attorney General for Environmental Protection (PROFEPA), 30–31
auto-demarcación (self-demarcation), 46, 48–49, 50–51, 52, 54, 56–57
Autonomous Territorial Government (COOTAD 2010), 97
autonomy of Indigenous groups: and cultural identity, 47; and drilling concessions in Peruvian Amazon, 68; and FECONACO mapping project, 73, 74, 76, 79; and Kichwa land management, 97–98; and mapping destruction of territory, 206; and Mapuce "zonal councils," 172; and Mapuche mapping project, 175; and Quilombola territories, 184–185; and repression of Mapuce people, 171; territorial identities of Mapuce people, 168
avifauna, 107
Awas Tingni, Nicaragua, 205–208, 209, 210
ayllu–aylluguna (family), 98, 104
az mapu (shape of the land), 167–168, 177

babaçu coconut breakers, 140, 142n3
Bako, Xto, 31
Baniuwa Indigenous group, 146, 153
Baré people, 146, 153

Barth, Fredrik, 147
Basque Homeland and Liberty (ETA), 170
Baxter, Alexandre, 152
Beija-Flor community, Brazil: author's research in, 145–146; conflicts over territorial claims, 148–151, 160; historical background, 146–148; and mapping workshops, 151–157, *152*, *154–159*
Belén community, 75
"Belo Horizonte," 149–151, *150*
Benancio Huenchupán community, 85–87, *88*, *89*, 90–91, *92*
bënegulaza (stories of ancestors), 20–21
Berard, Franco "Bifo," 29
Berno de Almeida, Alfredo Wagner, 190, *192–193*
biodiversity: and Cauca Valley management program, 117–119; and *cimarrones* of Jamundí, Colombia, 116; and drilling concessions in Peruvian Amazon, 68; and Kichwa collective life, 99; and Kichwa ethnocartography, 104, 105–109, 112; and Kichwa land management, 102; and Mapuche mapping project, 176; and Mapuche respect for nature, 166; and social polygraphy, 35, 42, 43–44
Bobonaza River, 105–106, 108
Boca de Nichare, 52
borders and boundaries: and Beija-Flor mapping project, 156; and Cartesian coordinate system, 6, 141, 177, 217–218; of Chile and Argentina, 169; and collective mobilization, 138–139; conflicts with oral cartographies, 29–30; and defense of multiethnic urban lands, 151; and definitions of territory, 204; and dispossession of Indigenous lands, 164; and espitemological boundaries, 218; and FECONACO mapping project, 73, 75; and implications of participatory mapping, 7–8; intra-communal boundaries, 73; and Kichwa ethnocartography, 99–100, 112; and land titling, 75; and mapping destruction of territory, 206; and maps as empowerment tools, 170–172; and Mapuce territorial fragmentation, 168; and Mapuche

Index   229

Lofs, 90; and Mapuche mapping project, 87–88, 90, 176; and Mapuche spirituality, 92; and "new social cartography," 131, 141; and oral mapping, 22–23; and reconceptualizing territory, 209, 210–213; and social mobilization in Brazil, 140; and territorial planning in Robles, Colombia, 121; and Ye'kwana-Sanema mapping project, 46–47, 50, 52; and Zapotec language, 22–23
Bourdieu, Pierre, 138–139
Brazilian Land Statute, 186
Brazilian Space Program, 185–187, 190–191, 192–193, 201n5
Brianezi, Thaís, 152
Bryan, Joe, 4–5, 12–13
bunde ritual, 124

Cajonos River, 26
Cajual Island, 183, 201n1
calendar maps, 40–41, *41, 43*
caminata (collective march), 101
Canadian International Development Agency (CIDA), 68
Canadian Petroleum Institute (CPI), 68
Canal Futura, 152–153
Caniullan, Victor, 167, 178
capacity-building efforts, 46, 49–51, 115
capital-intensive projects, 10
capitalism, 8
Cardoso de Oliveira, Roberto, 145
Carmen Paillao Vda. de Liempi community, 85
Caroní River, 45
Cartesian coordinate system, 6, 141, 177, 217–218
Cartografía cultural del Wallmapu, 86
cattle ranching, 118–119, 207, 210
Cauca River and Valley, 9, 11, 115–116, 117–119, 121–123, 126
Caura National Park, 57
Caura River, 45–46, 47, 52–53, 56–57, *58*
Cautín River, 86, 90
cemeteries, 123
Center for Anthropological Research (Guayana), 48

Centro de Investigaciones Antropológicas de Guayana (CIAG), 9–10, 46, 48–49
ceremonies and rites, 24, 90–93, 153
Chagres, Columbia, 115, 119
Charco la Torre, 122
Charco Redondo, 122
Chávez, Hugo, 49
Chesive community, 42
Chiles, Juan, 36–37, 42
Chinantec people, 24
ch'ixi, 213–214
Christmas celebrations, 124
chucha (*Didelphis marsupialis*), 127
cimarrones, 115, 117–118, 123, 126
citizenship rights, 219
civil society, 19
class divisions, 208
cochas (lagoons), 76, 78
Colapia S.A. (firm), 123
Colchester, Marcus, 46, 50
collective action: and collective resistance to extractive industries, 65–67, 69–74, 76–79; and criminalization of protest, 85, 174; ethnocartography as collective process, 104; and Kichwa defense of community lands, 101; and Kichwa land management, 97–113; and participatory action research (PAR), 115–117; and racialized categories in Brazil, 138–139. *See also* collective life
collective life: collective action, 5, 43; collective identities, 140, 151; collective memory, 44, 185; collective property, 49, 56; collective rights, 65, 68–69, 219; and commons, 28; and communality in Rincón Zapoteco, 24–26; and defining territory, 210–213; and demarcation of Mayangna lands, 206–207; and FECONACO mapping project, 75; and Kichwa knowledge production, 101; and Mapuche *nüxamkawün zugu,* 87; and Mapuche spirituality, 90–92. *See also* collective action; communality
Collor de Melo, Fernando, 186
colonialism: cartography as tool of, 6, 94; and conflicts with oral cartographies,

30; and dispossession of Indigenous lands, 164; and extractive industries, 28; and postcolonioal scholarship, 8; and Wallmapu lands, 10, 81; and Western academic influence, 5
colpas (hunting areas), 76
Comisión Verdad Histórica y Nuevo Trato con los Pueblos Indígenas, 84
commons, 28
communality: common use of lands, 140, 184–185; communal rights, 37; communal territory, 28, 123; community-based maps, 75–76; community labor in Mapuche culture, 92; and defining territory, 211; fabric analogy of, 26–28; and Mapuche philosophy, 166; and oral cartographies, 29–30; in Rincón Zapoteco, 24–26, 32; sketch maps of communities, 137. *See also* collective life
community mapping, 39
Confederación Mapuce Neuquina, 12
conflict maps, 121, 177, 195, *196–197*
"Conquest of the Desert," 81
Consejo de Ancianos de la Organización y de la Asamblea General Interétnica, 48
conservation practices, 7, 9. *See also* environmental damage and protection
Consolidation of the Amazon Region (COAMA), 39, 44n1
Constituent Assembly (Colombia), 35
Constitutional Charter of 1988 (Brazil), 185
"consulta previa" law, 67
contamination zones, 78
Copalyacu River, 75
coproduction of knowledge: and emergence of "new" social cartography, 142; and Forum on Participatory Mapping and Forests Rights, 4–5; and social polygraphy concept, 35; and territorial planning in Robles, Colombia, 116; and Ye'kwana-Sanema mapping project, 54, 57
CorelDRAW®, 177
Corporación Autónoma Regional del Valle del Cauca (CVC), 115, 118, 120, 127
CorpoVillapaz, 119
Corrientes River, 66, *69, 70, 72*, 77

Coulthard, Glen, 210–211
Council of Ancestors of the Organization and of the Interethnic General Assembly, 48
Council of the Kichwa Nation of Pastaza, 103
countermapping: counterhegemonic power of maps, 218–220; and defense of multiethnic urban lands, 151, 157, 160; and FECONACO mapping project, 76–79; and Quilombolas countermapping conflict, 187–191, 191–195, 200–201; and recent trends in social cartography, 1; and unexpected implications of participatory mapping, 7–8
crafts of Indigenous peoples, 117, 148, 153, 157
Creole culture, 169
criminalization of protest, 85, 174
Cruz, Ana Kátia Santana, 152
Cruz, Melquiades (Kiado), 4–5, 9
Cuenca del Corrientes, *69, 70, 72*, 75, 77, 79
cultural ecology, 205
cultural genocide, 93
cultural heritage, 43, *89*, 117
cultural identity, 29
cultural landscapes, 51–54
cultural mapping, 86, *89*, 93–94
cultural practices, 39
cultural reproduction, 40
cultural resistance, 23, 140
curacaguna (community leaders), 103, 104
Curamil Millanao, Alberto, 83
Curaray River, 105, 106, 108
Currumil community, 170
Cuyiñ Manzano survey map, 176
cyclical conception of time, 21, 40, 43

Daigle, Caroline, 5
dams, 122–123. *See also* hydroelectric projects
data collection, 73
decolonization, 5, 8, 94, 164
Decree 4.887 (Brazil), 187
Decree 7.320 (Brazil), 185
Dedejuimö Creek, 55
deforestation, 122, 157, 194

Deleuze, Gilles, 27, 32n12
demarcation process, 56, 171. *See also* borders and boundaries; land titles
Democratic Republic of Congo, 3
democratization of cartography, 78–79
demographics, 190
Department of Territorial Management, 103
Dessana people, 146, 153
development, economic, 57, 69, 83–85, 157
Diário Oficial da União, 201n1
Dias da Costa, Willas, 152, 156
Díaz, Floriberto, 24–25
dictatorship, 84–85
digital technology and media, 20, 28–29, 49, 73–74, 75, 178, 190
Dirección de Asuntos Indígenas (DAI), 48
Directorate of Indigenous Affairs, 48
discursive power of cartography, 8
dispossession of lands: and Awas Tingni, Nicaragua, 210; and backgrounds of volume authors, 5; and Brazilian *aldeias*, 145; and defense of multiethnic urban lands, 149; and deterritorialization of Mapuche people, 84; and history of colonialism in the Americas, 164; and impact of digital cartography, 28–29; and mapping destruction of territory, 204–208; and Mapuche mapping project, 174–175, 177–178; and reconceptualizing territory, 208–209, 214
Doña Alicia hydroelectric project, 82–83, 85, 86–87, 91, 93–94
dueños (spirits), 54

ecological damage, 57. *See also* environmental damage and protection
ecological-economic maps, 121–123
economic globalization, 211–212
economic power, 38–39, 99, 179
elders, 51, 57, 87–90, 123, 153. *See also* ancestral lands and knowledge
Electrificación del Caroní (Caroní Electricity Company; EDELCA), 45
El Playón, 52
enclosures of land, 27, 42. *See also* borders and boundaries

energy production. *See* hydroelectric projects; petroleum production
environmental damage and protection: and ancestral calendar-maps, 42–43; and Beija-Flor mapping project, 153–154; and biodiversity management in Cauca Valley, 118–119; and collective resistance to extractive industries, 65–67; and communality in Rincón Zapoteco, 24; contamination zones, 78; and defense of multiethnic urban lands, 149, 157; and deforestation, 122, 157, 194; and deterritorialization of Mapuche people, 85; and drilling concessions in Peruvian Amazon, 68–69; and ecological-economic maps, 121–123; and encroachments on Indigenous lands, 207–208; environmental impact assessments, 86; and FECONACO mapping project, 69–74, 72, 75–76; and Indigenous land tenure disputes, 153–156; and Kichwa ethnocartography, 99–100, 103–104, 105–109, 112; and Kichwa land management, 98, 102; mapping destruction of territories, 204–208; and mapping impacts of petroleum exploitation, 10; and Mapuche resistance to dam projects, 93–94; and Mapuche respect for nature, 166; and natural disasters, 207; and petroleum production in Peruvian Amazon, 77–78; and Quilombola countermapping conflict, 195, 200; and repression of Mapuche people, 172; and shining jaguar tale, 30–31; and social mobilization in Brazil, 139–141; sustainable practices in Brazil, 142n4; and territorial planning in Robles, Colombia, 127; and tools of social polygraphy, 42–43; and Ye'kwana-Sanema mapping project, 47, 57. *See also* biodiversity
Environmental Evaluation Offices, 78
epistemology, 7, 164, 166, 218
estuaries, 105, 106
ethnic identity: and Beija-Flor Indigenous Community, 147; and definitions of territory, 203–204; and ethnic conflict,

148–151, 153, 210; and ethnic mobilization, 145–146, 146–148, 153; ethnocartography projects, 97–98, 99–101, 103–104, 105–112, 112–113; and Kichwa collective life, 99

Europeanization, 169

evictions, 179, 207

ewütü (mountain), 56

expert-driven mapping, 3

expropriation of lands, 42, 77, 84, 145, 148, 160, 183, 185–186

extractive industries, 10, 28, 57, 83–85, 99–100, 102, 211. *See also* petroleum production

fabric of community, 26–28

faixalenses, 140, 142n4

Farias Júnior, Emmanuel de Almeida, 4–5, 11–12, 195

farming, 37

Federal Constitution (1988; Brazil), 138

Federal University of Amazonas, 146

Federation of Native Communities of the Corrientes River (FECONACO), 71, 75–76, 77–78

feminist science studies, 6

financial incentives, 30

fishing and fishery resources: and Beija-Flor mapping project, 147; and biodiversity management in Cauca Valley, 117; and expropriation of Quilombola territory, 187; and FECONACO mapping project, 76; and Kichwa ethnocartography, 104; and Kichwa land management, 101; and resistance to hydroelectric projects, 142; and territorial planning in Robles, Colombia, 121, 122; and traditional calendar-maps, 41; and Ye'kwana-Sanema mapping project, 48, 50, 55. *See also* pisciculture projects

food shortages and security, 76, 119

Forest Peoples Programme (FPP), 46, 48–49, 57

forest resources and rights: and Beija-Flor mapping project, 146, 153; and biodiversity management in Cauca Valley, 118; and communality in Rincón Zapoteco, 26; and defense of multiethnic urban lands, 157, 160; and deterritorialization of Mapuche people, 84; and drilling concessions in Peruvian Amazon, 68–69; and encroachments on Indigenous lands, 207–208; and FECONACO mapping project, 71, 77; and impact of digital cartography, 28; and impact of seismic surveys, 67–68, 79n1; and Kichwa ethnocartography, 100, 104, 105–108, *107, 108, 109*, 112; and Kichwa land management, 101–102; and mapping destruction of territory, 205–206; and Mapuche mapping project, 83, 175; and Mapuche spirituality, 91; and Quilombola countermapping conflict, 194; and Rights and Resources Initiative (RRI), 3; and shining jaguar tale, 31; and territorial planning in Robles, Colombia, 121, 122; and threats of dispossession, 204; and traditional Indigenous knowledge, 38; and Zapotec lands, 20–21

Forum on Participatory Mapping and Forests Rights, 3–4

frontier lands, 79, 81–82, 207, 209, 214

Fundação Nacional do Índio (FUNAI), 147, 160

Fundaminga Foundation (Fundación Fundaminga), 9, 35, 39–40, 43, *43*, 115, 120

Funecorobles, 119

Gaia Amazonas Foundation, 39, 42

García Pérez, Alan, 75

Gen (spiritual forces), 91

General Assembly of the Kichwa People of Pastaza, 102, 103

General Environment Law 19.300 (Chile), 86

Gen Kawello (Spirit Horse), 91

genocide, 169, 176, 180n7

geocultural territorial identities, 172–174

geographic boundaries, 138

Geographic Information Systems (GIS): and Beija-Flor mapping project, 156; and digitization of community knowledge, 28–29; and FECONACO mapping project, 73–74; mapping environmental impacts in Wallmapu, 10; and Mapuche mapping project, 82, 94, 165, 174–175;

and participatory mapping in urban areas, 12; and Quilombola countermapping conflict, 190
geological studies, 67–68
geopiracy, 19
georeferencing: and Beija-Flor mapping project, 156; and FECONACO mapping project, 71, 73–74, 76; and Kichwa ethnocartography, 104, 112; and Quilombola countermapping conflict, 190, 194–195, 200; and Ye'kwana-Sanema mapping project, 48
Geraldo, Antônio Tadeu Drumond, 148, 150, 157
globalization, 6, 28, 211–212
Global Positioning System (GPS) technology: and Beija-Flor mapping project, 156, 157; and defining territory, 203; and FECONACO mapping project, 71, 73; mapping environmental impacts in Wallmapu, 10; and Mapuche mapping project, 165, 175, 176; and Quilombola countermapping conflict, 190, 194, 200; and shining jaguar tale, 31, 212–213; and US-sponsored mapping in Rincón communities, 20; and Ye'kwana-Sanema mapping project, 48, 49–50, 55
Goldman Prize, 83
Gomes da Costa, Iranir, 156
González, Carlos, 4, 11
Google Earth, 156
Gran Cumbal, 36, 38
"grounded normativity," 210–211
Group for Socioeconomic Studies of the Amazon (GESEA), 190
Guachinte, Columbia, 119
Guattari, Félix, 27, 32n12
guillatun ceremonies, 90–92
Gvlümapu region (Chile), 82, 92–93

Hale, Charles, 12, 13
Harley, J. B., 6, 8
historical memory, 79
Historical Truth and New Deal for Indigenous Peoples, 84
Hobsbawm, Eric, 140

Hoffmann, Ava, 4
Horacio Gómez Gallo Presbyterian Educational Institution, 119
Hoti tribe, 47
Humala, Ollanta, 67
human rights, 13, 37, 85, 205–206, 211–212
Human Rights Observatory of Indigenous Peoples (ODHPI), 163, 174
hunting and hunting lands: and Beija-Flor mapping project, 147; and *cimarrones* of Jamundí, Colombia, 115; and FECONACO mapping project, 74–75, 76; and hydroelectric projects, Caura River basin, 45; and Kichwa ethnocartography, 104, 106, 108–109; and Kichwa land management, 101; and territorial planning in Robles, Colombia, 121–122; and traditional calendar-maps, 41; and Ye'kwana-Sanema mapping project, 47–48
Hurricane Felix, 207
"The Hydrocarbon Potential of the Santiago Basin" (report), 68
hydroelectric projects: on Caura River, 45; Doña Alicia hydroelectric project, 82–83, 85, 86–87, 91, 93–94; mapping environmental impacts in Wallmapu, 10; Tapajós River Hydroelectric Complex, 142; and Ye'kwana-Sanema mapping project, 51–52

ichilla yaku (estuaries), 105–106
iconography, 112
igkamapu, 92
imperialism, 6, 8. *See also* colonialism
Indigenous peoples. *See* traditional Indigenous knowledge; *specific groups and places*
Indigenous People United in Defense of Their Territories, 67
Indigenous rights, 24, 46, 67, 77–78, 173, 203, 210
Indonesia, 3
infrastructure projects, 75–76. *See also* hydroelectric projects
Institute for the Regional Ecodevelopment

of the Ecuadorian Amazon (ECORAE), 103
Inter-American Court of Human Rights, 203, 205–207, 209, 210
Intercultural Games, 141
International Labour Organization's Indigenous and Tribal Peoples Convention 169, 1, 86, 139–140, 187, 203
Itamatatiua community, 12, 183
ixofillmogen ("all forms of life"), 82, 86, 90–93, 93–94, 166
ixtle (fiber), 26–27, 213

Jabuti and Dabacuri ritual, 153
Jamundí, Colombia, 115, 117–120, *118*, 123, *124*, *125*, 127
José María Córdoba Educational Institution, 119
jüdü (mountain), 56
justice, 102

Kari'ña tribe, 46
kaxün kura, 92
Kichwa people: and collective action for territorial rights, 97–113; and collective resistance to extractive industries, 66; Commune of San Jacinto del Pindo, 109–112, *110*, *111*; and community life, 98–99; and drilling concessions in Peruvian Amazon, 67; history of ethnocartography, 99–101; Kichwa Life Plan, 109, 112; Kichwa Nation of Pastaza, 11, 97, 100–103; and land management practices, 101–103, 112–113; and participatory mapping projects, 103–105, *105*, 105–112, *107*, *108*, *109*; and reconceptualizing territory, 208–209
kimce (sages), 167
kimvn mapuce (Mapuche wisdom), 163, 164, 180n3
"king's book," 37
kinship ties, 117–118
Kinxikew, Pascual, 176
knowledge, traditional Indigenous, 163
Kokamas-Kukamirias people, 66–67
kultrün (Mapuche drum), 93

Kumaaka Creek, 50–51
Kurakautin region (Chile), 10, 82–83, 85, 87, 92
Kurantu (rocks), 92
Kusawedu Ewütü, 56
kuxan (pain, illness), 167
Kuyujani (mythic hero), 52–54, 56
Kuyujani Organization, 47–48, 48–49, 50, 56–57
kvme felen (good living), 164, 167–168, 174, 179

Lafkence (people from the lakes), 173–174
lagoons, 36, 38, 76, 78, 100, 102, 105–106
La Guinea wetlands, 127
Lamiña, Alexandra, 4, 10–11, 208–209, 211, 212
land grants, 87, *88*, 90, 94n3, *173*, 174. See also land titles
landless movement, 149
land management practices, 97–98, 101–103, 105–112, 112–113
land titles: and access to oil reserves, 100, 208–209; and collective resistance to extractive industries, 67; and countermapping, 77–78; and definitions of territory, 203; and deterritorialization of Mapuche people, 84; and FECONACO mapping project, 71, 75, 79; and "grounded normativity" in mapping, 210–211; and land sale disputes, 148–149; and mapping destruction of territories, 204–208; and Mapuche mapping project, 87; and multiethnic Indigenous lands, 161n4; and Quilombola countermapping conflict, 187; and repression of Mapuce people, 171–172; and social mobilization in Brazil, 140; and territorial protection of Quilombola lands, 201n1; and Ye'kwana-Sanema mapping project, 49, 56. See also demarcation process
land use maps, *136*
Lara, Susana, 174
Las Dos Agüitas, 122
La Selva, Lower Rincón, 30–31
Latin America, 3
Law 165 (Colombia), 118

Law 947 (Argentina), 169
lawen (Mapuce medicine), 91, 176–177, 180n4
Law of Agrarian Reform and Colonization (INDA; Ecuador), 100
laws and legal systems: and agrarian reform, 100; and biodiversity management in Cauca Valley, 118–119; and collective resistance to extractive industries, 67; and criminalization of protest, 85; and dispossession of Indigenous lands, 145; and genocide of Indigenous people, 169; and Kichwa ethnocartography, 112; and land tenure disputes, 148–151, 160; and maps as empowerment tool, 170–172; and opposition to hydroelectric projects, 86; Peru's "consulta previa" law, 67; and recent trends in social cartography, 1; recognition of multiethnic territories, 146; and repression of Mapuce people, 168–170; and social polygraphy, 37–39; and territorial autonomy, 68. *See also* land titles
Leal, Claudia, 3
lentic ecosystems, 106
Lewfü (rivers), 90
Liberia, 3
Liempi Colipi community, 85, 87
life plans (*planes de vida*), 66
Lima, Luis Augusto Pereira, 156
livestock production, 169. *See also* cattle ranching
llactaguna (human settlements), 106
llellipun (ceremonies), 91
LLILAS Benson Latin American Studies and Collections, 217
Local Earth Observation (LEO), 48
location devices, 31. *See also* Global Positioning System (GPS) technology
Lof Hueñivales, 82, 87, 88, 89, 90
Lof Kinxikew, 175–177
Lof Kolliko-Folilko, 82, 87
Lof Kontué, 82, 87
Lof Linares, 177
Lof Mapuce, 12
Lof Paichil Antriao, 165, 169, 174–175, 177
Lof Pu Lof, 177

Lof Quintriqueo, 165
Lof Radalko, 82, 83, 87
logging, 207–208
logko, 168
Lozano Long Institute for Latin American Studies (LLILAS), 3–4, 11–12, 217
Luis Carlos Valencia Educational Institution, 119

maci-machi (Mapuche philosophical leaders), 91–92, 167, 178, 180n4
madreviejas (marshes), 117, 118, 123–124
mainstreaming of participatory mapping, 7
makacsis, 42–43
mallines, 176
Mamuna, Brazil, 194–195
manchales, 76
Mansilla Quiñones, Pablo, 4–5, 10, 212
Mapuce Norgvbamtuleayiñ Education Center, 163
Mapuche Confederation of Neuquén (CMN), 163, 170
Mapuche (also Mapuce) people: and colonization of Wallmapu, 81–82; and development of mapping project, 82–83; and extractive development, 83–85; Maphuche Lofs (territories), 82–83, 84, 86–90, 90–92, 93; mapping environmental impacts in Wallmapu, 10; mapping Mapuche spirituality, 90–93, 93–94; *mapuce kimvn* (wisdom), 163, 164, 180n3; Mapuce Parliament (Gvbamtuwvn), 172; Mapuchezugun (language), 81, 90, 179n1; symbology of, 178–179. *See also* Wallmapu–Waj Mapu (Mapuche Territory)
Mapuche Territorial Alliance, 10, 82
Maranhão, Brazil, 185, 195
Marañón River, 66
Marín, Ricardo, 42
Marín, Robertico, 42
Maroon communities, 115, 117
Martínez Luna, Jaime, 24
Marubo people, 156
Mawaris, 55
Mayangna people, 205–206, 208

Mayuruna people, 146, 153
medicinal plants, 86, 91–92, 108, 124, 127, 153, 177
Melnyk, Richard, 148–149, 153, 161n4
menoko (springs), 93
mestizo communities, 52, 208
methodological issues, 200
Mexican National Institute of Statistics and Geography (INEGI), 19, 22
México Indígena (Indigenous Mexico) project, 19, 22, 212
"micro-zones," 74
migrant populations, 12
Military Geographical Institute, 99
military power: and colonization of Wallmapu, 81, 83; and cultural genocide, 93; and deterritorialization of Mapuche people, 87; and expropriation of Quilombola territory, 186; and Mapuche collective life, 92; and Quilombolas countermapping battle, 187–191; and unexpected implications of participatory mapping, 8
Miñce mapu, 167
Minchiare, 50
mineral resources, 102. *See also* extractive industries; petroleum production
mingas–mingako (community labor), 92, 100
mining industries, 84. *See also* extractive industries
Ministry of Defense (Brazil), 186
Ministry of Science, Technology, Innovation and Communication (MCTIC), 186–187
Miskito people, 205–208
Mixe people, 24
Mobil Oil, 67
módulo rural (minimum agricultural plot size), 186
Molla, Emilio R., 174
Monteiro, Arlene Glória Alves, 148–149
"Mothers of the Mountain," 76
Movement of Those Affected by the Base (MABE), 190, 194–195, 201n5
multiethnic lands, 145–146, 146–148, 148–151, 151–157, *155*, *156*, 160
multilingual coproduction of knowledge, 4

Municipal Organic Law #302 (Brazil), 160
Mura people, 146, 153
myths and mythical figures, 52–54, 55–56, 123–124. *See also* spirituality

Nadua, 51
Nahuel, María Laura, 4, 12
Nahuel Huapi, 175
Napo tropical forest, 68
narrative cartographies, 5, 22–23, 28, 190, 191, 212–213. *See also* oral tradition
National Constituent Assembly (Brazil), 138
National Indian Foundation, 147
National Institute of Colonization and Agrarian Reform (INCRA), 201n1
National Institute of Indigenous Affairs (INAI), 170–171, 179
nationalism, 169
National Law No. 26.160 (Argentina), 165, 171
National Office of Natural Resource Evaluation, 68
national parks, 57
National University of Comahue (UNCo), 171
nation-states, 29, 30
natural resources, 140, 185, 211. *See also* extractive industries; petroleum production
"nature-culture" concept, 212
navigation, 50
neoliberal governance, 13, 83–85
Neuquén Popular Movement, 171
Neuquén province, Argentina, 165, 168, 170–173, 176–177
Neutral Mapuce Confederation, 172
newen (strength), 166, 176
Newe Sogobia, 204, 214n1
New Social Cartography Project of the Amazon (PNCSA): and Beija-Flor mapping project, 145–146, 148, 151–156; and emergence of "new social cartography," 131, 140–141; and Forum on Participatory Mapping and Forests Rights, 3; and Quilombola countermapping conflict, 190; Wagner's work with, 11–12
ngenko (water spirits), 93

nguellipun (traditional prayers), 86
nguillatúe (cultural sites), 93
nguillatun (ceremonies), 91
Nicaragua, 205–208, 210
Nichare, 50
"nodes," 32n10
nongovernmental organizations (NGOs), 190
nonlinear time, 21, 40–41, 43–44, 178
Nossa Senhora do Livramento, Brazil, *132, 133, 134, 135,* 141
Nudo de los Pastos (Knot of the Pastures), 36
nüxamkawün zugu concept (collective discussion process), 87
Nvwken, Mapuche Territory, Argentina, 163–179

Oaxaca, Mexico, 9, 24
Offen, Karl, 219
official cartography, 65–66, 67, 71, 77–79, 165, 169–170
oil resources. *See* petroleum production
Ojo de Agua Comunicación, 32n3
Oliveira, Luis de, 152
oral tradition: and FECONACO mapping project, 73; oral cartography, 20–26, 30; oral histories and knowledge, 31–32, 153, 175; and Ye'kwana-Sanema mapping project, 57. *See also* traditional Indigenous knowledge
Organización Interétnica e Intercomunitaria Kuyujani, 47
Organization of Indigenous Peoples of Pastaza (OPIP), 100–101
origin myths, 53–54
Orinoco River, 52
Ortega, Daniel, 207
orthography, 49
Otherness, 214

"Pacification of the Araucanía" campaign, 81
Palenque Cinco, 119
palenques (self-sufficient communities), 117
palihue (cultural sites), 93
Palmares Cultural Foundation, 201nn2–3
palmichales (palm leaf collection sites), 76
pamba (plain area), 106–108, *108*

Pancho Curamil community, 85
pan-Indigenous identities, 12
Paragua River, 45
Paraguay, 209
páramos (mountain plateaus), 36, 38
Paraná River, 42
PARSEP Group, 68
participatory cartography: and Awas Tingni, Nicaragua, 205; and Brazilian *aldeias,* 145–146; and capacity-building efforts, 49–51; Cartesian approach contrasted with, 9; and collective mobilization, 139; and cultural identity, 46–47, 48–49, 57–60; and defense of multiethnic urban lands, 146–148, 148–151, 151–157, 160; definitions of, 19; and digital technology, 28; and ethos of collaborative research, 217; goals of, 7–8; and Kichwa collective life, 98, 100, 103–104, 106–112, 112–113; and Mapuche mapping project, 86–90, 91–93; and "new" social cartography, 141; and Nvwken, Mapuce Territory, Argentina, 163–179; and oral societies, 22; participatory action research (PAR), 115–116; and "radical" social cartography, 1–3, 5–6, 10, 13, 219–220; recent trends in, 1–4; and resistance to resource-extractive industries, 65–79, *69, 70, 72*; and scope of subjects studied, 9–13; and seismic surveys, 79n1; and social polygraphy, 35, *36,* 36–37, 43; and territorial planning in Robles, Colombia, 115–116, *116,* 120–121, 127; unexpected implications of, 7. *See also* social cartography
participatory research and development, 7
Pastaza, Ecuador, 11, 97, 100–101, *105, 107, 108, 109,* 112. *See also* Kichwa people
Pastaza River, 66, 100, 105–112, *107–109,* 112–113
peasantry, 35, 126, 140, 142n4
Pehuen, Miguel Melin, 10
Peña Márquez, Juan Carlos, 40
Pereira Júnior, Davi, 4–5
Pereyra, Petrona, 164
Pérez, Gaetano, 51

PERUPETRO company, 68
Petróleos del Perú, 67–68
petroleum production: and collective resistance to extractive industries, 65–67; and countermapping, 77–78; and drilling concessions in Peruvian Amazon, 67–69; and FECONACO mapping project, 69–72, 75–76, 79; and Kichwa lands, 99–100, 102; mapping impacts of petroleum exploitation, 10; and reconceptualizing territory, 209, 211; and seismic surveys, 67–68, 79n1
Pewence (*pewen* people), 173
Philippines, 3
photography in mapping projects, 38, 194, *194, 199*
Piciñam, Pety, 176
Pikunce (people from the north), 173
Pikunmapu, 93
Pimental, Brazil, *136, 137*, 142
pimuntuwe, 92
Pinduc River, 105
Pineda, Wendy, 4, 10
Pintoresco hydroelectric project, 83
pipilongo (*Piper tuberculatum*), 127
Pira Paraná River, 42, *43*
pisciculture projects, 10, 85, 119, 123, 126
Piscifactoría Colapia, 126
place names, 50–51, 73, 90, 94n3. *See also* toponyms
Plan de Manejo (Area Management Plan), 50
Plan of Territorial and Natural Resources Management of the Kichwa Nation of Pastaza, 109
Plantanoyacu River, 75
Pluspetrol Norte, 67, 78
political power: and ancestral relational maps, 38–39; and collective mobilization, 138–139, 139–141; and counter-hegemonic power of maps, 218–220; and countermapping, 77; and democratization of cartography, 78–79; and interethnic political agreements, 146; and Kichwa land management, 97; and politics of knowledge production, 6
pollution, 68, 71, 78, 119, 149, 153–154, 157.

See also environmental damage and protection
Popular and Intercultural Education Center (CEPINT), 163
postcolonial thought and scholarship, 6, 8
postrepresentational geography, 8
power relations, 19, 29, 209–210. *See also* political power
precious metals, 65
Projeto de Cartografia Social in Manaus, 217
Provincial Decree 1184/2002, 172
Provincial Deputies Block of the Movimiento Popular Neuquino (MPN), 171
public health, 45, 57
public interest, 185–186
Pueblo-Nación Mapuce, 178
PUINAMUDT, 67
punewen (respect for nature), 166–167
purinas (temporal family sites), 100
Pvelmapu, 85, 92–93

quebradeiras de coco babaçu, 140, 142n3
Quechua people, 66–67, 75, 77
Quechuas del Alto Pastaza community, 77
Quilape López community, 85–87
Quilombolas: and background of study author, 12; and collective identities in Brazil, 140; and conflict over Alcântara Launch Center, 185–187; and countermapping battle, 200–201; countermapping battle with Brazilian military, 187–191; and legacy of slavery, 183–185; and Quilombola countermapping conflict, 201n5; and territorial protection, 191–195
Quinamayó, Columbia, 115, 119, 124

race issues, 138, 208, 210. *See also* ethnic identity
Radcliffe, Sarah H., 8
Ragiñé ce (people of the center), 173
Ragiñ wenu mapu, 167
rainbow symbolism, 54–55
rakizuam (Mapuche Indigenoius knowledge), 82–83, 86–87, 90–91, 93–94
Ranger, Terence, 140
reducciones (small land allocations), 169

Regional Autonomous Corporation of the Valley of the Cauca (CVC), 115, 118, 120, 127
relational network maps, 38–39, 39–40, *40*, 121, 123–126, *125*
religious ceremonies, 86, 153. *See also* spirituality
remediation efforts, 75–76. *See also* environmental damage and protection
researcher-subject relationship, 131
reserve zones, 76
reservoirs, 122–123
resource extraction, 10
Revolutionary Armed Forces of Colombia (FARC), 170
ribeirinha communities, 142
Right Livelihood Award, 44n1
Rights and Resources Initiative (RRI), 3
Rights and Resources International, 217
Rincón de la Sierra Norte, 9
Rincón Zapoteco ("Zapotec Corner"), 19, 20–22, 26, 28
Río Blanco hydroelectric project, 83
Rio Preto da Eva, Brazil, 145–147, 149, 153, 157, 160–161. *See also* Beija-Flor community, Brazil
Rivera Cusicanqui, Silvia, 25, 213–214
river dwellers (*ribeirinhos*), 140
river ecosystems, 105–106. *See also specific river names*
Robles, Columbia, 115, *116*, 119, 120–126
Roca, Julio Argentino, 169, 174
Roldán, Roque, 219
rubber, 65

Sá, Ivan de, 161n4
sabios ("sages"), 48, 50–51
sacha (forest ecosystem), 105, 108
sacha runa yachay (Kichwa knowledge), 106, 109, 112
Said, Edward, 140, 141
Salamanca, Carlos, 3–4
Salazar, Antonio, 168–169
Saliva linguistic group, 47
Salto Para, 50, 51–53, 54–56
Salvajina dam and reservoir, 122

Sampaio, Joaquim, 148, 151
Sanema people: and Caura River hydroelectric projects, 45–47; Caura River territory of, *58*; and mapping project, 47–49, 50–51, 54, 56–57, 60
San Jacinto del Pindo, 109–112, *110*, *111*
Santa Cruz Yagavila, 23
Santa Isabel community, 75
Santos, Glademir Sales dos, 152
Santos-Graner, Fernando, 53–54
Sateré-Mawé people, 146, 147, 152, 153
seismic surveys, 67–68, 79n1
seismic testing, 68
self-demarcation, 46, 48–49, 50–51, 52, 54, 56–57, 73
self-determination, 25–26, 101, 102–103
semio-capitalism, 29
Serejo, Vilson, 200
Servicio Autónomo de Propiedad Intelectual (SAPI), 56
shamans, 54–56
shining jaguar tale, 30–31, 32n3, 212–213
Sierra Norte, Oaxaca, Mexico, 9, 24, 30, 212
Silva Monterrey, Nalúa Rosa, 9–10, 50
Simpson, Leanne Betasamosake, 208
sketch maps, *134*, *135*, *136*, *137*, *154*, *155*
slavery, 115, 118, 183–185
Sletto, Bjørn, 5, 217
Sobisch, Jorge O., 172
social cartography: and Brazilian *aldeias*, 145–146; and collective identities, 139–141; and collective mobilization, 138–139; and defense of multiethnic urban lands, 146–148, 148–151, 151–157, 160; emergence of "new" social cartography, 141–142; and ethnographic practice, 131, *132–137*; and Kichwa collective life, 103; and Mapuche mapping project, 82, 86–90; and Quilombolas countermapping battle, 187–191; radical social cartographies, 1–3, 5–6, 10–11, 13, 219–220; and resistance to extractive industries, 65–67, 69–74, 76–79; and territorial planning in Robles, Colombia, 115–128, *116*, *118*, *124*, *125*; and territorial protection of Quilombola lands, 185–187,

Index **239**

191–195, *196–199*, 199, 200–201. *See also* participatory cartography
socialist governance, 9–10
social maps, *88*
social mobilization, 83
social polygraphy: contributions to participatory mapping, 43–44; and critical dialogue, 39–43; described, 9; and nonlinear time, 40–41, 43–44; origins of, 35; as ritual conversation, 37–39; and traditional Indigenous knowledge, 36–37
social sciences, 8, 131, 138–139
socio-anthropological reports, *178*, *188–189*
sociocultural change, 73
Souza, Anderson José de, 149
Souza, Nadja Christine de Castro, 152
Spaces, Politics, and Societies, 4
spirituality: and Beija-Flor Indigenous Community, 146; and Beija-Flor mapping project, 153; and biodiversity management in Cauca Valley, 117; and *cimarrones* of Jamundí, Colombia, 115; and communality in Rincón Zapoteco, 24–25; and defense of multiethnic urban lands, 160; and definitions of territory, 204; and Indigenous resource use, 76; and *ixofillmogen* in Mapuche culture, 82, 85–86, 90–93, 93–94, 166–167; and Juan Chiles mythology, 36–37; and Kichwa ethnocartography, 104; and Mapuche mapping project, 176; and Mapuche wisdom, 163, 164, 180n3; and pan-Indigenous identities, 12; and reconceptualizing territory, 213; and relational network maps, 123–124, 123–126; and shining jaguar tale, 30–31; and social polygraphy, 37–39; and space-time relationship, 40–43, 43–44; *sumak allpa* concept, 11, 98–99; and *supay* (protective beings), 76, 102, 106, 108; and traditional calendar-maps, 41; and vision-quests, 76; and "Waj Mapu" concept, 164–165; and web (*yëxhaj*) symbolism, 26–27, 31; and Zapotec veneration of ancestors, 20–21
springs, 21, 93, 108, 122

state repression, 168–170
State University of Maranhão, Brazil, 12
Stocks, Anthony, 205
subsistence labor, 92
subterranean systems, 167
sugarcane operations, 118–119, 126
sumak allpa (forests and territories), 11, 97–99, 102–103, 105, 107–108, 112
Sumak Allpa Plan (Territorial Management Plan), 97
sumak kawsay (community life), 97–99, 105, 112, 212
sumak mirachina (communal economy), 99, 212
supay (protective beings), 76, 102, 106, 108
sustainable use of lands, 101, 117–119, 142n3. *See also* environmental damage and protection
symbology, cartographic, 48, 74, 141, 177, 178–179

Talisman Energy, 75
tambus–tambuguna (seasonal family settlements), 100, 106
Tapajós River Hydroelectric Complex, 142
technical capabilities, 97
Technical Identification and Delimitation Report (RTID), 201n1
Tecknica Overseas, Ltd. (TOL), 68
territories and territorial claims: and communality, 25–26; defining territory, 203–204; deterritorialization of Indigenous peoples, 32n12, 81, 83, 84, 90, 93–94; and FECONACO mapping project, 71, 73, 79; and mainstreaming of participatory mapping, 7; maps as tools of power, 19, 29, 170–172; Mapuche "territorial knowledges," 81–82; and recent trends in social cartography, 1; reconceptualizing territory, 208–210; and social polygraphy, 41–42; territorial identities of Mapuce people, 166–167; territorial model of nation-states, 30; territorial recognition, 49; and territorial reorganization, 28; territorial rights, 141; "territorial turn" in cartography, 219; and unexpected

implications of participatory mapping, 8; and Ye'kwana-Sanema mapping project, 46, 47–49, 49–51, 51–54, 57. *See also* borders and boundaries
terrorism, 85
textual cartography, 22–23, 30, 213
Tigre River, 66
Timba, Columbia, 119, 124
toponyms, 52, 53, 60, 176–177
traditional calendars, 41
traditional Indigenous knowledge: and agricultural practices, 123; and biodiversity management in Cauca Valley, 119; and Juan Chiles myth, 36–37; *kimvn mapuce* (Mapuche wisdom), 163, 164, 180n3; and Mapuce medicine, 91, 176, 180n4; and Mapuche mapping project, 82–83, 86–87; and Mapuche resistance to dam projects, 93–94; and Mapuche spirituality, 90; medicine and healers, 86, 91–92, 108, 124, 127, 153, 176–177; and social polygraphy, 37–39; and unexpected implications of participatory mapping, 7–8
transdisciplinary approaches, 4
translations, 4–5
Tujuumoto organization, 47
Tukano people, 146, 148, 151, 153
Tupé Sustainable Development Reserve, 141
turu (swamp), 106

Uchuputu Supay, 107
Uchutican, 108
Ukraine, 186
United States, 19–20
Universidad de los Andes, 3
Universidad del Valle, Cali, Colombia, 11
Universidad Nacional de Rosario in Argentina, 3–4
Universidad Nacional Experimental de Guayana (UNEG), 48–49, 57
University of California–Santa Barbara, 12–13
University of Colorado, Boulder, 12
University of Texas at Austin (UT-Austin), 3, 217

University of the Andes, 217
UNOCAL Corporation, 67
Urarina people, 67
urban areas, 12, 145–146, 146–148, 148–151, 151–157, 160
urcu–urcuguna (forested hills), 107–109, *109*
urku (hill), 106
US Army, 19–20, 212

Valdez, Cristina, 164
validating maps, 74–75
Velasco, Álvaro, 4, 9
Venezuelan Constitution, 56
VHF radio, 31
Villa La Angostura, Argentina, 175
Villapaz, Columbia, 115, 119
vision-quests, 76
Vitery, Alfredo, 4, 10–11, 208–209, 211, 212

Wagner, Alfredo, 4–5, 11
Wallmapu–Waj Mapu (Mapuche Territory): background of mapping project in, 163–166; and development of social cartography project, 82–83; and extractive industry, 83–85; mapping environmental impacts in, 10; and Mapuce philosophy, 166–168; and Mapuche mapping project, 86–90; and Mapuche spirituality, 93; participatory mapping project in, 174–178, 178–179; and reconceptualizing territory, 211–212; state control of, 81–82, 214n1; and state repression, 168–174
water resources: and Caura River hydroelectric projects, 45; and countermapping, 77; and deterritorialization of Mapuche people, 84–85; and ecological-economic maps, 122; and FECONACO mapping project, 78; and Kichwa ethnocartography, 108; and Mapuche ethnocartography, 90–91, 93, 94. *See also* fishing and fishery resources; hydroelectric projects
watunna, 55, 56
web-based technologies, 12
web (*yëxhaj*) symbolism, 26–27, 31

welulkawün wirin zugu (cultural sites), 93
Wenufoye (Mapuce flag), 178
Wenu mapu, 167
werken, 12
Western cartography, 74, 131
Western Shoshone (Newe) people, 204, 214n1
wetlands, 122, 127
wigka–wigkakezugu, 92, 168, 170, 173
Wijice (people from the south), 173
Winkiare (Wonkiare) people, 50
Wiyu (feathered serpent), 54–55
Wood, Denis, 209
workshops on participatory mapping: and backgrounds of volume authors, 5; and Beija-Flor mapping project, 146, 147–148, 151–156, *152, 154, 155, 156,* 160; and emergence of "new" social cartography, 141–142; and FECONACO mapping project, *70,* 71–72, 74; Forum on Participatory Mapping and Forests Rights, 3–4; and Indigenous mapping project in Peruvian Amazon, *69;* and Kichwa ethnocartography, 103–104; and Kichwa land management, 101–103; and Mapuche mapping project, 165, 174–179; in Nossa Senhora do Livramento, Brazil, *132, 133;* and Quilombola countermapping conflict, 187–188, 190; and social polygraphy, *36,* 38–39, 39–43; and territorial planning in Robles, Colombia, *116,* 120–122, 124–126, 126–127; and Ye'kwana-Sanema mapping project, 51–52, 54
World Rainforest Movement (WRM), 48, 49
written language, 31–32
Wynter, Sylvia, 212

xawümen (Mapuche boundaries), 86–90, 92
xawün (gatherings), 83, 86–87, 90
Xawvnko (union or confluence of the waters), 173
Xhidza language, 22–23
Xhuaban, 20–21
xufken mapu, 167

Yagaeche, 20–21
Yagavila, 9, 20
Yaijudumö, 53
yaku (aquatic ecosystem), 105, 108
yaku pata pamba (flooding site), 106–107, *107*
Ye'kwana people: Caura River basin territory of, *58;* and Caura River hydroelectric projects, 45–47; mapping project, 9–10, 47–49, 49–51, 51–54, 55–56, 56–57, 60
Yucuna Amerú community, 39–40, *40*
Yurutí del Vaupés Indigenous community, 36, 40, *41*

Zapotec people, 9, 22–23, 24, 30, 212
"zonal councils," 172–173
zoning practices, 71, 74, 109–110